DICTATIONS

DICTATIONS

On Haunted Writing

AVITAL RONELL

INDIANA UNIVERSITY PRESS   BLOOMINGTON

From P.

This book was brought to publication with the aid of a grant from the
Andrew W. Mellon Foundation.

Manufactured in the United States of America

Library of Congress Cataloging-in-Publication Data

Ronell, Avital.
Dictations, on haunted writing.

1. Goethe, Johann Wolfgang von, 1749–1832—Influence.
2. Goethe, Johann Wolfgang von, 1749–1832—Influence—
Freud.   3. Freud, Sigmund, 1856–1939—Knowledge—Literature.   4. Psychoanalysts—Austria—Biography.   5. Goethe,
Johann Wolfgang von, 1749–1832—Friends and associates.
6. Eckermann, Johann Peter, 1792–1854—Biography.
7. Eckermann, Johann Peter, 1792–1854. Gespräche mit
Goethe.   8. Authors, German—18th century—Biography.
9. Authors, German—19th century—Biography.   I. Title
PT2189.R66   1986   831'.6   85-42753
ISBN 0-253-31712-6

1   2   3   4   5   90   89   88   87   86

Vestibulum ante ipsum primisque in faucibus
Orci Luctus et ultrices posuere cubilia Curae.
　　　　　　　　Virgil, *Aeneid VI*

Knochen, Wolken, kurz alles führen Sie uns
höher herbei.
　　　　　　　Hegel to Goethe, 24 February 1821

The swing could indicate transmission noise
or "ghosts" caused by multipath interference.
　　　　　　　　　Playback Magazine

CONTENTS

INTRODUCTION ix

Part One 1

Textor's Children: On Being Stillborn 5
Herr M. 12
Incidentals 19
Learning to Like Spinach 25
The Nature of the Text 29
Very Good Heads 34
Anaesthetics 45
Analyzing with a Hammer: Irma 48
Led by the Nose 52
Double Danger 55
The Meeting Place 57

Part Two 63

Preliminary Remarks 65
The Pas de Deux or *Was* is Goethe 69
The Place of an Absence 88
Serving Time 91
Body Building 107
Taking Dictation or How to Talk-Write and Rewind 117
"Was sollte ich tot sein?" 123
" 'You're breaking my arm,' I cried" 127
Growing Out of It 135

The *Farbenlehre* or "When PAC MAN Eats a Power
Pill, the Ghosts Become a Transparent Blue Color"   139
"A City like Berlin"   146
Hypnotics   157
VOrGEfühL   161
Losing One's Quill   166
The Festival of Incorporation   175
A Ventriloquy Kästchen   187

NOTES   193

I would like to acknowledge the continued support of
Marguerite and Jacques Derrida, Samuel Weber and Maria Torok.

*Research for this book was conducted under the patronage of
the Alexander von Humboldt Foundation.*

INTRODUCTION

The enduringly powerful appeal of Goethe can be imputed to the fact that he crosses all generic boundaries. Inasmuch as he did not maintain himself within generic limits, Goethe entitled himself to the comprehensive name of writer: when he crossed a bridge to science or philosophy the result, as in the *Theory of Color* or the *Fragment on Nature,* was more or less than science or philosophy. Indeed, he established an original and surpassing authority, as if the writing of Goethe was to be a new genre. But above all, this mode of surpassing, of instituting a new genre, does not appear to imply, as in so many cases of literary innovation, any form of disaster. To the contrary, he has the bearing of a serene genius, an Olympian or more specifically, an Apollonian spirit who incessantly denounces that which is weary or sickly, dissociating himself from the unnecessary suffering of Werther, for example, or the Romantics. His story reads like the superior narrative of success; he has known but evaded the abyss. In this respect, Goethe, his oeuvre and destiny, became for posterity both an inexhaustible source of inspiration and a traumatism of sorts. An eternal summit dwarfing and paralyzing what comes under its shadow, he is like the culmination of a Bildungsroman, the great drama of mastery, after which there can be only a falling off. Through the towering and therefore indeterminate position that Goethe adopted in regard to the diverse genres of discourse, one could say that he anticipated and in part programmed this rich and painful heritage: at once ungraspable yet present as preeminent authority, he condemns himself primarily to being a legendary, or in other words, a fantasmatic figure.

Of the things that Goethe sought to control, the no-things are perhaps the most curious. One among these may provide us with an emblem of the specifically ambiguous spirit that drifts through Goethe's work, one which is always linked to the anticipation of unknown effects. The vapors, namely, and the weighty yet invisible atmospheric pressures which at one time fascinated him are quite similar to the development of the Goethe-formation itself. Goethe's insights on weather forecasting, while interesting as such, can be taken as an early figuration of what is required when analyzing Goethe's heritage. To a certain degree, Goethe has grounded a concept based on the possibility of estimating or calculating in advance—something that, while having become a familiar element in The News genre of the actual and present, hovers between science and its others in a kind of epistemological teetering. The sensible, invisible thing that Goethe thought to compute, to know in advance, as it advances, led in 1825 to "The Theory of Weather," which in the meantime has been assimilated to the delicate science of the Weather Forecast. One scientist has felt the need to stress the civilizing effect of Goethe's aerial inquiries (as if this were not a matter of course, in other words, as if his participation in civilizing discourses had to be stressed), crediting him with having "laid the groundwork for the close network of weather stations that now covers all civilized countries."[1] As everyone in those civilized countries knows, the weather forecast usually comes after the news, extending past the new to offer a reading of foresight that combines modern divinatory skills with a certain calculation of probability. At one time such a reader was called a weather prophet.

The weather prophet reads what is at once there and not there, what belongs to being and not to being, which is why we sometimes say that there is no substance to his predictions. His objects are no objects, but the nebulous texts of wind velocity, cloud formation, and vapors. He responds to the above; and while "The Theory of Weather" was not conceived in the same passion as his other scientific pursuits, it nonetheless manifests an interest on Goethe's part for deciphering a certain domain of immateriality—the nonsubstantializable apparitions on whose wings phantasms are sometimes said to be borne. As unfathomable life ("unbegreifliches Leben"), weather discloses itself to us in its rapport to the possibility of a future.[2] The same elements which are gathered up in the concept of weather forecasting sustain ghosts, dreams, and some forms of hidden, telepathic transmissions.

What was it, however, that was being forecast? If Goethe is to be considered a heroic figure who survived the dangers of self-loss and dispersion, outliving the genre of madness that was at the time so prevalent, then the survival and perpetuation of writing after Goethe is genuinely problematic. This is the sense in which Kafka describes Goethe as a "monstrous entity" ("entsetzliches Wesen") whose memory prevents him from writing; however, Goethe's nobility does not even allow for the possibility of a strong ressentiment. In Nietzsche's words, he may have been something, finally, of an "ennobling inoculation" whose first phase implies danger, a radical poisoning which eventually protects against the very poison whose concept it is.

The serene resorption of poison, a consciousness of the beyond-disaster, points to a difference, according to Blanchot, between

Goethe and Nietzsche, for Goethe willed everything including his rescue; he was guilty, so to speak, of diverting his course from the shipwreck he knew. Nietzsche, on the other hand, threw himself into catastrophe with the certitude "qu'en se perdant il accomplissait son destin" (in losing himself thereby, he fulfilled his destiny).[3] And though it may seem that in this respect Goethe owes one to Nietzsche, Blanchot reminds us of Nietzsche's love and admiration for Goethe, for his Apollonian force and his Dionysian dreams.

In this respect, it is possible that Blanchot has named for us a law of Goethe's singularity, namely, that he has been rescued from the catastrophe that he, like Nietzsche, knew. Goethe may never be forgiven for the rescue missions, the offers of support, that were organized around him while Hölderlin and Kleist fell. And Nietzsche himself rescues Goethe from countless catastrophes, for example, in his poem entitled "An Goethe" that begins by rewriting *Faust:*

> Das Unvergängliche
> Ist nur dein Gleichnis!
>
> [The nontransitory, eternal
> Is but a metaphor for you!]

Avoiding disaster, Goethe also programmed it. An early and strikingly concrete example would be Werther, who, prior to being repudiated by his author, was received in a psychotic mode, in many cases leading to suicide or hysterical mimesis. In the same vein Goethe repudiated the so-called madness of the Romantics which he had largely inspired.

There is then a double movement written into Goethe's bequest, at once leaving behind the image of a monstrously mastering figure ("entsetzliches Wesen")—a classical figure—that lays monstrosity to a provisional rest, so to speak, but also leaves open the chance of fury and breakdown. Supposedly written shortly after she had read *Faust,* Mary Shelley's *Frankenstein* repeats the story of demonizing powers which are played out in the context of successive restorations to health. Frankenstein's fiend learns to grasp the predicament of finitude, and to commit suicide, when he becomes a dangerously close reader of Goethe. Figuring on his limited reading list, *Werther* in a sense telecommands the monster's "auto"-destruction. Viewed under this optic, *Werther* can be said to out-monster the monster. Injections of agitated tranquility are introduced each time by doctors, simultaneously engendering and finitizing—resembling what we tend to call a father. Faust's father, too, was a doctor, one who caused his son a great deal

of anxious commemoration, as was Victor Frankenstein; and Wilhelm
Meister was to terminate his *Bildung*'s labor both as father and as a
surgeon-barber. Goethe, as Nietzsche has taught us, was also a doctor
whose remedies often proved to be toxic as well.

Goethe, indeed, as we read in Kafka, will also have been the name
of the serious writing block. He was for instance the source of paralysis
for an otherwise untroubled writer, G.E. Lessing. According to the
testimony of the Berlin Enlightenment figure, Johann Jacob Engel,
Lessing's masterpiece was to have been a work entitled *Doktor Faust*.
But from the moment Lessing was made aware of Goethe's project
bearing the same title, his own work faltered. In fact, Lessing soon lost
the pouch (*Kästchen*) containing the *Faust*-manuscript. The psychopathology of this type of paralysis—which Freud, in response to Goethe's
apparition, will term *Schreiblähmung*—is however widespread enough
among writers in and of the German language(s) to seem like a minor
syndromic habit. Yet it was a habit that crossed the channel at certain,
unpredictable moments. Lord Byron's dedication to Goethe of "Sardanapalus" stammers out the self-extenuation of the subject; addressing
Goethe, it forgets the author, cancels the title, stumbling over "literary" and nearly botching the self-designated "Stranger" who proposes
the work. The signator never really signs, in a sense perishing or
dashing himself out of the homage.

Dedication of "Sardanapalus."—

To the illustrious Goëthe a Stranger presumes to offer
the homage of a literary vassal to his liege=Lord- the
fi*r*st of existing writers;—who has created the literature
of his own country—and illustrated that of Europe,—
~~in Eng~~ The unworthy production which the ^author^*I* ventures to
inscribe to him—is entitled^Sard ~~Sor~~ "Sardanapalus."— -

Just as the prominence of Byron's addressee induces a number of
slips or lapses, Goethe's apparition has been regularly welcomed by
uncontrolled writings of the unconscious. One cannot be but dumb-
founded by the quantity of Goethe-dreams recorded by the most eminent representatives of European letters. Two exemplary and closely
related dreamers would be Freud and Eckermann, but the same motifs
recur for instance in Benjamin's imaginary memory of Goethe. Goethe

is simultaneously the ancestor who gives so much that it cannot be received and a father whose strength is felt to be so vital that it needs to be supported, while it also has to be assured without the need of any support. Walter Benjamin dreams and writes—as will Freud, as has Eckermann—of a dim link between Goethe and the internal architecture of a vestibule, a kind of dark recess or vault. The dream appears in his *One-Way Street,* "No. 113." Beginning in the cellar, it takes him to a vestibule ("Vestibule—A visit to Goethe's house. I cannot recall having seen rooms in the dream.") and ends in the Dining Hall:

> In a dream I saw myself in Goethe's study. . . . The side of the writing desk abutted on the wall opposite the window. Sitting and writing at it was the poet, in extreme old age. I was standing to one side when he broke off to give me a small vase, an urn from antiquity, as a gift. . . . An immense heat filled the room. Goethe rose to his feet and accompanied me to an adjoining chamber, where a table was set for my relatives. It seemed prepared, however, for many more than their number. Doubtless there were places for my ancestors, too. At the end, on the right, I sat down beside Goethe. When the meal was over, he rose with difficulty, and by gesturing I sought leave to offer him support. Touching his elbow, I began to sob with emotion.[4]

"I began to sob": To touch the limb of a very old Goethe, taking his gift, the table d'hôte, my ancestors, too, and the shock of offering your support to Goethe: as if Benjamin had dreamt Eckermann, on the eve of Goethe's decline.

The difficulty of which we have given some examples—that of writing after the master writer, and of avoiding the dangers which he had himself circumvented—originates, of course, in the impossibility of forgetting Goethe. His state of unending agitation (what in *Faust* he calls "das rastlose Streben") and the malaise one encounters in appeasing his phantom is part of Goethe's testament. Beginning with the three difficult days of his birth, Goethe, in a sense, never stopped negotiating his singular contract with death. He departed while signing it (his final gesture was to write a phantom text; his last letter traced in the air after hallucinating the flotation of Schiller's scattered letters on the ground, was "W"). Leaving as he was about to write, disappearing while signing, he remained without a sepulcher.

Not only did Goethe sense the impossibility of his own departure— when Herder died he wrote, "Da wo ich Herdern beneide, There I envy Herder where I hear that *he* will be buried"—but he rigorously denied the death that surrounded him, thus making himself vulnerable to later charges of *Todesneurose*. As the burial-envy expressed in the citation concerning Herder suggests, Goethe knew that he in some way was to be barred from a final rest. Nor would he allow his closest relations that peace. Thus Ernst von Schiller will have been made to play *fort-da* with his father's skull. He would have preferred, he claims, to have returned it to the womb ("Schoss") of the earth. However, he has been constrained by his Majesty's desire ("Wunsch seiner Königlichen Hoheit") to deliver the skull to Goethe—to place it in his hands. This was to be Goethe's way of assuring Schiller's presence at his side, of presenting him to his dinner guests and safeguarding him. Schiller's skull, then, which Goethe was to receive at the Weimar library, was exhumed in the Jakobsfriedhof. But in the last moment— it is a question of the last moment—his son intervenes and judges the elder Goethe too fragile for the transaction; he had seen him weeping: "Der König hat geweint," Schiller has written in the catastrophic moment of *Don Carlos,* majesty has wept.

One can imagine the scene of exchange unfolding; the son of the once buried facing the son of the undead. Ernst definitively detaching himself from the cranial reel that he would have preferred to enter in Mother Earth. And August speaking in the name of the father, the eternal living—at once living and more or less absent. Goethe writes a poem soon afterwards, as if he had been there to receive his friend.

And August von Goethe, who wants no doubt to settle his debt with Ernst von Schiller, writes to him soon upon his departure in 1827 to announce his participation in founding a society that will institute a memorial ("Begräbnis-Monument") "für deinen und meinen Vater," as though he were writing of a single father. August's legacy was in a sense caught up in this organization of a sepulchral space; yet he exposes his desire to recuperate a place of rest principally for Schiller, thus shifting the ground of a genuine paternity—and Schiller was for Goethe's son the only and true father of German letters. This, however, may only serve to confirm the immovability of Goethe's position as father.

While the fantasmatic position that Goethe occupies in posterity cannot be limited to that of a father—there are, as we shall observe, a number of shifts and reversals in the roles he assumes—this remains the position from which he exercises the most intelligible power. In what follows I shall attempt to analyze the most striking aspects of this ensemble of roles and remnants—what we might call the Goethe-effect. The exchanges between art, science, and aesthetics, which are part of the specificity of Goethe's works, created a place for an exem-

plary, if unheard of, discipline; psychoanalysis made Goethe its epony-
mous hero. And yet, the "influence" that Goethe exerted on psychoanalysis, on its birth and internal expirations, is by no means a simple
matter. While Freud recognizes in Goethe the source and seed from
which psychoanalysis was engendered, his relationship to the source
becomes increasingly more ambiguous and intricate as he establishes
his discipline. As infinite creditor, Goethe is bound to appear in troubled or troubling moments, collecting his due, exacting a price and at
times reminding Freud of a history of calculations that is better left
untold. What this suggests is that only certain elements of the rapport
between Freud and Goethe are admitted into the text of psychoanalysis while others necessarily remain concealed or partially unconscious.
As we indicated earlier, Goethe's apparition exceeds a notion of the
other's anxious receptivity, but is something of a trauma, a mark of
devastation which is particularly visible in Freud. In a more general
sense, then, Freud will have named, without naming, the eerie position
in which Goethe has left us in this day and age. There remains something unassimilable about Goethe, something that to this day cannot
be laid to rest. And so, like Freud, one makes every effort to consider
him as a mortal and finite figure; one counts his days, computes his
ages, divides them into finite periods—and one, like Freud, is still
haunted by Goethe's ghost.

As for Eckermann, he appeared to mark the place of a double in
Goethe, thereby paradoxically assuring his unicity. Secretly splitting
but fortifying Goethe's signature, Eckermann, who wrote under dictation, completed Goethe's oeuvre. The completion of Goethe however
implies the sacrifice of another: the disaster of Eckermann. Always
already condemned as parasite, Eckermann is the price to be paid for
Goethe's achievement. With the possible exception of Nietzsche, no
one has deciphered the other side of Goethe's signature, the hiero-
glyph of a counterfeit totality, as "Eckermann." This perhaps would
be one way to reconsider Nietzsche's beauty pageant of abject self-
knowledge, by reading the writing couple whose sustained encounter
takes place on the grounds of a catastrophe. In order to discover the
specific contours of this catastrophe, I have had to make use of certain
psychoanalytical methods, a practice which I believe is particularly
justified by the fact that some sources of psychoanalysis are under
Goethe's influence, still taking dictation from him.

If the texts of Freud and Eckermann are to be understood here as
exemplary of a certain writing under dictation, this is because the

voice which traverses them without belonging to them is, as the voice of an author par excellence, a particularly strong one. The ambiguity of Goethe's position for those who write in his shadow is no doubt discernible in a good many other similar cases. Often, however, the ambiguous effects of Goethe in themselves prove to be traumatizing. The ghost-writer of Freud and Eckermann's texts, Goethe is constantly reinvented by them; while his roles change with high frequency, he nonetheless continues to send them orders through more or less conscious channels of transmission and by means of a remote control system. What is specific to this mode of writing concerns not only its manner of producing a text dissociated from itself, and struggling against itself. But this writing takes as its point of departure the remoteness of the original author, the incalculable distance of the one who dictates. The resulting texts are bound to assume the function of a double, as in the case of Freud, who places his dreams at a distance in order to interpret them with Goethe or as in the testimony of Eckermann, which is deprived of a true signature; they give rise, though often unconsciously, to repetition and to correspondences with an original that would be "Goethe." However, at the same time, one discerns the playing out of a struggle and a shattering effect that disfigures at once the origin and the copy. This remoteness and quest of the author are no doubt readable in every text. But the cases which concern us have in this respect the privilege of supposing a primary gap between the text and the source; and this gap repels the source itself toward a place where it can take the form of a genuinely mythological constellation, enabling it to exercise from a distance an inordinate force: Goethe is no longer for Freud and Eckermann a simple text—if such a thing exists—but a text, amplified, so to speak, by myth and biography.

The strength of his influence gives rise to a particularly intense and altogether remarkable struggle precisely because of the primary distance: it is a strength that dictates. In return, the text dictated to Eckermann and Freud manifestly exceeds the limits of a literary work; in Eckermann's personal destiny placed at the service of Goethe as in the dreams and preoccupations of which Freud makes the very material of his theory, the text extends itself without preestablished limits and infests, beyond the oeuvre or the corpus, even the life and body of those who rewrite it. Where the remote presence of Goethe institutes a place of encounter for the literary and biographical, aesthetic and scientific, psychological and physiological problems—in the histories themselves of Freud and Eckermann—one is obliged, in order to follow the course of transmissions, to mix genres and enlarge the field of inquiry. The obtained contaminations are in a sense authorized by the very practice of the leading characters: by that of Eckermann, no doubt, who despite his reserve appears to invest Goethe with decisive powers of all kinds, and certainly by the practices of the scientist-poet and the psychoanalyst. The contaminations that have spread through the body of this commentary are in the first place controlled by the phenomenon at hand—by dictation—and attempt to come to terms with its magnitude and its paradoxes.

DICTATIONS

31 January. Nichts geschrieben. Have written nothing. Weltsch brings me books on
Goethe, that cause me a dispersed, absolutely inapplicable excitement, eine zer-
steute, nirgends anwendbare Aufregung.
Outline for an essay, "Goethe's monstrous
being" "Goethes entsetzliches Wesen." Fear
of the two-hour evening walk. . . . Furcht
vor
4 February. The total passion Der mich ganz
durchgehende Eifer, with which I read about
Goethe (Goethe's Conversations, etc.) and
which keeps me from any writing und der
mich von jedem Schreiben abhält.

> From Kafka's Diaries,
> 1912.

Part One

Of the tables and tabulations that were drawn up to compute the debts of psychoanalysis, perhaps no balance was more difficult to maintain than the columns devoted to "Goethe." An unimpeachable book-keeper, Freud left an opening, a sizeable margin of error, when settling his accounts. It would seem appropriate, then, to begin with the relationship in Freud of error to Goethe—the frontispiece to a work whose first chapter is titled "The Forgetting of Proper Names." The frontispiece ("By Permission of Sigmund Freud Copyrights") looks something like this:

THE PSYCHOPATHOLOGY OF

EVERYDAY LIFE

Forgetting, Slips of the Tongue, Bungled Actions, Superstitions and Errors
(1901)

> Nun ist die Luft von solchem Spuk so voll,
> Dass niemand weiss, wie er ihn meiden soll.
> *Faust,* part II, act V, scene 5

> Now fills the air so many a haunting shape,
> That no one knows how best he may escape.
> [Bayard Taylor's translation][1]

"Now": act V, scene 5; Life, Everyday; a haunting shape. It has not seemed necessary to name the author who makes an apparition under the heading of Superstitions and Errors and the varied activities of forgetting. Yet Goethe is made to remind the reader of something that cannot be altogether forgotten, something that spooks or haunts the text about to be opened, and in ways from which no one knows how best he may escape.

Nor should the history of this phantom citation escape us, for it will prove of some interest in the pages that follow. The editor's introduction tells us that Freud's "time was fully occupied by the completion of *The Interpretation of Dreams* (1900a) and the preparation of his shorter study *On Dreams* (1901a) and it was not until late 1900 that he took up

The Psychopathology of Everyday Life seriously."[2] This is when, in October of that year, he asks leave from Fliess (Freud, 1950a, letter 139) to use for the motto of his work the quotation from *Faust* which in fact appeared on its title page. "On January 30, 1901 (letter 141) he reports that it is 'at a standstill, half-finished but will soon be continued.'" The relay has begun. Freud borrows Goethe's ghost from Fliess, at once incurring a double debt, while "seriously" working on two works that deal at length with Goethe's spectre, which brings Freud back to Fliess and the problem of a writing standstill. By taking away the citation that appeared in Fliess's book, however, Freud was also transferring into his own account, and thus driving away the phantoms that were at that time supposedly haunting Fliess (*Interpretation of Dreams*). All of these relationships—of Fliess to Goethe to Freud to writing—as well as those listed in the subtitle to the *Psychopathology*—of forgetting to slips of the tongue to bungled actions to superstitions and errors—belong to a certain fantasmatic reading of psychoanalysis to which Freud's double indemnity returns us.

Freud may not be superstitious, but the *Psychopathology* is spooked; and it tells us as much, from the start (by letting Goethe, or rather *Faust,* do the talking). There is more to be said about the citational mode in which Freud meets "Goethe," which often amounts to a vampirization of sorts, a libidinal depletion.

But supposing the frontispiece to psychoanalysis, whether borrowed or not, were in fact openly inscribed as "Goethe"? How open could the inscription of the *Geheimrat*[3]—Goethe's official title—be? At the risk of divulging an already open secret, let us enter Freud's calculations at the point where he makes Goethe the origin of his desire, the beginning of a psychoanalytic drive.

If Goethe occupies a place of honor in the genesis and history of psychoanalysis, then Freud's testimony to this effect could be reasonably expected to suggest the specific terms of Goethe's membership in his large organization. Since the authority which Goethe exercises in Freud is largely of a fantasmatic order, however, it is very likely that any testimony Freud could give on this subject has been altered through secret negotiations he had had with himself, thus making it rather doubtful that what he has to say is strictly on the level. To assert Goethe's fantasmatic strength in these negotiations implies, among other things, that there is a certain probability of miscarriage in Freud's calculations of his unconscious debt to Goethe. Such a debt always falls due to a figure whose loss is as deeply desired as it is regretted; this is perhaps why the calculation of the debt is always linked in Freud to the calculations made from Goethe's death. One way of interpreting those aspects of Goethe's power over psychoanalysis of which Freud himself was not conscious, would be to attune one's ears to the telepathic orders that Goethe's phantom transmitted to Freud by a remote control system. Any gamble on a type of intertextuality that would deal with telepathic channels involves a risk, of course: for example, when one aims to exceed Freud's own calculations, the calculation at which one arrives could amount to a seemingly extravagant reliance on coincidence and chance. However, a case can be made for chance, just as it was made by chance, at least in terms of etymological transmission; that is to say, in this case, the calculation which takes into account some apparent coincidences in order to unmask them might turn out to be inexhaustible, always leaving an outside chance.

Textor's Children: on Being Stillborn

The mortality timer has been set. Freud calculates from the year of Goethe's death. But he says he really wanted to start from his birth, to return us to the issue of their birth. This difficult, belated birth which delivered Goethe into the childhood of the modern German language figures importantly, if uneasily, in Freud's preoccupations. But if the Goethezeit—the time or age of Goethe, his timing and aging—has to be newly recounted, this time it will not be without the aid of a well-instructed midwife, the *Hebamme* who was not entirely present at the bedside of the mother tongue. To engage a modern midwife who, to the chagrin of Goethe's maternal grandfather, was sorely lacking at the scene of birth, is to call on someone or something whose wisdom was gained from the experience of an equally traumatic birth. For if the psychoanalytic method is to be adopted for the purpose of inducing Goethe's birth at this time, it is not because psychoanalysis has conceived a foolproof method of assuring or controlling birth. Rather, psychoanalysis was born along similar lines of delay and deferral, somewhat like the Mignon of *Wilhelm Meister,* without a proper name or genre and as an androgynous body of uncertain harmony sharing the genetic makeup of art and science.

Yet Freud would calculate from the year of his death. On the face of it, there is nothing striking about such a calculation; so much, in

Freud's case, was borne up by death, including the proper name, "Psychoanalysis," which he patented, as if by chance, the year of his father's death. Even Freud's birth was calculated by his father, Jacob Freud, from the date of his own father's death. On the same sheet of paper announcing "Schlomo Sigmund" Freud's birth, the father had entered the details of the paternal grandfather's death: Rabbi Schlomo was buried on the eighteenth day of the month of Adar (23 February 1856). Psychoanalysis would retain this double movement which folds death upon life—*fort* upon *da*—while it would also prop up the number eighteen in order to strengthen the memory of its conception. And Psychoanalysis would utter the name of Goethe when dreaming of the first birth-spasms. For the time being, there may be no better way of commemorating the enormous labor pains of these fathers than to reach into the opening of their legacies.

While it could never be ascertained on whose side he really was, Goethe was often at Freud's side during critical moments. At not so critical moments, he would frequently appear in letters, conversations, and even in analysis sessions. Freud would habitually appeal to Goethe as a citational prop for his scientific investigations. His most frequent appeal for support, despite his predilection for *Iphigenie,* will have been to *Faust, Wilhelm Meister, Dichtung und Wahrheit,* or to what he simply terms "Goethe." On three imposing occasions Goethe manifests himself by name as the primary material for Freud's secondary revisions.

The first of these occasions concerns the case of the guilt-ridden patient who has forsworn his chronic masturbatory habits shortly after his father's death. He tends, however, to renounce his resolve, though "only upon rare and extraordinary occasions."[4] Freud explains that "it [masturbation] was provoked, he told me, when he experienced especially fine moments, or when he read especially fine passages." Freud will disclose only one such passage, and it might be noted in passing that he has taken the precautionary measure of repeating "he told me" within the indirect citation attributed to the patient. That passage, Freud's patient told him, can be found in *Dichtung und Wahrheit,* part III, book 11.

Now Freud himself returned to that especially fine work in "A Childhood Recollection from *Dichtung und Wahrheit*" (S. E. XVII, pp. 147–56) to review what he had, on a first reading, merely suspected, but which had recently found support in another patient's narration.[5] The issue in question brings Freud to Goethe's opening pages, to the pages which open on Goethe's life. With scrupulous attention to detail, Freud recalls these lines, passing over them without comment in order to arrive at the episode which depicts Goethe throwing the family pottery and dishware out the window to a chorus of "noch mehr!" ("do it again!").

Freud repeats the beginning of *Dichtung und Wahrheit* as follows: the constellation of stars proved favorable to Goethe's birth, with the exception of the moon (*der Mond*). Though Freud does not emphasize the point, his first name begins to split apart in this inscription, for this is the story of Goethe's triumph (*Sieg*) over the moon, which in a minor key pits the two aspects of Freud's first name against each other. The splitting of his name—into the literary and scientific, for instance—constitutes a hesitation in Freud's reading of Goethe, to which we shall later turn. Freud continues his recital: Goethe entered the world as though dead; it was only after great efforts were made that he was brought to life; "there follows a short description of the house," and so forth. Freud eventually glides home into an analysis of Goethe's relationship to his mother, basing the specificity of his findings on the beginning of the autobiography.

Freud will have begun with the second beginning of *Dichtung und Wahrheit,* with the scene of a troubled birth, skipping the *Vorwort* in which a Goethe that survives himself is celebrated as he attains to a transparency of consciousness. His fictive correspondent demands of Goethe an autobiography "precisely now, at the very time when knowledge is fuller, consciousness more lucid."[6] This guarantees that the text to follow will not only be agreeable and confer a new life ("neubelebend") on the author to the extent that he will work through what he had begotten ("jenes Hervorgebrachte"), but he will be able to elaborate it to the endpoint ("zu einem Letzten zu bearbeiten"). This request—with all the implications of birth, rebirth, and death that it carries—prompted him, Goethe maintains, to write *Dichtung und Wahrheit,* a work that will spring from a tireless crossbreeding of memory, observation, and reflection. However, Freud wastes no time on the elaborate establishment of the *Dichtung* mechanisms and proceeds to the seat of the perceived *Wahrheit* of the matter and matrix (the etymology linking *Materie, mater,* and matrix is Freud's idea, in another context).

The other beginning of the autobiography—which, incidentally was largely dictated to Goethe by Bettina,[7] who had lived with his mother—the one with which Freud begins, opens the First Book: "On August 28, 1749, midday at the stroke of bells, I entered the world in Frankfurt am Main. The constellation was felicitous"—with the exception of the moon, not to mention the apathy of Mercury and the sublime indifference emanating from Saturn and Mars. But "the sun ['die Sonne'] stood in the sign of Virgo, and was culminating for this day. Jupiter and Venus exchanged friendly glances. The moon, which happened to be full, exerted the power of its counterglow ['Gegenschein'], particularly as its hour had just come. It ['er': he] therefore opposed my birth, which could not come about until this hour had passed." In the first paragraph Goethe was born, although those celestial elements of an exclusively male gender are said to have tried to prevent his birth. However, in the second paragraph, "these good aspects which astrologists subsequently rated very highly may well have been the cause of my survival ['Erhaltung,' preservation]." For Goethe, in the second paragraph, was thought to be stillborn. In fact it took three days for his birth to come about. But Goethe did arrive in the world: he "kam für tot auf die Welt, und nur durch vielfache Bemühungen, brachte man es dahin, dass ich das Licht erblickte" ("[I] was taken for dead when coming into the world; only after going to great pains, did they manage to have me see the light of day"). Goethe was thus born dead, or taken for dead at birth, and will want to be born again (perhaps for the first time) at his deathbed. For who can avoid overhearing the uncanny bracketing of this bio-graphical closure that begins with a desperate struggle toward light and ends with the legendary cry for "mehr Licht!"?

The only proper name to earn the dignity of being mentioned close to the celestial powers, within the context of a painful, belated birth, will belong to Goethe's maternal grandfather, a gentleman whose first names are homonymic with that of the initially stillborn child. Johann Wolfgang Goethe was given the name of his grandfather, which is to say, of his mother. His mother's family name, or his grandfather's name, was Johann Wolfgang Textor. "This situation," Goethe continues "placed those around me ['die Meinigen'] in a state of distress but was nonetheless advantageous to my fellow citizens ['Mitbürger'] . . . and helped many of those born after me." Here we rejoin Freud's analysis where it turns out that, with the exception of his sister, Cornelia, Goethe's brothers and sisters all in fact died in infancy. But thanks to Textor's manipulation of the situation, or thanks to the effect that Goethe's first birth-death had on the maternal grandfather, the "fellow citizens" would at least be born without first dying. The grandfather saw to it that the *Hebamme* (midwife) would, in the future, be more alert to the business of birth. The figure of the *Hebamme* returns to Freud even as she absents herself.

However, Freud makes no mention of Textor. Why he had forgotten or repressed the one figure who might have furnished the gateway (*Tor*) to his own text—and who, as exemplary dream interpreter endowed with telepathic gifts (p. 40) might have enjoined Freud to read his fortune in this stellar configuration—is a matter for speculation. Did he simply eclipse the sentence or overlook it while transferring the passage onto his own pages? But as Freud's letter to Marie Bonaparte warns: after the appearance of one of his forthcoming books, one would no longer be able simply to say, "I forgot" (the princess's excuse for having missed a rendezvous with the analyst). Especially not when Freud's expressed intention in this essay was to trace the contours of the young Goethe's jealous proximity to his mother, the ramifications of which involved the child's hostility toward her other children, his evanescent siblings. Freud's forgetfulness takes a more radical turn, however, if we recognize that the scene he resists recurs in his own writing when he himself assumes the role of maternal grandfather to the young Ernst's game of *fort-da*.[8] For was not Goethe performing before Textor an original version of *fort-da* with death-life in his mother's bed—little Ernst played the game of revenants under his mother's bed—and quite literally, at the portals of the female cavity? This scene is delivered to the maternal grandfather, be he Freud or Textor, for critical observation. It is the moment signalling the retreat of the paternal name (Textor dissolves into Goethe, Freud into Halberstadt), and Goethe's name, which combines the grandfather's name with that of the father, bears the mark of the nominal *fort-da*. Freud's motivation for playing *fort-da-fort* with the narrated event of Goethe's birth may have something to do with this uncanny revival.

While it now seems necessary that Freud omit mention of Textor in order to save his analysis from the abyssal pull of the uncanny—*Dichtung und Wahrheit* ineluctably poses Textor, the first reader-analyst of Goethe's birth, as a double for the dream-interpreter and the condition of a déjà lu—it seems equally strange, though on another register, that Freud should remain silent on another major term in the autobiography, and one that in certain ways also doubles for the Freud who in *Civilization and its Discontents* had opposed his laborious grappling to Goethe's effortless commerce with truth and writing.

What about Goethe's father, the father whom Freud for once preferred to ignore, as if he were Dora's mother, a mere psychotic housewife? Though he monitors the retreat of the mother's name, the father remains a place of non-encounter for Freud despite the abundantly troubled references made to him in the opening of *Dichtung und Wahrheit.* Freud slips by the first image of the man who was in some way responsible for Goethe's seeing the light:

> Unfortunately, one still held to the educational principle according to which children were to be weaned early on from all fear of the ominous and invisible; they were to become accustomed to terror ["das Schauderhafte"].

Das Schauderhafte, as it turns out, is another name for Goethe's father. We now approach the scene which, since Freud, has become classical, when "we children were supposed to sleep alone, but when this became impossible,"

> then Father, garbed in a reversed dressing gown and thus disguised enough for us ["in umgewandtem Schlafrock und also für uns verkleidet genug"], would plant himself in the way and scare us back into our place of rest. The resultant evil-gotten effect can be imagined by everyone.

How should one overcome the fear, Goethe continues, "which clamps one between a double horror ['Furchtbare']? My mother, always bright and cheerful," and so on.

So Goethe's father, by a mere robe-reversal, "was thus disguised enough" to frighten, literally to mortify, Goethe? What sort of phantom, appearing in the guise of an Oedipal nightmare, had Goethe seen that night, which Freud would not see? The father's first gesture in this family romance—and this point should be stressed—is "to frighten us back to our place of rest." The first image of the father rising out of the autobiography, then, reproduces the motif of something doubly frightening, something barely disguised (in other words exposed) but forceful enough to push back the child into his place of rest (*Ruhestätte*), a resting place: a burial place. Will Goethe have blamed his father for an all too early death, or for calculating his son's existence from the date of death (*Sterbejahr*)—as, coincidentally, Freud will do? (In a later episode baby Goethe stages his father's shaving accident by suddenly blaring a forbidden Klopstock verse.)

The natural father is associated in an important way with the particular concept of writing to which Freud alludes in his *Unbehagen* or *Civilization and its Discontents.* Not only does Goethe feel compelled to supplement the initial image of mortification with the fact that the father had forced his mother to write in the early years of their marriage (before Goethe came to her rescue), but more to the point, he uncovers a father who himself writes, but slowly and with laborious precision.

And precisely which book does this father belabor? Its title is *Viaggio in Italia,* which can be translated into Goethe's mother tongue—and, in a sense was, very quickly, by Goethe—as *Italienische Reise.* According to official records this work was completed in 1740, a good nine years before Goethe's birth (Prima edizione, 1932—the centenary of Goethe's death). Nonetheless, Goethe imagines that his father had spent most of his time during Goethe's youth "auf seine italienisch verfasste Reisebeschreibung, deren Abschrift und Redaktion er eigenhändig, heftweise, langsam und genau ausfertigte" ("on the portrayal of his voyage, which he wrote in Italian and whose transcription and drafting he drew up singlehandedly in serial succession, proceeding slowly and with precision")—which may give some pause for thought. All we know is that the father's text has been largely retraced by his son both in a discursive and experiential manner. Among other things, it was Goethe's father who first paid special homage to *Jerusalem Delivered* when he followed the trail of Torquato Tasso in Ferrara. In terms already suggested by Eissler's psychoanalytic study of Goethe, "the parallels between the (Italian) journeys of father and son are sometimes uncanny." However, the relay of debt from father to son turns into a site of death and devastation when Goethe's own son undertakes an Italian voyage and perishes in Rome.

Freud will himself retrace some of these motifs, as if reentering Italy under some sort of hypnotic guidance. In his book, Goethe will always be associated with those issues converging on Italy, writing, delay, and birth/death. But before entering in turn this dark continent, there is yet another family resemblance lording over their relationship. The fact that Goethe's family bore a striking resemblance to Freud's own family has already received some critical attention (which in itself is not a reason to omit it). Let us recall some of the common traits: the rather formidable age difference between Goethe's mother and father happens to be the same as the one between Freud's parents—the two mothers were youthful, separated by about twenty years from the fathers. The Goethe and Freud families also chanced upon the same number of children, with the same span of time separating the first-born males and their siblings (fifteen months); details of these and similar coincidences can be found in Max Schur's *Freud, Living and Dying.*[9]

These coincidences were surely remarkable enough to have inspired "A Childhood Recollection" largely shared by both men. However, Textor in particular seems to have disrupted facile identifications, though his may be the name and the opening to a far deeper cohabitation of spirits. The almost stillborn child is still being born, which is why the question of his *Sterbejahr* continues to have some currency. In order to throw some light on these issues, we might begin with Freud's *Italienische Reise*. As we cross the border into Italy, we might wonder whether Freud's omission of Textor also meant to suppress the point he had made in the *Traumdeutung* concerning "an architectural symbolism for the body and the genitals," where it is suggested that "every gateway ['Tor'] stands for one of the bodily orifices ('Körpereröffnungen') ('a hole') ('Loch')" (p. 352).[10] This takes us rather directly from a cavity to the mouth of a Venetian canal.

Herr M.

When Goethe escaped into Italy, he traveled under the pseudonym of Herr Möller. Freud takes another route but eventually meets up with a certain Herr M. His meeting is intercepted by preliminary problems which his letters to Fliess expose. Although it is unusual for Freud to be arrested with anxiety on the subject of his own work, his letters make references to the problem of writing paralysis he encountered in Italy. A letter of 15 October 1897, gives focus to Freud's dream of neurotic impotence. In this dream he has seen the skull of a small animal which he associates with "your wish that I find a skull on the Lido to enlighten me, as Goethe once did."[11] If Freud failed to discover enlightenment on the Lido, he will eventually discover that Goethe opposes evil not to God, but to the Libido. However, "the whole dream was full of the most mortifying allusions to my powerlessness as a therapist." Elsewhere, at "the climax of my life as a citizen," Freud will speak of Goethe's psychotherapeutic prowess (Goethe-Prize, 1930). However, the connections that emerge here with regard to the waning power of his therapeutic prowess concern the inosculating channels, which Freud does not pursue, uniting finitude and Italy with a largely paternal figuration. Whether Fliess's wish that Freud be Goethe—that Freud seek more light, Goethe's light, that according to an internal logic Freud die in the land of a father's fatherland—betrays a sadistic calculus with which Fliess may have tried to total Freud, this is not yet in the reckoning. Rather, at this point, what exacts an account is the way Freud himself perceives in Goethe a mortifying portal to his text.

To grasp the degree of mortification that Freud suffers at the hands of Goethe, for whom Italy and Fliess are often agents, the portals of another text, the *Traumdeutung,* must first be entered. This is the work to which Fliess has lent his authority as "first audience," "highest judge," and "representative Other." A dream appears under the heading of "Another Absurd Dream that Plays with Numbers." It is flanked by two other dreams whose framing effects should not be left out of the picture. The first frame, the anterior portal, runs like this:

> If only I had been the second generation, the son of a Professor or *Hofrat* [Aulic Councilor], I should certainly have moved upwards faster. In the dream I made my father into a *Hofrat* and Professor. . . . Fifty-one is an age that seems to be an especially dangerous one to men; I have known colleagues who have died suddenly at that age, and amongst them, one who, after long delays, had been appointed to a Professorship only a few days before his death [an allusion to Fliess's theory of periodicity in which male and female periods are computed, $28 + 23 = 51$].

Passing over this profession without commentary to reach the other end of the central dream, one finds the beginning of a dream immediately following: "The scene was in front of a gateway ['Tor'], double doors ['Doppeltor'] in the ancient style (the Porta Romana, as I was aware during the dream itself)." Treating these two excerpts as preface and postscriptum respectively—they are more than two, as the arithmetic and doublings suggest—treating them, then, by not treating them, let us bring the focus to the narration of another absurd dream:

> One of my acquaintances, Herr M., had been attacked in an essay with an unjustifiable degree of violence, as we all thought—by no less a person than Goethe. Herr M. was naturally crushed by the attack. He complained of it bitterly to some company at table; his veneration for Goethe has not been affected, however, by this personal experience. I tried to throw a little light on the chronological data, which seemed to me improbable. Goethe died in 1832. Since his attack on Herr M. must naturally have been made earlier than that, Herr M. must have been quite a young man at the time. It seemed to be a plausible notion that he was eighteen. I was not quite sure, however, what year we were actually in, so that my whole calculation melted into obscurity. Incidentally, the attack was contained in Goethe's well-known essay on "Nature."

This dream will enjoy a rather unique place among Freud's intimate revelations insofar as he will have it published on three occasions between 1900 and 1901 in the *Traumdeutung* (*Interpretation of Dreams*) as well as in *Über den Traum* (*On Dreams*). Before proceeding to Freud's interpretation of this dream, let us make a quick observation on the energy loss or gain from German to English. In general, the distinguished and only complete collection of Freud's work has kept surveillance over the German like a sovereign linguistic superego. The English of the Standard Edition is almost blameless in its forceful economy and precision; it has even gone so far as to smooth out some apparent wrinkles in Freud's diction, though these are very few. The Standard Edition, as its title suggests, is the model to which some French and Anglo-American writers on Freud refer, so it might be worthwhile to consider what befell the dream as it crossed the frontier into "our" language.

In the first place, Herr M. was "naturally crushed" ("vernichtet," destroyed, exterminated, eradicated); "his veneration for Goethe had not been affected" ("nicht gelitten," did not suffer); "I tried to throw a little light. . . . It seemed to be a plausible notion." Here Freud shifts to the present tense, writing, "Ich suche mir die zeitlichen Verhältnisse. . . . Es kommt mir plausibel vor. . . . " ("I am looking for the temporal relations. . . . It seems plausible to me that. . . . ") "I was not quite sure what year we were actually in": "Ich weiss aber nicht sicher, welches Jahr wir gegenwärtig schreiben" (I however do not know for sure [in] which year we are presently writing). "The attack" ("der Angriff") suggests onslaught, offensive, from *angreifen,* to seize, grasp, take, or catch hold of: fig., to corrode, eat into (as acid), break into, affect (an organ), strain (nerves); related to *Griffel,* stylus (a style or needlelike marking device, in entomology, a small, rigid, bristle-like anal organ).

What sort of calculation was Freud making in this very German dream, and why does it run into obscurity (*Dunkel,* a term often associated with the unconscious)? Because he is dealing with calculations of a specifically temporal nature, it should be noted that, in the first place, Freud shifts tenses within the narration of the dream.

Freud argues that the dream offers "einen logischen Zusammenhang wieder als Gleichzeitigkeit." A dream is like a system of writing (*Schriftsystem*), and Freud's example for this will be that "ab" means that the two letters are to be pronounced as one syllable. Samuel Weber has analyzed with rigor and elegance the issue of systematic rewriting (*Umschreiben*) in Freud's work. He points to Freud's emphasis on the synchronic moment of simultaneity (*Gleichzeitigkeit*) and spatiality (*Verräumlichung*) while he also addresses the problem of the inadequacy for Freud in a (synchronic) subject (*Sache*) and diachronic language—the problem of exposition.[12] Freud repeats now and again his conviction that precisely this simultaneity guarantees the closure of a dream. For this reason he calls for an art of exposition (*Darstellungskunst*) that would come as close as possible to disclosing the essential immediacy of the dream's trajection. This will not have been the first time that the psychoanalyst calls for some kind of art to enter his discourse. The care with which he has argued justifies our being afflicted in some elementary sense by Freud's somewhat disruptive grammatical temporal relations which themselves seek to expose the "absurdity" of the temporal relations within the dream. The commentary immediately following the r.*rration of the dream aims "quickly" to "find a means of justifying the nonsense in the dream": "Wir werden bald die Mittel in der Hand haben, den Blödsinn dieses Traumes zu rechtfertigen" ("We shall quickly take hold of, seize or have in hand the means by which to justify the nonsense of this dream"). This is how Freud goes about seizing those means and justifying the dream content: A certain Herr M., whom he had gotten to know among some company at table, had not long before asked him to examine his brother who was showing signs of mental paresis (*paralytische Geistesstörung*). When seeing the patient, Freud had asked him the year of his birth and made him do several minor calculations so as to test his memory; the patient, "incidentally," passed these tests quite well. At this point Freud recognizes "that I myself behaved like a paretic in the dream. (I do not know for sure [in] which year we are writing.)" Freud now sums up other recent sources that made their way into the dream: an editor of a medical journal, of whom he is a friend, had just printed a "devastating" critique (*vernichtende Kritik*) of the latest book by his friend Fliess. The critique was written by a young reviewer (*Referent*) of meager judgment. Freud intervened on behalf of Fliess, soliciting a response from the editor, who regrets the incident but cannot promise redress (*Remedur*). Whereupon Freud severs relations with the journal, expressing the hope that "our personal relations would not be affected by the event" ("dass unsere persönlichen Beziehungen unter diesem Vorfall nicht leiden wurden": lit., would not suffer). In this version of the commentary, Freud proceeds to "the third source of the dream." But in a subsequent version to be found in *On Dreams* (S.E. 5: 622) he adds with untroubled certitude, "this was the true source of the dream." "The third source of the dream" was, then, a recent account given by a woman on the subject of her brother's psychic illness ("von der psychischen Erkrankung ihres Bruders"; implying the process of falling ill). She had explained to Freud how her brother had broken out in a frenzy with cries of

"Nature! Nature!" Doctors attributed this outcry to the young man's intensive reading of "Goethe's striking essay" on this subject ("jenes schönen Aufsatzes von Goethe," that beautiful essay by Goethe) and to overwork in his studies—(Freud stops the sentence here in the other version)—of natural philosophy. Freud "preferred to think, however, of the sexual sense in which this word is used even by the less educated people here"; the fact "that the unfortunate young man subsequently mutilated his genitals ['Genitalien'] seemed at least not to disprove me." The young man was eighteen at the time of his outbreak. Freud notes that his friend's book deals with the chronological data of life and shows that the length of Goethe's life was a multiple of a number of days that has a significance in biology. He remembers a sentence from yet another unkind critique of Fliess's book: "One wonders whether the author or the reader himself is mad." ("Man fragt sich, ist der Autor verrückt oder ist man es selbst.")

"So it is easy to see that in the dream I was putting myself in my friend's [Fliess's] place (I looked . . . to shed some light . . . temporal relations). I, however, act like a paretic and the dream indulges (*schwelgt*, also debauches) in absurdity. Thus, the dream-thoughts (*Traumgedanken*) were saying ironically: 'naturally, the madman is a fool, and you're the brilliant ['genial'] people who understand it so much better. [The S.E. erroneously translates "Ihr seid" into "it's *he* (Fliess) who is the crazy fool."] Perhaps, though, it's the other way around ['umgekehrt']?' " And the other way around, Freud tells us, is generously given in the dream-content, insofar as Goethe attacked the young man, "which is absurd" whereas "it is still easy for a young man to attack Goethe, who is immortal ['unsterblich']"—in the other version Freud replaces the "immortal" with "the great Goethe"—"insofar as I calculated from the year of Goethe's *death*, whereas I had made the paretic calculate from the year of his *birth*."

Freud, however, has also promised the readers of the *Traumdeutung* "to show that dreams spring only from egotistical motives" (he will later change his mind on this). Thus, he must justify (*rechtfertigen*) the fact that he had made his friend's problem (*Sache*, subject) his own and put himself in the place of his friend who, Freud asserts, takes the place of Herr M. in the dream. But "my critical convictions while I am awake do not suffice. Now, however, the story of the eighteen year old ['die Geschichte des 18-jährigen Kranken'] and the different interpretations of his outcry, 'Nature!' come into play in terms of the opposition which my claim for a sexual etiology had, in the case of the psychoneurotic man, against the claims of most doctors." "I could say to myself: 'The kind of criticism that has been applied to your friend will be applied to you—indeed, to some extent it already has been.' And now I may replace the 'he' in the dream-thoughts with 'we': 'Yes, you are right, it's *we* who are the fools.' " ("Ich kann mir sagen: So wie deinem Freunde, so wird es auch dir mit der Kritik ergehen, ist dir zum Teil auch bereits so ergangen, und nun darf ich das 'Er' in den Traumgedanken durch ein 'Wir' ersetzen. Ja, ihr habt recht, wir sind zwei Narren.") "There was a very clear reminder in the dream of that 'mea res agitur!' in Goethe's small, incomparably beautiful essay." And this is how Freud concludes his commentary: "for when at the end of my high school days I was hesitating in my choice of a career, it was hearing that essay read aloud in a public lecture ['in einem populären Vortrag': in a popular lecture] that decided me on taking up the study of natural science ['der mich schwankenden Abiturienten zum Studium der Naturwissenschaft drängte'; *drängen:* to urge, thrust, push]."

Finding the means for justifying this lengthy exposition may not be so quick as it was in Freud's case. The interpretation of his dream dispenses a prescription explicitly recommending the application of "different interpretations" to the eighteen-year-old's diagnosis. However, this diagnosis may also require a prognosis from another point of view, for it could be that another eighteen-year-old boy was occupying Freud's mind the night of the dream. In order to approach this and other enigmas that linger persistently within Freud's text, I shall limit my interpretation of the dream and commentary, taken together, to two major possibilities, the first of which would be reducible to a sort of "anxiety of influence." The first interpretative stage is admittedly of somewhat less concern to us than the second, but hopes to clarify what follows.

Freud's asserted goal in the commentary is to justify his having made his friend's subject (*Sache*) his own in the dream. Indeed, one might ask whose dream this will have been. Was Freud dreaming Fliess's unconscious? For it is known that Freud could not entirely approve Fliess's book, and could have easily caused his friend, the professed "reader of his mind," a good bit of anxiety on this subject. Is Fliess being employed to blot something out (elsewhere Freud exposes F.'s relationship to *Fliesspapier* or *Löschpapier:* blotting paper)?[13] In his commentary Freud places his desire and failure to write, calculate, or clarify (*aufzuklären*) close to Fliess's name. Considering that this follows upon the evocation of genitals to approach the issue of genius, we are reminded of something that the nexus gathering together enlightenment, writing-paralysis, and genius recalls. Does it not recall Freud's other dream, reportedly provoked by Fliess's wish, in Italy? Was not the issue already linked to the issue of genius? The word in German for Italy is *Italien*. The problem of *geni*us, the shock of influence and impotence which Freud associates with both Fliess and Goethe, is linked in some specific way to a genre of *Gen-Italien* (genitalia).[14]

In the commentary, Freud, however, joins genius with a concept of irony when he quotes the dream as speaking "ironically," though it is not clear which part of the quotation should be taken as ironic, nor whether dreams do in fact speak irony. The first part of the quotation deals with the relation of fools and madmen to genius. The irony would be, as Freud interprets it, that in fact he and Fliess are the fools to Goethe's critical genius. But the quotation goes on to ask whether the relationship would not be "the other way around?" Now if this part of the quotation were to be in the service of irony, then the sense of the dream's irony would appear to turn the other way around, thus making Goethe the madman or fool—the *Tor*—and allowing Freud and Fliess to accept the attributes of genius. In any case, he appears to assert a relationship of unsheathed brilliance travelling between Goethe, himself, and Fliess. In fact, Freud, who is anxious to blend Fliess's figure into his own, claims "it was easy to see that in the dream I was putting myself in my friend's place." The quick and easy pace with which Freud draws near his goal tends to produce an effect of breathlessness.

In the same quick spirit, Freud asserts that he must supplant "him" (Herr M.) with "us" (Freud and Fliess). Which "us" is more convincingly convened? Freud reveals time and again that it is naturally his friend Fliess with whom he identifies, thus effectively deflecting the criticism that has been dealt in the dream to Fliess toward himself. If, however, we bear in mind, as alas we must, that *two* friends figure in the dream-interpretation, then a helpful confusion might ensue; namely, another pattern of identification emerges taking place between Freud and the other friend, the exterminating editor, *against* Fliess. In this respect, it is important to note that the phrasing of Freud's relation to criticism ("so wird es auch dir mit der Kritik ergehen") could well be taken to mean: your critique (of Fliess) will also follow along these lines and, to a certain extent, has already done so; that is, you, Freud, are attacking Fliess with unjustifiable violence in Goethe's *Fragment*. Freud, who may not have found a skull on the Lido as Goethe once did or who may not be enlightened as Goethe was, can nonetheless obtain the backing of his friend, the editor; he can now crush the mindful Fliess in the nature of Goethe.

Put another way, and with less violence, Freud would here be borrowing the authority of Goethe's name in order to criticize Fliess,
however fragmentarily.

Such an interpretation concurs with the fact that the two doctors put
an end to their friendship in August of the same year as the publication
of this writing. This prospect is further betrayed by Freud's interpretative language: the editor, he says, cannot promise redress. Not only
does the Latin word, *remedur,* communicate in every sense with the
single other Latin event in this text, *mea res agitur,* but it also belongs
less to the sphere of critical judgment than to that of curative procedure, to Freud's "natural science." In other words, the editor-friend
has recourse to Freud's language in order to attack Fliess, and the
actual relationship about to be severed presently reigns between Freud
and Fliess. Freud's identification with the other friend appears to fulfill
the requirements for discovering the egotistical motor to his dream. If
it were Freud's unarticulated and unarticulable desire to destroy Fliess
and his book containing chronological data on Goethe's *Lebensdauer*
(lifespan, durability), he would be taking the part of Goethe and attacking Fliess in the name of the immortal name. Indeed, this would
be the symbolic accomplishment of Fliess's wish that Freud be Goethe;
but it was clear from the start that in this triangular arrangement one
of the members would be committed to a sacrificial movement initiated
by the imaginary couple, be it pronounced as Fliess and Goethe, or
Freud and Fliess, and so on. The attack would originate with the
coupling of Goethe/Freud (Herr Möller/Herr M.), but the victim's
(Fliess's) "veneration for Goethe(/Freud) would not suffer"; that is,
Freud would not suffer.

Incidentals

The triangulation of Goethe: in the dream and commentary Goethe is
formulated according to three overt references or phases. In addition
to the genital phase I have suggested, there now come variations on
the phases of orality. Following Goethe's censorial attack, Freud inserts his conclusive "incidental" remark: Goethe's *Fragment über die
Natur* decided the wavering (*schwankenden,* swooning) young Freud to
take up what he here calls *natural* science. Everyone knows that the
age of a high school graduate is about eighteen, and a quick glance at
Ernest Jones's chronology of Freud's life bears out the hypothesis that
Freud was indeed eighteen around the time he began to receive emis-

sions from the eighteenth-century genius.[15] In some way, then, the
eighteen-year-old who cried "Nature!" upon reading the same *Fragment* prior to mutilating himself, bears some relation to Freud himself.
The work of tying together the interpenetrating issues of self-mutilation and Goethe must be left to the second interpretation. Suffice it to
say, so that the so-called reader will not be left too unsatisfied, that
well before the *Traumdeutung,* Freud writes to Martha Bernays that he
has burned his papers and most of his letters on the occasion of
Goethe's birthday anniversary. Here, Freud prefers to think that
Goethe is in no way implicated in the young patient's outcry, despite
the latter's intensive work on the decisive *Fragment.* Freud's preference lies instead with the *popular* meaning of the word, and with
substituting his sexual etiology for the reference to Goethe. This substitution, as Freud reminds us in his commentary, amounts to something of a scandal. Now the scandal, which Freud does not properly
name, may lie in the fact that "Nature" can mean both semen and
menses, male and female discharge—or, if we were to transpose this to
the contextual filter of Freudian ideology, it suggests the specific sexu-
alized modes with which Freud has identified Goethe, namely, masturbation and mutilation. Engendering will of course be another issue.

So in the commentary Freud pushes Goethe back, laying him to rest,
and allows only a very mediated encounter between the eighteen-year-
old's predicament and Goethe. The tone of his decisive move suggests
that he is protecting something, and shows him to be less concerned with
protecting Goethe's name in this context than his own. For the same
writer who demonstrated such fervor in refusing the connection between Goethe's *Natur* and its popular meaning claims to have been
aroused around his eighteenth year by a popular reading of the *Fragment.* Freud has chosen a slightly slanted formula for designating "public" lecture. The fact that Goethe's words were imparted to Freud in an
open lecture, publically transmitted by Carl Brühl, "destinerring" until
they were deposited in Freud's ear—in other words, and among other
things, the fact that Freud at no point refers to ever having read the
Fragment, in his Sophia edition of Goethe or elsewhere, will be of some
consequence. The precise place where the editors chose to deposit this
text, its chronology in print—but here we are getting ahead of ourselves,
that is to say, of Freud.

Jones genially agrees with Freud that Goethe's dithyrambic piece
exerted an immeasurable influence on the dream-interpreter; but
Freud signals a desire to be shaken awake ("meine kritische Überzeugung im Wachen reicht hierfür nicht aus"), thereby introducing a rich

antisemantics in *Überzeugung:* over-engenderment or as in the case of
the *Über-Ich,* super-engenderment, the one suggesting excess, the
other a system of constraints. (If Freud writes that his understanding
when he is awake is insufficient, is he asleep or awake when knowing
his unknowing or somnambulance?) An anasemic reading of this line
yields something like this: In my waking state I cannot read the critical
question of engenderment; this dream to which I cannot attain in
waking is about engenderment (*über Zeugung*), a kind of sadistic engenderment (*Über-Zeugung*) whose witnesses (*Zeugen*) must not be
asked to testify (*zeugen*); and thereby they must not return to the root
of testifying, to the testicles. The cutting of (*kritische*) the testicles to
which I in my sleep bear witness . . . and so forth. But I am protecting
(*wachen*) my deposition and that which certifies me—my *Zeugnis,* the
Zeugung and *Zeug,* the *Überzeugung* which I protect from criticism
and other cuts. Protecting and protected, I am convinced (*überzeugt*)
that this critical cut cannot be read by me when I awake. And if we
resemanticize the sentence, neutralizing it to the normative peace that
it seeks in Freud's text, we can be sure only of this much: both the
dream and Psychoanalysis are shown to return to Goethe's *Natur* as
the source of their engenderment.

If Freud's commentary is exemplary of a psychoanalytical method,
we should also be attentive to something whose fruition is however
intended for the second interpretation. This would involve the out-
cries, "Nature!" lodged within Freud's exposition of his dream and
commentary, and their epitactic function: Herr M. of the dream was
naturally crushed by Goethe's attack which itself must have been naturally produced when Herr M. must have been eighteen; and with a
touch of irony, "naturally you are the geniuses." The periodic appearance of Nature, in its adverbial and other disguises, goes through
something like a menstrual cycle within the text at moments which
cannot however be restricted to "natural" processes or deductions.

In his commentary, Freud naturally refrains from giving a reading of
the primary inclusions that his relationship to Goethe assumes. And
yet the dream proper—that is, his rendering or translation of the
dream—points to the first manifestations of a union in which anxieties
of dependency and identification, as well as neighboring ones of debt
and guilt, are not spared.[16]

In the other version of his commentary to be found in *On Dreams,*
Freud will add that the "nonsensical character of this dream becomes
even more glaringly obvious if I explain that Herr M. is a youngish
businessman, who is far removed from any poetical and literary inter-

ests." Herr M., who turns out to be Herr Me in the first version, had
been far removed from Freud's interests, from Freud's business, and
yet it will be he who holds the honors for being eradicated by Goethe's
Natur. However, this other version further produces a vocabulary of
senility—"senile dementi," "feeble-minded," "fossil." Maria Torok
has argued that Freud links his father's sudden senility to the public
exposure of his businessman-uncle's fraud—the exposure occurs in a
'popular reading,' in fact, of newspaper journals.[17] According to
Freud, his father turned gray-haired overnight at the news of his
brother's arrest (Freud will spend a good part of his life trying to erase
the fraud from Freud). It is perhaps useful to be aware of this encroaching businessman ("far removed from any poetical and literary
interests") when situating Goethe's entry into the scene of traumatic
debt and progenitorship. Particularly since the fraudulent and nonsensical character of the dream becomes so "glaringly obvious" when
Freud veers away in this remark from a specifically poetical text. For if
Maria Torok's reading is right, then Goethe's position in this text is
already linked to devastation, to the sudden aging or zap-senility af-
flicting Freud's father. The unpoetical taint was witnessed by all, becoming a social or popular event in Vienna when Freud himself was
about ten years old. The reference to senility in *On Dreams* is also a
bit removed from poetical and literary interests insofar as it is linked to
the university; Freud ushers in the fossil in the context of there being
"no age limit in the German university," which inspires the dream of
the analyst's paralysis.

It appears that to some extent the immortal Goethe had been
granted an unterminal tenure at the university or that he would be
absolved of any such problem of aging. However, it is precisely the
question of aging or biological chronology, *Lebensdauer,* which inspires the reference to Goethe. Freud prefers to calculate from the
date of his death, and we should add that he utters the death penalty in
the same sentence which claims the poet's immortality; *unsterblich*
(immortal) and *Sterbejahr* (year of death) create a conceptual syn-
tagma around the name of Goethe. Who or what was Freud putting to
rest as he writes this year? It is "still" easy for a young man to attack
Goethe, the commentator asserts. But Freud himself is no longer a
young man at this writing. Goethe was considerably younger than
Freud—he was thirty-two—when the *Fragment* was written. (Freud is
now forty-three. Eighteen years before the publication of this writing,
Freud had entered the General Hospital of Vienna, and about eighteen years before that, he had entered the *Gymnasium* or high school.)

At the time of writing the *Traumdeutung,* however, Freud was desperately seeking to gain entrance into the university, which in some sense designates itself as the domain of agelessness while it also sets the mortality timer. In this connection, consider the host of metaphors designating the parasitical, feeble-minded *old* men inhabiting the university in conjunction with the *young* reviewer (*Referent*) of meager judgment who had attacked Herr M. We seem to have before us, at the midpoint of Freud's life, a match in which the age-limits with respect to the university, are pitted against each other in a race toward feeble-mindedness or degeneration—the one being precocious, the other, advanced. In Freud's dream, the figure of the young reviewer dissolved into the image of Goethe who attacked the figure of the youngish businessman or, according to Freud's account, Fliess and himself. From whose *Sterbejahr* was Freud calculating: Goethe's or his own? We know, thanks to Fliess's studied calculations, that Freud was scheduled to die in 1907, an eventuality which Freud took very seriously. Would not Freud then be the de-generation of Goethe (at the very least in terms of Fliess's notions of *Lebensdauer*), or at least slip into the place of one of those Goethe children who, to Freud's lucid horror, died without Goethe's taking note of the event ("A Childhood Recollection from *Dichtung und Wahrheit*")? But "degeneration" can be made to mean something else as well, as Werner Hamacher has argued: "Degeneration—this means not merely downfall, but also deviation from the form of genre or genus."[18] De-generation, then, means a kind of indebted and, as such, always guilty structure of individualization, a breaking off from the source implying a moment of monsterized self-abhorrence. Degeneration and degenitalization: this is what participates in the question of a *Sterbejahr,* a closure without end. Ironically, and even naturally, however, the literal sense of a calculation involving each *Sterbejahr* could have been one and the same, since Freud's *Lebensdauer* will have equalled that of Goethe, notably, by surpassing the eighty-two-year deadline.

To go back to school, however, it might be asked what the university has to do with Freud or Goethe or a possible relation of the two. While genius only rarely resides inside the university (the invention of genius would seem to prohibit entry), it is the case that, in his lifetime, Goethe was responsible for opening university doors and urging merit promotions for many of his contemporaries—Fichte, Schelling, and Hegel would be three of several names to mention in this context; Schiller would be another.

To some extent the immortal Goethe remains inaccessible to the problematics of an aging or mortality with which Freud appears to associate the university, for he was never more alive than after the date of his death (cf. *Totem and Taboo* on the dead father). The decisive moment, as with all thoughtful mobilization, takes place prior to entry. The university, as something to be entered, provides a kind of immunized zone, a place for undaunted fossilization, free from the crush of exogenous attack. For the analyst, therefore, Goethe may always be located at the portal of the university—the situation in which Freud now finds himself—because it was here, prior to his initial entrance into the university, that Freud claims to have engendered psychoanalysis from the seed of Goethe's *Natur*. This would have something to do with that scandalous sexual etiology with which Freud interprets "Nature," one that uncovers his "feminine side," as he was fond of remarking to Fliess. It was at the originary moment of entering the university, a moment susceptible to reproduction and in itself always conceived as reproduction, that Freud received Goethe's legacy. Was he enfeebled, made unsteady (*schwankend*), by the enormity of this gift at the moment of conception? Freud tends to impute considerable significance to the time-span culminating with this moment. In "Some Reflections on Schoolboy Psychology" ("Psychologie eines Gymnasiasten," 1924), moved by an encounter with a former teacher, he writes:

> At such moments as these, I used to find, the present time seemed to sink into obscurity and the years between ten and eighteen would rise from the corners of my memory, with all their guesses and illusions, their painful distortions and heartening successes—my first glimpse of an extinct civilization . . . my first contact with the sciences. [S.E. XII, p. 241]

Once again years sink into obscurity, from which memories, or peculiar angles of memory, soundlessly protrude. However, at the time of this writing—the writing of the *Traumdeutung*—Freud seeks reentry into the university; he is having dreams of neurotic impotence and "Goethe's skull"; he dreams, he writes, of the young, immortal, or at least great Goethe's attack on him; years later he will send his daughter, Anna, to accept in his name, at Goethe's birthplace, the Goethe-Prize, for he is himself feeling "too feeble" and his prosthesis will have made reading the acceptance speech impossible; he presently writes his early, immortal, or at least great work, and piecing together his signature, he is underwriting Goethe's attack. There is an inescapable pull in the direction of institution, career, public approbation (which can also come from a grave), a concept of primal debt, and mortality. In order to throw some light on this particular formation in Freud, let us consider briefly another dream that Freud recounts and comments.

Learning to Like Spinach

Slipping into a taxi, Freud is carried further along in his negotiations with a concept of *Urschuld*. The cab driver, whose face Freud does not see, turns out to be Goethe. Driven by Goethe, Freud dreams another type of calculation whose protagonist appears in the illumined eyes of a taximeter (S.E., p. 637). In the commentary Freud remembers having left a party the night of the dream in the company of a friend. The friend had offered to hail a cab and see Freud home. " 'I always prefer taking a cab with a taximeter,' the friend said, 'it occupies one's mind so agreeably; one always has something to look at.' " When they had settled into the cab and the driver set the meter (which immediately displayed a first charge of sixty hellers), Freud "carries the joke further." " 'We've only just gotten in, and already we owe him sixty hellers. A cab with a taximeter always reminds me of a table d'hôte [this table figures in the dream]. It makes me avaricious and selfish, because it keeps on reminding me of what I owe. My debt seems to be growing too fast, and I'm afraid of getting the worst of the bargain; and in just the same way at a table d'hôte I can't avoid feeling in a comic way that I'm getting too little, and must keep an eye on my own interests.' I went on to quote, somewhat discursively:

> Ihr führt ins Leben uns hinein,
> Ihr laßt den Armen schuldig werden.[19]

End of quote (how many sets of quotation marks should one care to place around Freud citing Freud reciting Goethe?). In the context of accumulating debt and guilt (*Schuld*), Freud goes on to cite Goethe "somewhat discursively." The debts start multiplying here, beginning with the friend who offers the cab ride and whose *délicatesse* dictates that he promptly direct Freud's attention to the meter, thus ushering us from the table d'hôte to a notion of parasitical desire which in turn invites Goethe's participation. The taximeter, while occupying the friend's mind so agreeably, reminds Freud of what he owes, or perhaps of a debt he might have forgotten—in any case it produces a destination organized around a concept of owing. Freud acknowledges the debt somewhat discursively—that is, by changing courses to accommodate another discourse which also reminds him of a debt: to that discourse which, in a haunting way, knows and names nothing less than Freud's debt.

His commentary appears to have satisfied its interpretive hunger when Freud asserts: "Thus I was reminded of the duties of parents to their children. Goethe's words gained a fresh meaning in this context." Thus Freud names the debt that he feels he had originally forgotten, namely, the debt that parents have toward their children. His own debts or duties are recalled to him only after he is reminded by Goethe of the primal debt that children incur. While Goethe's words gained (a fresh meaning), Freud only has increasing charges to contend with; his debt seems to be growing faster, and Freud is naturally afraid of getting the worst of the bargain. In the dream as well as in the sources attributed to its content, the issue of debt emerges at the table; the matter of eating should be retained here, as well as the context of Freud's somewhat discursive citation, the Harp player's song in *Wilhelm Meister,* which begins: "Wer nie sein Brot mit Tränen ass. . . ." ("He, who has never eaten his bread with tears. . . .")

Freud returns at this point to the family table, and while no one was crying over bread, one of the Freud children has had to master or learn to like spinach. Freud recalls in his commentary that on the evening of the dream his child had refused to eat spinach, just as he had as a child. Eventually Freud Sr.'s "taste changed and promoted that vegetable as one of my favorite foods" (p. 639). Can it be said that Freud's multiple slippages from child to father and back were engaged by Goethe?

Those who have had to swallow spinach, a species of the goosefoot, in the presalad days or prior to Popeye's propagandistic efforts to make of it the fiction of a desireable substance, may recall the serious revulsion inspired by this slimy mucosity. Learning to eat spinach and to like it, in other words learning to swallow one's disgust and therefore also the parental injunction to "EAT YOUR SPINACH!" to the point of embracing "that vegetable as one of my favorite foods" situates Freudian spinach as a vital ingredient in the formation of the superego. Spinach controls the difference between child and parent, the parent within the child of emerging Superego in a drama beginning with the second course of *desgoust.* In many ways, learning to swallow one's disgust constitutes the main course in Freud's tables of knowledge. Which ought to turn the tables on Goethe.

We can now be mindful of the fact that taste is given to change, disgust can be swallowed, and what was once judged unappetizing can later be promoted to a favorite and cited as such. In matters of aesthetic taste as well, as in the case of an eighteen-year-old who listened to a popular Goethe with some degree of apprehension and the forty-four-year-old who incorporates Goethe into the body of his oeuvre. Whichever meter has been ticking in Freud's unconscious and continues to tick in his discourse, Freud is not drawing interest in this bargain. Either as parent or child.

We have seen Freud link Goethe to a notion of originary debt or guilt ("Ihr bringt ins Leben uns hinein. . . ."), and we know that Goethe is headed for the dirty business of *Totem and Taboo,* where great fathers are murdered and great sons consume the father only to be cursed with the anxiety of radical guilt. Can Goethe (and Freud) be saved from this fate? Well, in *Totem and Taboo* Goethe intervenes at the moment of execution to save himself—and Freud. Here is how superego (which, as we saw, is engendered by the son through identification with the father) saves his skin:

> Was du ererbt von deinen Vätern hast,
> erwirb es, um es zu besitzen.

> What you have inherited from your
> fathers, acquire it to make it yours.
> [Freud, citing *Faust* I, i]

Since Goethe intervenes here in his exemplary manner in order to give a sound interpretation of the birth of the superego, he escapes being repudiated by Freud or murdered as the father. On the contrary, Freud cites him as someone who had intuited the systematized theory underlying *Totem and Taboo,* as someone whose truth had to await metapsychology in order to be discovered and interpreted: thus psychoanalysis becomes father to Goethe. And we have already seen Goethe name his debt to psychoanalysis: *"Ihr führt uns. . . ."* ("you bring us [back] to life"), we, these impoverished lines, in order to name our debt. Goethe names a debt, and it is not unthinkable that Freud would see himself as a cause for Goethe's admission. This would amount to just one of Goethe's belated births.

But if Freud agrees to be Goethe's creditor, to place himself in the position of Goethe's father, he is now forever running the risk of being attacked, crushed, destroyed, and consumed by his guilty (*schuldig*) son. For if psychoanalysis is the father of Goethe's intuitions, then that

which surpasses or astonishes Freud in Goethe's text is equivalent to a
neglect of debt with respect to psychoanalysis, or to Goethe's murder
of the father. Like the archetypical victim of the animated design—or
the dream-victim—Freud will have made himself exceedingly vulnerable to successive attacks (*Angriffe*).

Now that we have, or rather, Freud has saved Goethe from the jaws
of *Totem and Taboo,* let us return to the epicures of the family table
and to the taximeter which continues to tick. The issue was spinach
and Goethe, and whether Goethe had begotten Freud's discursive
style. Or perhaps the immortal Goethe, demoted to the great Goethe,
has already been shown in Freud's commentary to be indebted discursively to Freud. For Freud is reminded of his parental duties, which he
had somehow forgotten. This is perhaps the context in which Freud's
earlier "confusion of temporal relations" should be considered. Let us
take Freud at his word. He is reminded by Goethe of his parental
duties, of his duties as enmothering father. It is a commonplace of
Freudian criticism, and of Freud's own Freudian criticism, to recognize
Freud as the genitor of psychoanalysis. "For Psycho-analysis is my
creation," and "I have come to the conclusion that I must be the true
originator of all that is particularly characteristic in it," are some of the
terms Freud adopts in *On the History of the Psycho-Analytic Movement* and elsewhere. It may well be this child, psychoanalysis, toward
whom Freud pleads guilty in connection with Goethe: guilty of a certain abandonment, of abandoning his "own" stock, style, and discourse in favor of the adoptive child; guilty of leaving the desired
purity of psychoanalysis at critical moments in its development in order
to visit with those "incomparably beautiful pages" of poetry. Freud
pays calls on poetry when he wants to be minding psychoanalysis;
these calls are paid highly, as he reminds us: "Goethe's words gained."
Indeed, the charges made against Psychoanalysis would often be
unsparing in singling out Freud's mythological scientificity at crucial
junctures of his theoretical elaborations.[20] Wouldn't Freud need to be
constantly reminded of his parental duties to psychoanalysis and,
therefore, somehow *need* to start calculating Goethe from his *Sterbejahr* within his first great text? In order to protect the child of whom
Goethe reminds him, Freud will inscribe the date of death, presently.

In a footnote to another dream, Freud makes a statement on the
subject of Herr M. that seems otherwise senseless. This dream, he
notes, is concerned with the problem of birth and death ("Geburt und
Tod wie in dem kurz vorher erfolgtem Traum von Goethe und dem
Paralytiker," p. 342). In yet another passage (*Traumdeutung,* p. 332),

Freud quickly refers to the dream once more, expressing what presents itself as a most peculiar desire: he alleges the dream shows that Goethe should be treated as a madman ("dass Goethe behandelt werden soll, als sei er ein Verrückter"). But Freud, pitting Goethe against himself, adds that this dream-thought had followed the principle of reversal (*Umkehrung*) and contradiction. What remains clear is that either Freud or Goethe must be eliminated—or treated. At this point, however, the elimination of one risks paralyzing or devitalizing the other. Whether the treatment to which Freud subjects Goethe be clinical or discursive, Goethe—the madman who left Charlotte von Stein because, as he confides to Herder, she showed too lively an interest for interpreting dreams—will always return to Freud.

The Nature of the Text

The second interpretation, which forms a "plausible" couple with the first, begins where we left off, or so it seems. As everyone knows, Freud tampered with his first name. In 1870, he had his name changed back from Sigismund to Sigmund, thus leaving the *mund* intact.[21] In any consideration of Freud's biography, this should, and no doubt has, become a matter of unsettling irony. For it is also well known that the part of his body destined to suffer gradual and painful decomposition would be concentrated around the area of his mouth (*Mund*). In her book on Freud, Helen Puner goes as far as binding his subsequent illness with Freud's violent fall at the age of two, which left him with a life-long scar along the jawbone (*Freud, His Life and His Mind*, 1947). Her etiology has since been refuted, for as Jones pointed out four years later, the cancer began on the right side whereas the wound was inflicted on the left side of the jaw. Puner, however, is certainly right in drawing our attention to the concrete mark of that early traumatism and in isolating, as her flair for continuity forces her to, the jaw area as a particularly fragile and enduring point of reference. Freud would have been beardless without that mark, Puner is careful to remind us. But it would not be until eighteen years after the *Traumdeutung* that the first cancerous manifestations emerged in the form of a palatal swelling. Indeed, the entire area around his mouth, and its many names, proffers a generous opening for speculative intervention while it also presents a screen—a certain pilosity, as it were, that would require our shaving the text.

This protuberance as well as this aperture continue to produce their effects in our interpretation as they may have, in some uncanny way, in Freud's dream of Goethe's attack. In order to remain within the precinct of that pain, its many covert appearances, perhaps it would be useful to begin by pointing to certain sounds that the German "mouth" lets out. They are *munden,* which means to please, as in matters of appetitive taste; *münden,* to flow or empty into; and *mündig,* coming of age, in the sense of no longer being a minor. The delicate tissues of genius, maturity, influence or confluence of spirits will be provisionally grafted onto the physiognomy of our subject. Remembering that Freud feels attacked by Goethe's genius, let us invoke the etymological intimacy of genius, generation, genitals, and genre. *"Mea res agitur,"* Freud recalls, "this concerns me," or literally this is about my "thing" (and Goethe). If it were possible to discover the *Remedur* for clearing up the general obscurity surrounding Freud's concern, this would require us to admit, at this point, the word *Angriff* in its medical sense— meaning that the unspeakable would need to be uttered, if only for experimental purposes: Goethe attacked or affected an organ, but this "did not change my veneration for Goethe" and "I hoped that our personal relations would not be affected by the event." Indeed, these frightfully personal relations appear to be constituted by the event (*Vorfall*) and, it must be assumed, in the mode of suffering. Goethe's unjustifiably violent *Angriff* through the *Fragment* naturally destroyed something, naturally too soon; ironically, " 'he' which I must change to 'we' " are *genial.* The attack was *ungerechtfertigt:* unjustified, of course, but also finished unjustly (*ungerecht-fertigt*) or, if we mutilate a bit—and this concerns Freud—unfinished with justice (*un-gerecht-fertigt*). Now to meet the attack.

By almost universal agreement, Goethe's unfinished dithyramb on Nature can be classified as one of his early ventures into the natural sciences. Lionel Trilling goes as far as naming this piece an important and "elegant disquisition on Nature," though I wonder whether scholars have not been prejudiced by the force of Goethe's signature when they read the piece, which is neither markedly scientific nor especially poetic for that matter. There are, however, other discursive ventures more plausibly attributable to Goethe's pen, but we shall return to these in a moment. In his commentary, Freud refuses to interpret the "Nature!" of the self-mutilating eighteen-year-old close to Goethe— and not only because when he was himself eighteen, Freud had listened, in a popular setting, to the resonances of "Nature" in the mode of the *Mindergebildeten* (this is the term on which he bases the "popular," sexual meaning of Nature)—that is, as a self somewhat lesser formed and informed than the self "writing this year." In the narration, Herr M. was naturally crushed by Goethe's attack. The taste of Goethe's critique is bitter. Freud's temporal calculations run into obscurity (*Dunkel*). Nonetheless, the dream will be interpreted by the dreamer in terms of genius and genitals, both of which are troubled. Freud dissociates self-mutilation from Goethe first by splitting the meanings of "Nature," then by severing the manifest link between the eighteen-year-old patient and Goethe. This eighteen-year-old, who comes to resemble Freud, subsequently mutilates his genitals. Freud's other patient masturbates to *Dichtung und Wahrheit*.[22] If these two types of affinity to Goethe were presented in the form of an option, one would certainly prefer to evacuate Freud's name from the site of the first case, particularly since few have claimed to recover more pleasure in Goethe's "incomparably beautiful pages" than the analyst.

But however inclined we may be to invest Freud's reading of Goethe with a principle of pleasure rather than with one of irrepresentable sufferance, we must nonetheless ask ourselves why he eliminated Goethe—the Goethe-*Fragment*—from the context of mutilation, favoring instead the sexual "meaning" of "Nature" and its sexual interpretation. And even if the patient's self-mutilation manifestly invites a diagnosis dealing with sexuality—the attribution of sexual meaning to a symptom—the symptom itself seems to be more urgently bound up in Goethe's text than with a sexual question. If something is being repressed when Freud effaces Goethe here, would it not be a certain link between Goethe and the phantom of (self-)mutilation?

The binding terms of Freud's early engagement with Goethe, and his secretive espousal of his text have barely come to the fore, though it should be possible to assume that the bitter taste of Goethe's crushing genius will stay in Freud's mouth, if only to travel to the genitals and back. It is known that at the time of writing the *Traumdeutung*, Freud was suffering from a boil on the scrotum and, as the dream in which he dissects his own pelvis displays, Freud was very much focused on the greater genital area of his body including the pelvic girdle. He was also at this time producing the insights which led him to believe in the veracity of Aristotle's assumption that dreams tend to harbor a sort of alert system for nascent illnesses (*Traumdeutung*, p. 36). His own formula for at least three likely dream sources is listed in part I, C, of the *Traumdeutung* as: 1) External Sensory Stimuli (*Äussere [objektive] Sinneserregung*), 2) Internal (Subjective) Sensory Excitations (*Innere [subjektive] Sinnesregung*) and 3) Internal Somatic Stimuli (*Innerer [organischer] Leibreiz*). Bearing in mind the place of these dream-incubators, and

particularly the third of these, let us travel with Freud, if only momentarily, from the site of mutilated genitals back to the intact part of his
name, to his mouth and text.

It cannot of course be ascertained whether the mutilation of the
maxillopalatal region was consciously felt by Freud some time before
the first cancerous symptoms actually emerged from a state of latency;
nor can it be ascertained which came first—the symptom or the identification of the symptom, the text that fabricated the disease or the
disease that infested the text. This is where Goethe offers his prosthetic hand. For another of his scientific ventures in which he had
made a mark for himself—now for a more plausible type of *mea res
agitur*—involves his discovery of a specific articulation of the jawbone,
the *os intermaxillare* ("Ein Zwischenknochen der obern Kinnlade"),
written, incidentally, at about the same time as the *Fragment über die
Natur*. To state this very summarily, Goethe had discovered that belt-
way of Freud's body which would be vulnerable to incessant mutilation. It was perhaps Goethe's most passionate discovery, surpassing in
personal investment and importance any of his previous pieces of writing, including *The Sorrows of Young Werther*. It seems, indeed, that
all of Goethe's systems were stimulated by this *os* which, let it be
remembered, also means an opening, as a mouth, or an entrance, as
the orifice of the vagina. Goethe's agitation was so marked that he
produced this unique and extraordinary confessional delicacy: owing to
this discovery, he writes to Charlotte von Stein on 27 March 1784, "I
am so joyous that all my bowels are stirred" ("Ich habe eine solche
Freude, dass sich mir alle Eingeweide bewegen"). In a sense, then,
Goethe has already arranged for a shuttle mechanism to travel between the upper maxilla and the lower stations of the body.

If Freud has been struggling to protect the name of Goethe from
contamination by the episode of self-mutilation, he may have been doing so to insure his own name, which bridges not only the gaping memory of his body's somatic history, but also of that body of discursivity
which he named Psychoanalysis. For it should not be overlooked that
Freud prefers to name his discursive body here and in numerous other
contexts a *natural* science (as opposed to "philosophy," which is associated with the figure of the stricken eighteen-year-old). Indeed, the
dark moment in which he is presently writing requires him to elaborate a
mode of fragmentation that contains within it, like a potential explosive,
the possibility of mutilation. The fragment, Freud explains, is the fundamental mode of dream, and the dream-interpretation must proceed

delicately by fragment. Yet some of the words ushered in to put a handle on the fragment could easily tip over into mutilation. What about the sentence, "the dream is a conglomerate which for the purposes of investigation should be once again *zerbröckelt*" (broken up, pulverized, *Traumdeutung*, p. 451)? How easily and how persistently will the fragment efface mutilation? At any rate, we can begin to perceive a general strategy linking, however cautiously, the fragment, Goethe's *Fragment*, psychoanalysis, mutilated genitals, and the jaw. Will it not be one of the great ironies of psychoanalysis when, in the moments it succumbs to extreme fragmentation, it will call on the fetishized name of the *Fragment* to hold together an edifice eternally prone to collapse? It will engender the fragment—as its paternity, its source, its child, as citation and absolute debt—constantly, obsessively to dissimulate its fear of mutilation. Freud and Psychoanalysis, as Freud and Psychoanalysis constantly remind us, are to name one and the same thing (in *"Selbstdarstellung"*—the quotes around this title have too often been forgotten).

But what had Freud and Psychoanalysis actually read when they said they were reading Goethe? Or, in the terms set out by Freud, what was read to them, by what means of transmission did a voice carrying "Goethe" reach a place in Freud of internally wavering fidelity?

Let us suppose that when Freud remembers the *Nature-Fragment* as the source out of which Psychoanalysis is generated, his memory is partially controlled by a question that the *Fragment* itself emits, but leaves unanswered: "And the mother, where is she?—" ("Und die Mutter, wo ist sie?—"). Could Psychoanalysis conceivably have written itself into the dash of this linkless question? On some level, it could be argued, there will be no mothers in Freud. Not merely because the inaugural text, the *Traumdeutung*, is memorialized as the father's ensepulchered sign, but also because there are to be no mothers in the sense of the real, the resistant or even in terms of what Lacan will understand as the Symbolic order. The *Fragment* proposes an originarily Imaginary posing of the mother, a self-constitution prior to the incursion of language: "She has no language nor has she discourse; but she creates tongues and hearts through which she feels and speaks" ("Sie hat keine Sprache noche Rede, aber sie schafft Zungen und Herzen durch die sie fühlt und spricht"). Mothers, as in *Totem and Taboo,* are structured as mothers-in-law, removed and removing from themselves, creatures of substitution par excellence. In this sense, Mother not only doubles for Psychoanalysis as substitutive activity, but has the drive to save herself from herself, that is, from Psychoanalysis: "A mother, as she grows older, saves herself from this by putting herself in her children's place, by identifying herself with them; and this she does by making their emotional experiences her own" ("The Horror of Incest"). Fathers, on the other hand, linked as they are to the concept of themselves cannot save themselves, they cannot appropriate to themselves the children which they become, but can only be cut off.

The question continues to be raised: Und die Mutter, wo ist sie?—Mothers, abject withdrawal symptoms of phenomenological anxiety: they are there to show what is not, producing what is not as a perceptible object (the little boy in Freud *sees* what she does not have). Like Dora's mother, "nothing could be got from her." An opening, a gap, a kind of prior mutilation that saves itself. Where is she?—a question whose blaze momentarily illuminated Freud's omission of Goethe's maternal name when analyzing the autobiography. Where is she, the feminine, what is her place, what does it want? This no doubt has become a generic question by now, to which Freud responds precisely in terms of a certain nowhere and nothing of genitals, a radical suspension of the fixity of genre—the place, in fact, from where a petrifying Goethe may have arisen. Thus when Freud speaks of "the oppressive descent" to the realm of the Faustian Mothers, it becomes necessary to follow him down.

When Freud recalls an early disclosure made by Charcot, he also remembers forgetting it: "Mais dans des cas pareils c'est toujours la chose génitale, toujours . . . toujours . . . toujours!" Charcot is quoted as having said this at a Parisian party. "I know that for a moment I was almost paralyzed with amazement and said to myself, 'Well, but if he knows that, why does he never say so?' But the impression was soon forgotten" (*On the History of the Psychoanalytic Movement*). Almost paralyzed, almost petrified, the truth of M, Medusian speechlessness. And particularly when it is not a *chose;* not always, anyway, *an sich.*

Very Good Heads

The supposed inspirational source of psychoanalysis, its founding text—or Goethe's supposed *Fragment*—has borne up well under the pressure of time.

This *Fragment* continues to head theoretical references to Goethe and, as recently as 1974, for instance, initiated a 300-page volume of essays on Goethe.[23] The time has come to let Goethe attack the *Frag-*

ment. Here is what he has to say, four years before his death, about Freud's presumed source of inspiration:

> Jener Aufsatz ist mir vor kurzem aus der brieflichen Verlassenschaft der ewig verehrten Anna Amalia mitgeteilt worden.
>
> That essay has been recently imparted to me from the epistolary legacy of the eternally venerated Duchess Anna Amalia. [*Erläuterung*, p. 48]

Goethe's *Fragment* issues, then, from the legacy of Anna Amalia. (The names Anna and Amalia may have had a special familial resonance with Freud, since Anna was the name both of the sister who married his wife's brother and of the daughter who assured the continuance of the paternal lineage. Amalia is the forename of Freud's mother, who died two weeks after the bestowal of the Goethe-Prize in 1930.) Goethe writes:

> Dass ich diese Betrachtungen gefasst, kann ich mich faktisch zwar nicht erinnern. . . .
>
> I cannot remember having in fact written these reflections. . . . [*Commentary*, p. 48]

Whereas Goethe cannot remember having written the *Fragment*, Goethe scholars are divided on the issue of the *Fragment*'s authorship. Many scholars at least have worked under the assumption that Goethe had in fact written the piece; nonetheless, the 1975 edition of the *Hamburger Ausgabe* and other authoritative sources attribute the *Fragment* to Georg Christoph Tobler, the Swiss writer who had borrowed Goethe's copyist on the occasion of his visit to Jena. What Goethe does remember, however, is that in the years "to which said essay might be attributed, I was principally occupied with comparative anatomy." In those years, Goethe adds, he was actually working on the *Zwischenkieferpublikation:* on the jawbone, his first and, for a long while, most secretly guarded discovery.[24] He had, at the time, been trying to excite the curiosity of "very good minds" ("sehr gute Köpfe": lit., very good heads) with his scientific discoveries but no one seemed terribly interested. "And, as with so many other things, I had to quietly pursue my own path."

Freud would of course experience similar disappointment in the reception of his first substantial scientific discoveries, and he makes no bones about this situation, for example, in the foreword to the second edition of the *Traumdeutung*. Freud colors his anger with his mordant

Witz when referring to the "good heads" of his professional circle and states that no thanks are due to the interest shown by them; indeed, the need for a second edition of "diesem schwer lesbaren Buch" owes nothing to these readers. The *Traumdeutung* was too difficult for psychiatrists and philosophers. It is to the vaster circle of cultivated and inquisitive readers (*Gebildeten und Wissbegierigen*) that Freud owes the second coming of his work.

Whereas Freud published his anger over the indifference towards his work, Goethe publishes that he quietly went on to pursue his scientific projects in an atmosphere of marked hostility; his pursuit was no doubt nourished by his pathological antipathy to Newton. It is striking that Goethe's *Commentary* on the *Fragment* should place this text with two other scientific works. Besides the work on the jawbone on which Goethe actually comments here, there is the one whose subject matter was revealed to him in Venice on the Lido: "In the year 1790, the origin of the skull from the vertebra was revealed to me in Venice" (p. 49). This is where we met Freud and Goethe for the first time, at the Lido, with Freud contemplating a small skull. Freud had claimed to have followed Fliess's wishes at that time. But he could have just as easily been observing Goethe's injunction and articulated wish in the *Zwischenkieferknochen* essay: "My greatest wish is that my readers may themselves find the opportunity to take the skull in hand" (p. 188).

It will be remembered that Freud, though having fulfilled this wish, was not graced with the revelation of a text at that time. Goethe, on the contrary, "verfolgte nun eifriger die Konstruktion des Typus, diktierte das Schema im Jahre 1795 an Max Jacobi in Jena und hatte bald die Freude von deutschen Naturforschern mich in diesem Fach abgelöst zu sehen."[25] Freud's own scientific revelation—the revelation of his text—will come about exactly one hundred years after Goethe's dictation to Jacobi. This is the moment in which Freud writes these famous words to Fliess: "Do you actually believe that one day one will be able to read on a marble plaque attached to this house: 'Here, on July 24, 1895, the secret of dreams was revealed to Dr. Sigm. Freud?' The chances for this to happen are as of yet very slim." At Freud's later inference that the *Traumdeutung* rose up as an epitaph on his father's tomb, it is difficult to forego mention of the precise grounds of Goethe's discovery, one hundred years earlier. Goethe's servant, Goetze, had recovered the skull from the Jewish cemetery at the Lido and brought it to his master's attention. Thus dawned, through this odd coupling of a god and an idol, a discovery that would long haunt Freud, and whose phantom he had sought at the same site as Goethe.

As for Goethe's text, it is quite conceivable that Freud would have at some point after his school years, or even earlier, read the *Commentary* (*Erläuterung*) which usually accompanies the *Fragment über die Natur*. Or at least he would have known about it from Jacob Bernays, Martha's uncle and noted Goethe scholar who had written, among other things, *Zur Kritik und Geschichte des Goetheschen Textes* (1866). Bernays may have made Freud aware of Goethe's substitution in the *Commentary* of the texts on the *Zwischenknochen* and *Schädel* for the *Fragment*. Even if this were not the case, or Freud had not gathered this information from his own elaborate readings of Goethe, or from the Viennese Goethe Society, by the time he was writing the *Traumdeutung*—and Fliess had written *Die Beziehungen zwischen Nase und weiblichem Geschlechtsorgan,* etc., whose first page refers to the *Morphologie* (containing these texts)—Freud was certainly keenly aware of the import, if only for Goethe, of Goethe's scientific discoveries. But to tell the truth, when you open Freud's copy of the eleventh volume of his *Sophie of Sachsen,* 1893 edition, you see, in the first part, on the first page, the *Natur-Fragment.* And on the second page you see Goethe's disclaimer. A few pages later, you find the essay on the Z w i - s c h e n k i e f e r, where the word is italicized, with spaces like missing teeth. The eleventh volume is titled *Zur Naturwissenschaft.* (This may explain why Freud emphasized having heard and not seen the *Fragment,* although of course he did see and read the volume.) It is then entirely within the realm of Freudian logic to consider the *Fragment on Nature* as somewhat of a screen memory, a *Deckerinnerung* for Goethe's text on the jawbone. Like the son in Kafka's *Judgment,* Freud will try to cover (*decken*) the father's corpus only to witness its monstrous revival in the form of an enlargening organ.

To bring to light some of the components of the rapport between Goethe's scientific discovery and the genesis of Freud, we first note the context of Goethe's scientific pursuits.

Shortly after *Iphigenie,* in 1780, Goethe was tiring of his political duties as *Geheimrat.* He writes to Charlotte von Stein: "Wieviel wohler wäre mir's, wenn ich von dem Streit der politischen Elemente abgesondert, den Wissenschaften und Künsten, wozu ich geboren bin, meinen Geist zuwenden konnte." ("How much better I would feel if I were relieved of the polemics of politics. Then I could turn my thoughts to the sciences and arts—which is what I was made for.") Although this is the time that coincides with his discoveries of *Torquato Tasso* and *Wilhelm Meister*—in short, when he conceives the "classical" period of his poetical career—Goethe, a good six years

before his Italian voyage, considered himself to be born as much a
scientist as a poet; in fact, his letter to von Stein would seem to place
his scientific drive ahead of his poetic aspirations. Curtius for example
notes that "not until his middle period did Goethe discover that he was
actually born to be a writer [of poetic works]." Until as late as 1791,
Goethe was intent on making his mark principally in the sciences and
considered his artistic bent a "wrong tendency." His attitudes toward
his texts are revealing: Goethe was not the least concerned about
losing possession of his copies of *Götz* and *Werther,* but he did everything to hang on to the text of the *"Knöchlein"* and assert its priority.[26]
In a letter to Lavater he asserts that the *Knöchlein* was for him the
fundamental text. Whatever the priorities, this double identity which
Goethe claims for himself cannot have been foreign to Freud, who at
once incorporates and problematizes the painful inevitability of the
double nature, the double genre, indwelling in his own discourse. Thus
Freud writes in the preliminary note to the *Traumdeutung:*

> With the communication of my own dreams it inevitably followed that I
> should have to reveal to the gaze of strangers ["fremden Einblicken"]
> more of the private aspects ["Intimitäten"] of my psychic life than I
> liked, or than is normally necessary for any writer who is a scientist
> ["Naturforscher"] and not a poet. Such was the painful but unavoidable
> task.[27]

The *Naturforscher* is, however, forced into the role not merely of
Poet, but of arch-poet precisely "so that I would not have to renounce
the marshalling of evidence for my psychological conclusions." Yet,
when Freud does make a discovery, the evidence of its truth will
frequently be said to hark from the poets. When, for example, writing
on sexual repression in *Selbstdarstellung,* Freud, in order to found the
nasty theory of infantile sexuality, states: "The results established confirmed what poets and keen observers of human nature had always
maintained." Freud's evidence or "Nature" will often, in such cases,
resemble Goethe and Schiller's idea of nature in their aesthetic writings: a prior poetry. The language of Freud's exposition further recalls
Goethe's language in *Dichtung und Wahrheit* when he explains this, for
example: "Childhood was supposed to be 'innocent' ['unschuldig'],
free from sexual lust, and the struggle with the demon 'sensuality' was
supposed to arise only at the Sturm und Drang period of puberty."
Besides its appeal to the *demon* of sensuality and to the literature of
the Sturm und Drang period from which Goethe's name is indissociable, this passage reads much like a recollection from Goethe's *Selbst-*

darstellung, Dichtung und Wahrheit, in which he explores his own case of "infantile desire" for his sister, (compare the section beginning with "that interest of youth, that awe before the awakening of sensual drives," part II, book 6).

From another point of view, in the third foreword to the *Traumdeutung,* Freud predicts that future editions of his text will require a deeper investigation of the poetic resources on the one hand and scientific depth on the other. In the subsequent forewords, Freud will begin to enmesh the two discourses (if they are indeed two) and refer to scientific material as *Literatur.* Indeed, the book proper begins with the bigeneric heading, "Die wissenschaftliche Literatur der Traumprobleme" ("The scientific literature of dream problems") and the first paragraph of *Traumdeutung* ends conveniently with two words which have occupied us here:

> Having gone thus far, my description will break off, for it will have reached the point where the problem of dreams merges into ["einmündet"] more comprehensive problems, the solution of which must be considered ["*in Angriff genommen,*" lit.: taken in hand] in terms of other material.

The time has indeed come for us to prepare a solution for this material and to adjust the issue of Goethe's attack. The attack, the solution, the mouth, the jaw: do these features properly belong to Freud or Goethe? These features of a common text, of a doubly redoubling identity on both parts—on the part of the scientist and the poet—belonging to neither the one nor the other exclusively, this text begins or ends with the morphology of inaugural discoveries. I shall isolate a few sentences of Goethe's discovery without commentary for the moment:

1. Dieser vorderen Abteilung der oberen Kinnlade ist der Name os intermaxillare gegeben worden. Die Alten kannten schon diesen Knochen und neuerdings ist er besonders merkwürdig geworden. . . .

2. Der Knochen, von welchem ich rede, hat seinen Namen daher erhalten, dass er sich zwischen die beiden Hauptknochen der oberen Kinnlade hineinschiebt. Er ist selbst aus zwei Stücken zusammengesetzt, die in der Mitte des Gesichtes aneinanderstossen.

3. Sein vorderster, breitester und stärkster Teil, dem ich den Namen des Körpers gegeben, ist nach der Art des Futters eingerichtet. . . .

4. Die zweite Sutur, die sich im Nasengrunde zeigt, aus den canalibus naso-palatini herauskommt und bis in der Gegend der conchae infe-

rioris verfolgt werden kann, hat er nicht bemerkt. Hingegen finden sich beide in der grossen Osteologie des Albins auf der Tafel I mit dem Buchstaben *M* bezeichnet.

5. Und so beschliesse ich diesen kleinen Versuch mit dem Wunsche, dass er Kennern und Freunden der Naturlehre nicht missfallen und mir Gelegenheit verschaffen möge, naher mit ihnen verbunden, in dieser reizenden Wissenschaft, soviel es die Umstände erlauben, weitere Fortschritte zu tun.[28]

1. This frontal section of the upper jawbone has been given the name *os intermaxillare*. The Ancients already knew this bone and recently it has become especially noteworthy. . . .

2. The bone of which I am speaking derives its name from the fact that it is placed between the two primary bones of the upper jaw. It is itself composed of two parts which are joined in the center of the face.

3. Its foremost, widest and strongest part, which I call the body [of the bone], is determined according to the type of food intake. . . .

4. The second suture, which is located in the base of the nose, arises from the *Canali naso-palatini* and which can be traced as far as the area of the *Concha inferior,* was not noticed [by Vesalius]. On the other hand, both are found in Albin's great osteology on plate 1, designated by the letter *M.*

5. And so I conclude this small venture with the wish that it might not prove displeasing to connoisseurs and friends of natural philosophy ["Naturlehre"] and that it might accord me the opportunity to be more closely bound to them and, as far as circumstances permit, to make further progress in this enticing ["reizenden"] science.

Thus Goethe makes his contribution to science, a science that cuts as deeply into the Freudian body as one dare imagine. But could Freud himself have imagined this uncanny link—one that privileges the initial *M,* as in Herr M., explores the buccal cavity to fix on the jaw, is preoccupied with modes of food intake (as Freud will have to be for a good part of his life), and insists on naming and renaming the traumatized area—as early, say, as the time of his *Matura*?

I am certainly not the first to connect the name of Fliess with that of his young friend, Fluss, to whom Freud was writing at the time of his exams. Freud was first, as usual, to draw attention to the jarring compatibility of the names of his most vital friends: Fluss, Fleischl, Fliess. Before there was Fliess there was Fluss, and before Fluss (also "river") dissolved into Fliess (also "flowing," "secretion"), there was Fleischl (also "flesh," "meat"). And though we shall have to cut Fleischl out of the picture, his name should resonate in the suture of Fluss and Fliess. The remains of Freud's correspondence with Fluss date from 1872–74. At this time Freud is preparing his *Matura,* reading for the first time Sophocles' *Oedipus Rex* (of which he will be required to translate thirty-three lines), very much taken with Fluss's sister, signing his letters alternately Sigismund and Sigmund Freud, commenting on his exams, deciding on a career and quoting Goethe. At the threshold of maturity (or martyrdom, as Freud says, referring to the *Reifeprüfung,* alias *Matura*), Freud switches processes by substituting the natural for the legal process, abandoning his earlier goal of becoming a lawyer— herein he outdoes Goethe who was obliged by his father to study law at Leipzig. By 1874, he writes a letter of apology to Fluss with the intent of acquitting himself for having missed a rendezvous:

> Es war eine letzte schwächliche Eruption eines vormals mächtigen Kraters, ein letztes Zücken aus einer Gegend meines Leibes, die seit langer Zeit in offenem Aufruhr gegen die Ruhe und Ordnung in meinem Organismus steht—ich meine mein Gebiss. Ich bin in dieser Hinsicht in einem peinlich traurigen Dilemma; lebt der Mensch um zu essen, so lebe ich, um mir die Zähne zu verderben, d.i. an Zahnschmerz zu leiden. . . . mein Leben ist dann mit Notwendigkeit an den Zahnschmerz verknüpft, den ich folglich bei Lebzeiten nicht mehr loswerde—ein ebenso trauriges Schicksal und Ihres Mitleids ebenso würdig. [6. Marz 1874]

> It was the final, feeble eruption of a formerly powerful crater, the last spasm from an area of my body ["Leib"] which, for a long while, has been in open revolt against the peace and order in my organism—I am speaking of my denture ["Gebiss"]. In this respect I'm in an embarrassingly sad dilemma; if man lives in order to eat, then I live in order to ruin my teeth, that is, in order to suffer from toothaches. . . . My life is, then, necessarily bound up with the toothache, of which, it follows, I shall nevermore in my life rid myself—such a sad destiny and as such worthy of your sympathy. [6 March 1874]

Regardless of how witty Freud could be with respect to the seedy neighborhood of his mouth (Freud was also witty when the Gestapo stampeded through his apartment),[29] he was certainly aware of the area in which his body had chosen "openly" and "necessarily" to revolt against him. Perhaps it is unnecessary to trace the itinerary of Freud's pain, or to emphasize the duration of the symptoms that had been forming around the maxillo-buccal region. Nor would it seem necessary at this point to make the connection, as Goethe does in the *Zwischenkiefer* study, between the mouth and nose and, in this connection, to remind anyone of Freud's experiments with cocaine, his

addiction to cigar smoking, nor to mention that Freud had considered
Fliess, at least initially, merely as "a throat, nose and ear specialist."[30]
Officially, Freud's problems begin in 1923, under the diagnostic heading of epithelial cancer, requiring surgical intervention in the form of
the resection on the level of the *maxillaris superioris* (which figures in
Goethe's essay under "Corpus," p. 186). The details of Freud's operation are dreadful enough, and leave one wondering why he had submitted himself to the butchery of a declared enemy without mentioning
the illness or operation to his family. Details of this and subsequent
operations—they were thirty in number—can be found in a recent
clinical report by Dr. Sharon Romm who reconstructs the histopathol-
ogy of Freud's cancer in *The Unwelcome Intruder* (1984) and in Max
Schur's earlier *Freud: Living and Dying* which characteristically begins
with a quote from Goethe.[31] Schur is the physician whose injection
brought Freud his final rest. Suffice it to say that his wife and daughter
found Freud slumped in a chair, bleeding profusely at a run-down
clinic on the wrong side of town. By tragic coincidence, Freud and his
grandson, Heinele, were operated on the buccal cavity at the same
time. The child died on 19 June 1923, leaving Freud as the guilt-ridden
survivor of the double operation.

Schur promotes the hypothesis that Freud likewise had a relationship
of "guilty survivor" to the author of *Die Beziehungen zwischen Nase
und weiblichen Geschlechtsorganen*. Should this be the case, then
Freud's survival, as any survival inevitably does, carries the seed and
afterlife of his own death. In order to place the deposited seed with
some exactitude, however, we might first examine the opening and
closure of the *Traumdeutung*. While giving birth to psychoanalysis as a
discipline, this work will also leave a residue of traces indicating
Freud's future disease, whose localization—the *maxilla* or *Kinnlade*—
Goethe studied in the double and phantom of the *Fragment über die
Natur*. The originary moment of the *Traumdeutung*'s genesis could
thus be interpreted by means of a dream containing a foreboding or
premonition of the disease. But what position does psychoanalysis take
toward such dream-contents? The closure of the *Traumdeutung*, its
Lösung or solution, appear to have foreseen and foretold all the modalities of this question:

> Und der Wert des Traumes fur die Kenntnis der Zukunft? Daran ist
> natürlich nicht zu denken.

> And the value of dreams for supplying an awareness of the future?
> Naturally, one cannot think of such a thing.

Naturally, Freud estimates, this value is not thinkable. Then why does Freud think the unthinkable at the end of his thought? And why does he continue to think the unthinkable to the end? The slight hedging with which Freud initially proceeds to un-think the unthinkable should not escape us:

> Man möchte dafür einsetzen: Kenntnis der Vergangenheit. Denn aus der Vergangenheit stammt der Traum in jedem Sinne.

> One might say instead: they supply an awareness of the past. For dreams are derived from the past in every sense.

The dream descends from the past *in every sense.* Yet Freud does not show himself averse to adding this qualification, at once timid and assertive:

> Zwar entbehrt auch der alte Glaube, dass der Traum uns die Zukunft zeigt, nicht völlig des Gehalts an Wahrheit. Indem uns der Traum einen Wunsch als erfüllt vorstellt, führt er uns allerdings in die Zukunft; aber diese vom Träumer fur gegenwärtig genommene Zukunft ist durch den unzerstörbaren Wunsch zum Ebenbild jener Vergangenheit gestaltet.

> Nevertheless the ancient belief that dreams foretell the future is not wholly devoid of truth. By picturing our wishes as fulfilled, dreams are after all leading us into the future. But this future, which the dreamer represents as the present, has been molded by his indestructible wish into a perfect likeness of the past.

Freud thus makes provisions for the futural dimension of dream to flash before us, but only within a horizon circumscribed by a repeatable past. Nonetheless, this movement which blends the future into the past does admit, however cautiously, a certain filtration of the future or fortune-telling elements of dream. This ambivalence, it has been shown, hovers on the frontier between science and its others, be these poetry, superstition or telepathy.[32]

At this frontier and time, it makes sense to conclude our interpretation of Herr M.'s dream; to that end, it seems indeed necessary to take into account the possibility that the last page of the *Traumdeutung* leaves open. To proceed in the manner of Freud himself, we might first reassemble some of the fragments that make up the dream-content. In this dream, Goethe violently submits Freud to an operation both critical and surgical in nature. Freud identifies one of the instigators of the dream as the eighteen-year-old who had read Goethe's *Fragment.* Another source is given as Freud's own reception of this

Fragment, which he remembers as having taken place at a critical point in his development. Let us reconstruct the events.

At the age of eighteen, Freud is in the process of choosing a career. During this period he recognizes the first manifestations of pain on the inside of his mouth, whose development he anticipated in a letter to Fluss. At this point he is incited by a public reading of Goethe's *Fragment* to opt for a career in the natural sciences; Goethe's text is thus perceived by Freud as the seed from which his future discoveries will be engendered. This is also the age in which Freud decides on the variations around the *mund* of his first name. About twenty years later, while writing his magnum opus, Freud faces another decisive step in his career in which Goethe once again makes an altogether striking appearance. Freud begins openly to attach a good deal of anxiety to Goethe's name. In the first place, Freud, troubled by his double nature of scientist and poet, also dreams of a discovery at the Lido that might respond to Goethe's injunction or in some way satisfy his demand. He develops a theory of dream that retains the imprint of necessary fragmentation and germinates precisely in his analysis of Goethe's attack. The disappointment he experiences in his scientific career reflects to a large extent the sorrows of Goethe in the same field. Freud is at loose ends over the fortune-telling aspects of the dream.

As for Goethe, his intervention in the history of psychoanalysis proves to be as painful as it is paradoxical. The violence of his attack appears to be linked to an act of mutilation and even to the self-mutilation of the patient with whom Freud is associated. To the multiple determinations that make Goethe's attack intelligible we can add the possibility of reading Freud's recollection of the *Fragment on Nature* as a screen memory behind which another essay on nature, written at the same time as the *Fragment* and to which Goethe attached the highest value, can be discerned. This would be the essay in which Goethe names and treats the *Zwischenkiefer* of the upper maxillary. If Goethe should then appear to Freud as an unappeasable phantom, this is not only due to the double trajectory that his genius had forecast—the same could have been said of Leonardo da Vinci—but also, most cruelly, because Goethe had put his finger on Freud's indelible wound, placing the affected area under the sign of his victim in Freud's dream (*M*). When Goethe delivers his sentence, he pronounces with equal gravity his support and condemnation of Freud. But he will also try to abandon Freud to his lot by refusing to underwrite the text which, according to Freud, he had sired: indeed, Goethe has withdrawn his signature from the founding text on which Freud and Psychoanalysis counted so heavily.

In this somber light, one could read the *Traumdeutung* according to the terms retrospectively suggested by Freud himself, as an epitaph for a father whose irremediable loss gives rise to desperate calculations but who nevertheless continues to infest Freud's text and body, where he has deposited the seed of death. This is where Fliess comes in, for he will have made explicit the synonymity of Goethe with catastrophe and death as early as the dream of neurotic impotence, for example, when he sent Freud to seek Goethe's "light" on the Lido. However, it should suffice to remain within the context created by the dream of Herr M., where Fliess is shown in the light of his speculations, which turn out to be as "mortifying" as the dream of the Lido: Freud identifies the book under heavy attack by Goethe as the one dealing with Goethe's *Sterbejahr*. According to Fliess's calculations of the same genre, Freud was to die in 1907. The chronological data with which Fliess computes Goethe's life span will thus provide the grounds for legitimating his sentencing Freud to death. Despite Fliess's sadistic statistics, Freud and Goethe will have had the same *Lebensdauer*. But if Fliess and Goethe do cooperate in any way, it is largely by setting the mortality timer for Freud. Under the circumstances, Freud will have to stave off Fliess's as well as Goethe's frontal attacks, and he will have to screen himself and his text from their acts of mutilation.[33]

For Freud, then, Goethe intervenes as the name of the *Sterbejahr,* as the instance from which the deadline must be calculated. This is as true of the dream in which Goethe attacks him as it is of the one in which a taximeter imperturbably reminds Freud that the time for settling accounts is nearing. For us, too, the stakes are high and the calculations difficult, all too difficult. In order to appreciate them, one has to renounce safeguarding or even saving the text from the pressure exerted by a question of timing and, perhaps necessarily, of bad timing. The question involves knowing at which point calculations must begin in order to account for the apparition of a syndrome, a complex, or even of what we call a cancer.

Anaesthetics

If the operation to which Freud has been submitted is too dreadful because too real (in the sense of being disruptive of certain imaginary and symbolic modes in critical perception), and if Goethe has been brought in to give his light to Freud's unspeakable afflictions, it is because the proliferation of Freud's disease cannot be stopped—

certainly not with Goethe, where things began to split. Nor can the fragile opening from which Freud's growth issues be blocked or silenced. This opening of many names speaks to us in different voices. One is the *Traumdeutung* itself, on whose inner limits scattered references to Freud's future disease mercilessly proliferate.

Consider for instance Freud's demonstration of the "Dream as Wish Fulfillment" in chapter III, where he devotes merely three sentences to interpreting a dream about the opera. He tells of the circumstances surrounding a certain patient's dream. This patient had just undergone an unsuccessful operation of the jaw ("einer ungünstig verlaufenen Kieferoperation"), and had acquired the habit of throwing her cooling apparatus ("Kühlapparat") on the floor. Freud is called in by her doctors to bring this woman to her senses. He dutifully reproaches her for her poor behavior, but she explains that this time she had thrown away her apparatus as the consequence of a dream. In the dream she found herself sitting in a loge at the opera and showing lively interest in the performance ("in einer Loge in der Oper und interessierte mich lebhaft für die Vorstellung"). A certain Herr Meyer, whom the woman knew only remotely, appeared to her in the dream. He was in a sanitorium, and his mouth was causing him great pain. Obviously, this man was in need of her postoperative apparatus. She had therefore thrown it away in her sleep, so that this Herr M. could make proper use of it. Freud translates this dream by staying in the vicinity of the mouth, without however marking the proximity of his analytical language to the dream-content: it "sounds like an exposition of a manner of speech ["klingt wie eine Darstellung einer Redensart"] which presses forth from the lips in an uneasy situation ["die sich in einer unangenehmen Lage über die Lippen drängt," is driven from the lips—as the apparatus was]: I really can think of greater pleasures [than keeping this thing on my mouth]. The dream points to this greater pleasure, that is, attending the opera ("Ich wusste mir wirklich ein besseres Vergnügen"). But does this dream really expose no greater logic than that of "greater pleasure"?

For heuristic purposes, Freud limits his concern to demonstrating "disguised wish fulfillments" ("Verkleidete Wünscherfüllungen," the title of this section), but in so doing he wraps up a three-sentence interpretation in a disguise, in the trappings of wish fulfillment. Freud could certainly think of greater pleasures than granting this dream the interpretive investment or rigorous dismantling which it appears to invite. He shuts the woman's mouth quickly, closing on the third cadence—as if anticipating the trismus (increasing difficulty in opening the jaws) from which he would greatly suffer. The cipher *three* figures importantly in Freud, as in the Oedipal triangle, to be sure, or in notions of "Thirdness" subsequently elaborated by Lacan and his various triangular mathemes. However, *three* as a limiting concept also tends to function as a referential calculus of Freud's disease or, more generally, of an incomputable probability.

But what in its most easily reducible form does the dream tell? In the first place chapter three's woman was feeling no pain; she found herself in a private box at the opera, feeling especially alive during the performance, "showing a lively interest." It seems very likely that the dream translates a matter of life and death. The woman, as we know, had recently been under anaesthesia (i.e., feeling no pain) in an operating theater; the interest she showed in what was performed upon her was no doubt "lively." The two shows—the incapacitated, mute show ("the woman showed . . . ") and the performance for which her body became the site—were, so to speak, live, staged on the terms of recovery. Watching this operation from a condition of partial encasement, she was also in some way departing. The operation took place in a *Loge,* which Freud translates without apparent pause into "uncomfortable *Lagen,*" meaning, in his usage, "situation," but which also prepares the ground for the past tense of "to lie down," as in "we laid" (*wir lagen*). *Loge* is chained as well to the archaic form, *Löge,* which in modern German is *Lüge,* the lie. Here is what my dream scanner shows: the operation was a lie, a failure; the victim—*Opfer* reinscribes *Oper*—was feeling no pain, though she was vividly aware of the representation (*Vorstellung*) before her. She could now dispense with her apparatus; from her private box, silenced and insensible, she would no longer have any need for it. Instead, she passes it on to Herr M. Years later, Freud allegedly attempts to do away with his own apparatus in a similar manner.

Following the opera or operation, following the scene in the *Loge*—the phallic "L" once again slipping in and out of a woman's mouth, the logic of which Freud locates in a manner of speech—an illusion is dislodged. There may be no beyond the pleasure principle for her, the dream erases the memory of future painlessness. Freud does not care to dwell on pain (as in the famous Irma analysis). His own problems had been settled long ago in a letter to Fluss; he remains silent in the silhouetted face of his destiny, or before the pain which issues from the mouth—for example, from an unsuccessful operation of the jaw.[34]

But a botched operation also implies a botched interpretative oeuvre, which is perhaps why the operative principle in Freud's wish fulfillment would be to keep apart the opera as operation and the opera as oeuvre. He, for one, knew of greater pleasures in his work than to look into the mouth of the opera and to inspect its loggia, its great jaw. This was precisely where the woman was cornered after her unsuccessful operation, when she threw her apparatus away in favor of another representation. Freud, too, dispenses with his analytical apparatus in favor of a different type of representation or exposition for this dream. We now leave the loggia of the opera for another great hall in which the *Apparat* dissolves into a most peculiar *Präparat*.

Analyzing with a Hammer: Irma

While the *Traumdeutung* closes with the hypothesis that illuminated our way through the cavernous premises of a "wish fulfillment" dream, it opens with a mutilated entry about another dream—another mouth or cavity which communicates in a vital sense with the female cavity. At the end of the opening dream and commentary, Freud writes: "I have now ended the [I]nterpretation of [D]reams ['ich habe nun die Traumdeutung vollendet']." This opening will therefore also have been a closure, and will continue to open and close like one of the mouths it investigates.[35] Freud himself calls this opening a *Mustertraum* (model or exemplary dream; *S.E.:* specimen dream). It is a monstrous dream, impregnated with the future and marked with the agonies of guilt and birth: *natura*. It is the dream whose inscription Fliess is known to have mutilated. But the mutilation is multifaceted. Fliess certainly compelled Freud to excise substantial portions of the dream for publication purposes; he had also received Freud's patient whose name appears in the entry as "Irma," but whose actual name was, it now appears, "Hammerschlag." Freud's substitution of *Ir* for what it conceals would be a story in itself—one which he only intimates at several junctures of his commentary, for example, when writing of diagnostic error (*Irrtum der Diagnose*, pp. 114, 119). The story of the maltreatment to which Fliess subjected Irma is no longer a secret: Freud had referred Irma to Fliess, who then operated on her nose, on the bone. In the course of the operation, Fliess had inserted a tampon in Irma's nose, which he later forgot to remove. As a consequence, Irma was afflicted with a serious infection which almost cost her (and Freud) her life. This, then, is the story of Irma's infection which Freud, however, calls Irma's injection. To Freud's dismay and astonishment, Fliess was cavalier about his error and failed to see the need for Freud's fuss over the matter.

Fliess's double mutilation of the Irma episode returns to Freud's pages as the hind-thought (*Hintergedanken*) of the event (*Vorgang im Traum,* also "operation" of the dream). Let us retain the *Vor-gang* here, for everything takes place behind the preface (*Vorbericht*)—behind the hall, the passage, the colonnade of a Belle Vue or a canal. By now we are removed from the canals of Venezia drifting toward another topography of the canal on whose bridge the nose, with its extension into the buccal cavity, very literally continues to perceive the trail of Goethe.

Now the dream narrated as Irma's injection takes place in a large cavity, "eine grosse Halle," a type of vestibule where Freud or rather "we" are receiving many guests, among whom (*unter ihnen,* under whom) Irma is soon sighted. Freud receives Irma and the others. His word for this reception is *empfangen,* whose other strong meaning in German is "to conceive, become pregnant." Irma, as we later discover, is a young widow; in the commentary Freud will substitute his wife for Irma, without however linking up the obvious: Freud is treating a young widow, maybe his own wife, on the event of his wife's birthday (*Analyse,* p. 113). The reception takes place, according to the commentary, in some great hall resembling Freud's summer residence, Belle Vue. But what is the *belle vue* which Freud cites in a dream connecting his wife's birthday with Irma's injection? He tells us in so many ways, without ever saying so. The first motive assigned to the dream is that he wanted to respond orally to Irma's letter. His response takes the form of reproaches (*Vorwürfe*), for Irma has not yet accepted his "solution" ("*Lösung*" is placed in quotation marks)—or, since Freud himself lifts the word out of its comfortable context, the young widow has not yet accepted his "unravelling," "dénouement" ("*Lösung*").

Freud's principal gesture consists in taking the young woman aside to tell her, "If you are still in pain, then it's really only your own fault ['Schuld,' guilt, debt]." *Lösung* also means redemption, ransom; Irma has not yet accepted his ransom, which is why she is at fault and strangely in debt. She replies in the dream, "If only you knew the pain I am suffering in my throat, stomach, womb ['Leib,' also 'body']; it's choking me ['zusammenschnüren,' to lace or tie up, to wring]." Freud is frightened by this profession of pain: "I think, in the end I have overlooked something of an organic nature" ("ich denke, am Ende übersehe ich da doch etwas Organisches," I am overlooking something organic). Wanting to redeem himself from the charge of oversight, he takes Irma into custody and looks. Freud now escorts the young widow to the window and actually looks into her throat. "At this, she shows some resistance, as do women who wear prosthetic devices ['wie Frauen, die ein künstliches Gebiss tragen']. I think, she does not need it, however." Freud, who will himself wear and endure a prosthesis as a consequence of his cancer, thinks to himself that this young widow— also his wife—does not need art or artifice (*künstlich*).

In the commentary that follows, he does explain the dream as having something to do with his own health; but when localizing the trauma- tized area, he places or displaces the pain to his own shoulder, which is frequently cramped after long writing sessions. In the dream, however, "the mouth then opens easily" (*"der Mund geht dann gut auf"*), per- mitting him to discover, on the right side, a large spot, and elsewhere he also spots scab formations "upon some remarkably curly structures which were evidently modelled on the turbinal bones of the nose." He immediately calls over another guest, Dr. M., who, pale and limping, joins the couple to concur with Freud's opinion: they are undoubtedly faced with an infection. Dr. M., by the way, is "beardless along the chin" ("ist am Kinn bartlos"), as Freud might have been without his ineffaceable wound. They both are aware that Irma had recently re- ceived an injection of *"Propylpräparat . . . Propyl,"* etc. The needle with which the injection had been administered was also probably unclean, impure ("Wahrscheinlich war auch diese Spritze nicht rein").

It may be recalled that when Lacan analyzed this dream, he applied the tripartite formula for propyl to the three women whom Freud names in the commentary. Speaking of this "vraie tête de Meduse," he recognizes at the base of the throat "l'abîme de l'organe feminin d'où sort toute vie," and so forth,[36] which is one way of looking at it— though the dream can be said to take other turns as well, and particu- larly since Freud insists on a kind of dildo-logic, anxiously surveying something that is not entirely there, not entirely male or female ("like women who need an artificial prosthesis"), being insertable, detach- able, something that he can impute to an unknown future.

When analyzing the dream, Freud merely attaches a footnote to the passage dealing with Irma's mouth:

> I suspect ["ahnen," to have a presentiment or premonition] that the interpretation of this piece ["Stück"] of the dream has not been car- ried far enough in order to pursue the whole of its hidden meaning ["Sinn"]. . . . Each dream has at least one spot at which it is unfath- omable ["unergründlich"]—a navel, as it were, that is its point of contact with the unknown.

This note of presentiment could not have found a more ominous opening. Nonetheless, Freud does make his allowances and concedes that the dream may have some bearing on the future in terms of wish fulfillment. With respect to this dream he, however, announces its result thus: "that I am not guilty" ("Das Ergebnis des Traumes ist nämlich, dass ich nicht schuldig bin"). So it seems that on one level the result and resolve of the dream eliminates the premonition of the future. On one level, that is.

The *Muster* or monster dream requires Freud to peer at formations taking shape on the right side of the mouth, proximate to the maxillary, and to localize his sense of guilt and the name which he attaches to that guilt in the mouth, the *Mund*. At this juncture we recall that German provides other names for designating the area of the jaw and mouth, namely *Rachen* and *Schlund*. *Rachen* means "yawning abyss" as well as "throat," "jaws," "cavity of the mouth"; *Schlund* means "pharynx," "throat," "esophagus," as well as "gorge," "abyss," "crater" (compare Freud's letter to Fluss on "crater"). The dream, as Freud repeatedly asserts, is not limited to the inspection of Irma's cavity, but allows him to exercise his vengeance (*Rache*) and to expiate his guilt (*Schuld*). Everything in the dream points to the conjunction of this threesome which designates the area of future devastation, including the tripartite formula, Trimethylamin.

Now, in the analysis of the dream, Freud claims that he has been exercising a double revenge, the one against his friend who had given him an odiously smelling liquor and the other against Irma, the disobedient patient with whom he identifies his wife as well as his daughter, Mathilde. The word he uses to designate "disobedient" is *unfolgsamen,* and can be broken down into *unfolg-samen:* the semen that does not follow. We know that Freud's reference to his wife does not limit itself to the event of her birthday, but includes the fact of her present, unwanted pregnancy—that is, unwanted by Freud. Thus, we approach the abyssal moment of the dream whose cavity is conceived not only as mouth and nose, but as the womb and its unwanted secretions: we are before two horrors of future engenderment, consigned to the cavities of the nasal-palatal region and the womb. And right now Fliess's nasal secretions also preoccupy Freud—Fliess who, as Freud reminds us (p. 122), had opened up (*eröffnet*) the terrain, upon which those secret relationships between the nose and the female organs take form. As Freud does not remind us, Fliess's book holds birth and abortion to amount to the same phenomenon. Fliess could have caused Freud discomfort on yet another count, for it is he, Freud's "first public" and "highest judge," whose censorial injection into Freud's dream left Freud with the consequences of impurity—the impure stylus—on the threshold of Freud's first substantial work of maturity. The preparation of this work, as of the propyl injection, had been submitted to Fliess's judgment. With this injection, we are introduced into the bottomless moment, the omphalos in Freud's analysis, which begins: "with a preparation of propyl . . . propylen ['Mit einem Propylpräparat . . . Propylen'] . . . How did I ever get to that? ['Wie komm ich nur dazu?']"

Led by the Nose

On the same evening as the dream, Mrs. Freud had opened a bottle of liqueur whose label read *Ananas* (pineapple). And now we come to the third part of Fliess's intervention or title. This Fliess, who initially was no more than an ear-nose-throat doctor, secretes from yet another cavity, that of the ear, which will now communicate with the mouth and nose, as Freud begins to trace an oto-erotic zone. The liqueur had been given to the Freuds by their friend, Otto. This gift of *Ananas,* Freud suggests in a footnote, should not be read entirely innocently; for one thing, "it incidentally contains a remarkable echo ['Anklang'] of Irma's family name" (p. 120). Because Freud asks his readers to attune their ears to the resonances of this remarkable word, he can be overheard also to quietly announce that he has been leading us by the nose: in spoken language, *Ananas* resonates homonymically with *an der Nase* (*an-der Nas*), as in *an der Nase führen* (to lead by the nose; to lead astray). Or perhaps Freud himself is being led by the nose, by Irma, by Fliess, by his pregnant wife, and now by Otto. Otto's liqueur produced a strong smell of fusel oil, thus inducing Freud neither to taste nor "pay for" it (*kosten,* to taste, to cost). Otto is always giving things away and Freud hopes that someday a woman will cure him of his habit. In any case, Freud will not smell, let alone taste or support this man's offering. But it will offer a key for the interpretation of the dream. Freud had substituted *Propyl* for *Amyl,* the scent of the *Ananas:* "I certainly undertook a substitution; I dreamt *Propyl* after I had smelled *Amyl,* but such substitutions are perhaps only admitted in organic chemistry." Organic chemistry indeed.

In pathology, amyloid degeneration is a change of structure by which amyloid is formed and deposited in the tissue or organ affected. This is the albuminoid developed in diseased degeneration of various animal organs. In botany, albumen is the substance that surrounds the embryo in many seeds; it is also, for instance, the white of an egg. Albumen is thus the endosperm or perisperm. Freud himself mentions albumen, or egg white, but in the context of a sinister joke prompted by Dr. M. and a colleague. These two doctors visit a gravely ill patient, at which occasion Dr. M. feels called upon to play a diagnostic joke. Dr. M. tells his colleague that he has found egg white in the patient's urine. But the colleague would not be led astray ("liess sich aber nicht irre-machen," p. 120) and responded calmly: "That doesn't matter, Herr Colleague, the egg white will be expelled! ['ausscheiden,' eliminated]." Freud cites this example to expose his scorn for colleagues ignorant of hysteria, and explains that it had worked itself into his dream in the form of the guest whom he consults when looking inside Irma's mouth. But whether we are speaking of urine or sperm, it all comes down to the discharge of the male organ contaminated with properties of the female organ—something Freud does not say. This discharge will contain something like albumen, covering the egg, which, as Freud remembers, can be eliminated or, we might add, removed, from the vagina, the limit (*Scheide*). In his dream and commentary, then, Freud eliminates (or represses) the amyloid or the diseased organ and the prospect of birth to replace them with another type of birth, bringing to light another type of child. This is the dream of the double birth of the *Traumdeutung*, the dream of Irma's injection that will engender the exemplary and initiating dream-text after which the *Traumdeutung* will have reached fruition, "completion." And it is Irma, formerly Emma, who, on the event of his wife's birthday and Freud's *Sterbe-jahr*—for Irma is a young widow—will act as midwife and wet nurse to the dream of dreams, the story of the semen that did not follow. Others have already mentioned the inversion of Emma which produced *Amme*, midwife and wet nurse, while elucidating Freud's marked attachment to his own wet nurse.[37] We are back at the scene of Goethe's double birth and of Freud's repression of Textor, who had intervened in the education of the *Heb-amme*, the female figure of *Aufhebung*—the wet nurse who lifts the (stillborn) child into existence. Let this scene be projected on a backdrop while we continue to pursue Freud's *Amme*, who brings the *Traumdeutung* into this world.

Freud receives and conceives Irma or *Irrmama* at the threshold of the third part of his book. But according to his description, Irma is received and conceived in a *grosse Halle*. As vestibule or cavity, as architectural or anatomical structure, *Halle* is never quite inside nor outside the body, quite like a mouth or vagina. Nor is the narration of

Irma's injection qua dream either quite inside the body of the *Traum-deutung* or part of the somewhat external, preparatory pages that lead into the analysis of dreams. In fact, the Irma dream, while making up the last part of *Die Methode der Traumdeutung* with its principal emphasis on methodology, and while holding the rank of Freud's *Muster-traum,* somehow introduces or introjects, without entirely belonging to, the subsequent chapters demonstrating the varieties of dream and dream-analyses. At once the threshold and the completion of the *Traumdeutung,* it arrives before the interpretation of dreams actually begins; it neither belongs to the history that precedes the *Interpreta-tion,* nor does it take part in the section devoted to *Dream.* It begins as a *Vorbericht* (preliminary report or preface), in which we learn that Freud had begun to dream his great vestibule as a *correspondance manquée:* his dream will have been, within the dream, the response to Irma's unanswered and perhaps unanswerable letter. And before it begins as a *Vorbericht,* Freud is citing a letter from the "great philoso-pher-poet, Fr. Schiller."

I shall cite Freud's citation in its entirety, not only because it insists on the architecture of creation, on holding down the *fort,* as it were, and guarding the doors—the *Tore*—but also because this is how Freud has chosen to have the portals to his text guarded. The guardian will not be the grandson of Textor, and with good reason, but the post will be relegated to his great friend, the *philosopher*-poet, whose corre-spondence with Goethe makes up one of the noblest interpretations of German Idealism:

> The ground for your complaint seems to me to lie in the constraint imposed by your reason upon your imagination. I will make my idea ["Gedanken"] more concrete by a simile. It seems a bad thing and detrimental to the creative work of the mind if Reason ["Verstand"] makes too close an examination of the ideas as they come pouring in—at the very gateway, as it were ["an den Toren schon"]. Looked at in isolation, a thought may seem very trivial or very fantastic; but it may be made important by another thought that comes after it, and, in conjunction with other thoughts that may seem equally absurd, it may turn out to form a most efficient link. Reason cannot form any opinion upon this unless it retains the thought long enough to look at it in connection with the others. On the other hand, where there is a creative mind, Reason—so it seems to me—withdraws its guards from the por-tals, and the ideas rush in pell-mell, and only then does it look them through and examine them in mass.—You critics, or whatever else you may call yourselves, are ashamed or frightened of the momentary and transient extravagances which are to be found in all truly creative minds and whose longer or shorter duration distinguishes the thinking artist

from the dreamer. You complain of your unfruitfulness because you reject too soon and discriminate too severely.

1 December 1788
[S.E., 103]

"And nonetheless," Freud adds and repeats "such a 'withdrawal of the guard from the portals of Reason' as Schiller calls it, is by no means that difficult." Freud generally appeals to Schiller, the philosopher, the poet, for encouragement and approbation. Schiller's correspondent, the scientist, the poet, who in a certain sense is also Freud's correspondent, invariably arrives on the scene to judge and attack.

Double Danger

Though this era precedes their deep friendship, Goethe is very present in the letters Schiller wrote around December 1788. Since Freud was leafing through Schiller's correspondence with Körner, we might do well to follow his cue with the aim of establishing a more telling context for the letters written around that time. On 14 November 1788, Schiller writes of his hope that "Goethe would be the third man" in a project linking Wieland and himself. At the time, Schiller is also seeking an appointment as professor of history at Jena; he is counting on Goethe's help, but with a good deal of reserve. By December, Schiller is in Goethe's debt, and shows himself susceptible to feelings of hostility (and admiration) for the great creditor. His letter to Körner of 24 December discloses a plausible motive for Schiller's ressentiment: "Goethe lives from the revenues of his large capital, which seems to be in such solid standing that no external contingency or scarcity could cause him any concern over its decrease."[38] A year later, we find a letter the complement and inversion of which Freud published. Here Körner adopts the role of cheerleader, encouraging Schiller on the subject of genius:

> I cannot entirely subscribe to the comparison you made between your-self and Goethe . . . I greatly doubt that Goethe has more genius than you. He may have more technical skill ["Kunstfertigkeit"] in some fields, however; and you can gain on his advantage ["und in diesem Vorzug kannst du ihm abgewinnen"], even in the dramatic field.

Since Freud has cited at such length Schiller's reassuring anatomy of inspiration, let me add here Schiller's response to Körner:

I have to laugh. . . . This person, this Goethe, is just in my way; and he
so often reminds me that fate has treated me harshly. How easily was
his genius carried by fate, and how, until this very minute, must *I* still
fight! [9 March 1789]

The philosopher-poet provisionally sounding and signing off on the
scientist-poet; civilization had its discontent.

These are the letters to which Freud refers us at the portal of the
Irma dream. They were written, for the most part, while Goethe was
in Italy. At the time Goethe was happily sending off letters that begin
like this: "This week was full of diligent activity. Anatomy and perspective are advancing, even if one always hopes to do more than one
really does" (to Charlotte von Stein, Rome, 19 January 1788). Later,
years later, in another letter Goethe responds to Schiller's letter to
Körner of March 1789, telepathically, as if it were Goethe's task, and
only his, to clear the passageway. Making Schiller his own, appropriating Schiller in his own way, Goethe designates the path which he had,
according to Schiller, obstructed:

> The greater part of your letter not only contains my thoughts and
> convictions, but the letter also develops them in a manner that I myself
> would hardly have done. The designation of the two paths that our
> investigation has taken, the warning before the double danger that be-
> falls one when an example is derived from a portrait, the consequences
> thereof, and even the words and expression is of the kind that I could
> have signed. . . .

Then, as if he were preparing to enter with Schiller the Propylaeum of
which so much would be said and written, Goethe adds:

> Since we both admit that we do not yet know in a clear and determined
> fashion that which we have discussed, but that we are rather search-
> ing. . . . Leonardo da Vinci begins his work on the plastic arts with
> these singular words: when a pupil has perfected himself in perspective
> and anatomy, then he may seek out a master.

By 6 January 1798, Goethe will be grateful to Schiller, for "you have
brought me a second youth, and you have remade me into a writer
["Dichter"], which I had as good as given up."

We have passed the threshold of friendship and knowledge which
began as an exchange of letters—and, on Goethe's part, somewhat of
an exchange of Charlotte von Stein for Schiller. They are inventing a
third man, the couple seeks a master by way of Leonardo; they launch

the *Briefwechsel* to which Freud responds in the *Traumdeutung*. Freud is to meet them at the Propylaeum.

The Meeting Place

To find the way to the underbelly of the *Propyl*-solution in the text of Irma, I propose that we enter with Freud the great *Halle* on the occasion of another birthday and letter which, on the face of it, is an *open* letter, a kind of carte postale, reinscribing the earlier thematics of an Italian voyage along the lines of finality and powerlessness: "My powers of production are at an end," Freud begins, ending: "I myself have grown old and stand in need of forbearance and can travel no more." Nonetheless, Freud is still Goethe-bound.

The letter, written in January 1936, is occasioned by Romain Rolland's birthday. Freud's title: "A Disturbance of Memory on the Acropolis." To his French correspondent Freud explains that he and his youngest brother would normally vacation together in the late summer. In 1904, when Alexander and Sigmund Freud visited Trieste, they were presented with the long-desired prospect of spending some time in Athens—three days, to be exact. As the certitude of seeing the Acropolis increases, they inexplicably find themselves in "remarkably depressed spirits." The entire letter is taken up with investigating the causes of this depression. Freud's text proves rich in allusion to French terms such as *déjà vu, fausse reconnaissance, déjà raconté,* and so on: yet he has difficulty determining why he would be *triste* at Trieste. The sense of *déjà raconté* which he mentions may not appear to join up with the name of Goethe per se, but Freud does illustrate the sensation of encroaching joy and present sorrow as "an example of the incredulity that arises so often when we are surprised by a good piece of news, when we hear we have won a prize, for instance" (S. E. XXII, p. 242). This would comprise the only apparent allusion to "Goethe."[39] For although Freud was repeatedly nominated for the Nobel Prize in literature, of all things, the only award of considerable prestige that would ever be granted to him was the Goethe-Prize in Frankfurt, just three years before his books were burned in Berlin. Freud writes of the "too good to be true" effect of this visit and of the disbelief associated with hope that one would live long enough actually to view the Acropolis. The sense of a double consciousness or split personality, of guilt and inferiority assails him as he reconnoiters the Greek military ensemble. He describes this as

the experience of derealization which emerges as a sort of propylaeum of defense for the ego:

> It will be enough for my purposes if I return to two general characteris-
> tics of the phenomena of derealization. The first is that they all serve
> the purpose of defense; they aim at keeping something away from the
> ego, at disavowing it. Now, new elements, which may give occasion for
> defensive measures, approach the ego from two directions—from the
> real external world and from the internal world of thoughts and im-
> pulses that emerge in the ego. [p. 245]

In order to urge the point, Freud cites the lament of the Spanish
Moors *Ay de mi Alhama,* which tells how King Biabdil received letters
(*cartas*) announcing the fall of his city, Alhama: "he determines to
treat the news as *non arrivé*: the King threw the letters in the fire and
killed the messenger." In so doing, "he was still trying to show his
absolute power." This passage suggests itself as an allegorical reading
for the genesis of the Irma dream, insofar as the dream is said to arise
from Freud's concern about the relativization of his power (*Autorität*)
and from his anger toward the messenger, Otto, who informs Freud of
Irma's fallen state (*Vorbericht*). But the messenger is somehow
adopted by the unconscious; thus only the dream itself secures a certain fictional "arrival of the message"—in fact, it begins, we may recall, as a compensatory form of epistolary exchange.

When he himself arrives at his troubling destination in Athens, Freud
is in awe of the fact "that I should have come such a long way." For
when he was a mere schoolboy "the limitations and poverty of our conditions" appeared to preclude the possibility of his ever travelling this
far. Freud remembers that he "might that day on the Acropolis have
said to my brother 'and now here we are in Athens, and standing on the
Acropolis! We really *have* come a long way!' " He also remembers that
just as he was about to be crowned Emperor, Napoleon remarked to his
brother at the threshold of Notre Dame, "What would Monsieur notre
Père have said to this, if he could have been here today?"

Past this apt comparison, Freud arrives at a solution for

> the little problem of why it was already at Trieste [that] we interfered
> with our enjoyment of the voyage to Athens. It must be that a sense of
> guilt was attached to the satisfaction of having come such a long way:
> there was something about it that was wrong, that from the earliest
> times had been forbidden. . . . It seems as though the essence of suc-
> cess was to have got further than one's father, and as though to excel
> one's father was still something forbidden. . . . The very theme of
> Athens and the Acropolis in itself contained evidence of the son's supe-
> riority. [p. 247]

It should be remembered, however, that his father "had been in business, he had had no secondary education, and Athens could not have meant much to him." Thus moved by filial distance Freud names the symptom "filial piety."

One can hardly wish to engage Freud in a debate on a subject so properly his own. But it does seem odd that he would not have had occasion to feel such pangs of filial piety prior to Athens, say, in Venice or Rome or even in America, where he was honored by no less an institution than the university. As for the father in question, it seems reasonable to suppose that Freud had excelled him considerably just by travelling to Berlin, for example, or simply by crossing the Vienna streets over to the Rathausstrasse and opening his practice with the title of Herr Doktor Freud. It seems that Freud had already crossed the paternal threshold long ago, when receiving his Matura, for instance, which he had already termed, at that time, his "Martyr."

Perhaps the single other figure who had reason to stir in Freud a feeling of deep filial piety was Goethe. Of course, the closest he ever came to Athens was through Lord Byron's catastrophic voyage to Greece. Goethe knew about Greek art, of which he wrote imposingly, mostly through literature—Winckelmann would be a prime example—and through his friends Mayer and Moritz. Thus beyond or along with his own father, Freud was no doubt excelling another, very powerful Monsieur notre Père, the one who had been his judge and aggressor since at least the time of his Matura. Indeed, Goethe may have recalled to Freud, as he was standing before the Acropolis, the name of Napoleon which, at least on that side of the Rhine, was culturally entwined with that of Goethe, whom the emperor met privately in 1808.[40] Perhaps, too, the source of the phantom reference which Freud makes in the open letter to the Frenchman, and which can be linked to his sense of *déjà raconté,* is to be found in the corpus of a father who foretold this moment in a celebrated essay whose history has been marked by a long series of interceptions before reaching its self-addressed destination at the Acropolis. It is entitled "Einleitung in die Propylaen" ("Initiation [or Entrance, Introduction] into the Propylaea"). We are standing before the father complex and the solution of the *Geheimrat,* whose preparation had begun in Italy, long ago, but this time consolidating in *Tri*este: before the third gate—the propylaeum—of the Acropolis.

In his essay Goethe names his debt to a past whose grounds he would never tread: "What modern nation does not owe its artistic formation to the Greeks; and, in some disciplines, who more so than the Germans?" The richness of this essay can scarcely be gathered up in a few remarks, but for our purposes it will be necessary to mark just some key moments in a work which, in the first place, gives focus to the exchange of ideas and letters ("Ideen- und Briefwechsel"), to the meeting grounds for the arts and sciences, to the framing of judgments, indeed, to the need for bringing questions before a higher authority or court.[41] The essay makes claims for a psychological-chronological procedure ("psychologischer-chronologischer Gang"), speaks for the transference of the self into works of nature and art ("in die höchsten Werke der Natur und Kunst überzutragen"), struggles with great models ("grossen Mustern"), situates comparative anatomy and imputes to the genuine artist a capacity to penetrate the depths of his own mind ("in die Tiefe seines eigenen Gemüts zu dringen"). This text consecrates a ground of speculation whose highest priest and cultivator would be Freud; it initiates themes that would reach maturation under Freud's tutelage, and one finds Freud treating and retreating from many of these themes in his oeuvre, the way a master accepts and abandons certain disciples. But the particular enticement that this essay offers for our study unfolds in the beginning of the initiation to the Propylaea:

> The young man who begins to feel the attraction of Nature and Art believes that active ["lebhaft"] striving alone will enable him quickly to penetrate to their innermost sanctuary; but the man discovers that even after lengthy wanderings, he is still in the forecourts ["Vorhöfen," also "vestibules"].
>
> Such a consideration has occasioned our title. Rung, portal ["Tor"], entrance, vestibule, the space between the inside and the outside, between the sacred and the prosaic: only this can be the place where we shall commonly dwell with our friends.
>
> If there is someone for whom the word Propylaeum more specifically recalls that structure through which one arrived at the Athenian citadel, then this, too, is not contrary to our intention. But one should be careful not to impute to us the effrontery of endeavoring to conceive such a work of art and splendor here. Under the name of the site ["Ort"], let one understand what might have transpired only there: let one await interlocution and discussion that, perhaps, would not be unworthy of that place.

This moment of Goethe's solicitation speaks for itself, and speaks for Freud, I believe. It is the unlived memory of the Acropolis, the remembered dialogue that Goethe would never travel far enough to hold; it is perhaps the paternal spirit with whom Freud uneasily communed that day in Athens, remembering indeed his schooldays, but blotting out the image of "the youth attracted by Nature and Art," the young man strangely drawn by Goethe's Nature to erect an "edifice" which, according to the *Traumdeutung,* "is still incompleted."

We have at once discovered and returned to the space between the inside and the outside, the portal, the mouth, the text, the anatomy of the *Propylaen,* the forgotten injection into the initiating *Mustertraum.* The Irma dream had already brought us somewhere near the third gate of Freud's inaugural work. We were at the end of the second chapter, searching for the *"Propylpräparat . . . Propyl,"* how did Freud ever get to that? This would be one passageway, or to speak in the manner of Freud and Goethe, one portal, entrance, vestibule.[42] The Irma text is constituted in and by that vestibule, and besides being the second chapter, it is also the third gateway to the text. For the *Traumdeutung* begins with an unacknowledged chapter, if one agrees to count the section containing the prefaces. And though we have emphasized the opening in terms of initiation and birth, this moment resembles the two processes only insofar as birth, like initiation rites, cannot be conceptually limited to the bringing about of something. But something is usually removed, and usually from the body, be it the child who formerly filled the womb or, as in the rite of circumcision—to take just one example—a part of the male organ. This emptying or loss usually makes up the entrance fee; it is the fee that life pays to death at the macabre festival which Freud will call *fort-da.*

One can never lose sight of the fact that the *Traumdeutung* as such is profoundly concerned with and even built on the notion of a *Sterbejahr*—one that is by no means restricted to Goethe, though he may be its unique point of articulation. Freud is himself reminded of the centrality of the *Sterbejahr* when he writes the second preface to the *Traumdeutung* in the summer of 1908, and traces the work's genesis to the trauma or *Trauerarbeit* (mourning—literally, work or oeuvre of mourning) over his father's death. Though the period in which Freud began writing his great work coincided with his abandonment of the trauma theory, the transference from *Trauma* to *Traum*-work remains engraved in his project. The *Traumdeutung* not only contains the first seeds of the Oedipus complex, but also shows Freud's entire perspective on literature to be shaped by the haunting event of the Father's Death. This comes to light in Freud's interpretation of Sophocles, to be sure, but also in his interpretation of *Hamlet* whose origin Freud assigns to the death of Shakespeare's father in 1601 as well as to the untimely end of his son, Hamnet. It is of little importance whether Freud was correct in his assumptions; what is important is that these deaths make up an integral moment—a kind of invisible matrix—for his overall strategy. Freud introduces his interpretation of *Hamlet* by way of Goethe, whose binary scheme opposing the pensive with the active Hamlet Freud lays to rest. The word employed by Goethe and Freud for "action" in this case is *Tat,* which resounds death—*Tod*—in hushed tones, particularly when one considers Freud's spelling of death as *Tot*—the adjectival dative of which would be *totem,* as in *Totem and Taboo.* Indeed, *Totem* is the work which ends with Faust's beginning, allowing us to hear the beginning as the end, the deed as the dead: "In the beginning was the Deed" (*Tat,* I, iii). Swaying from *Tat* to *Tot,* the beginning of Freud's deed and legacy is already entangled in the active movement from "a-a-a" to "o-o-o," from *da* to *fort,* to which Freud, as occasional father to Goethe and grandfather to himself—for sons become the father of the father, he tells us in *Totem and Taboo*—earnestly commits us.

When citing a certain line from Shakespeare's *Henry IV,* Freud would make a curious lapsus of which a good deal has been said. Quoting, "Why thou owest God a death (V,i)," Freud would repeatedly replace "God" with "Nature." Was Freud thinking of Goethe's "Nature" each time he put this citation to paper? Did Psychoanalysis owe a death to its begetter and child, to its dreadful initiator whose mark would sear Freud's corpus for good? The memory of a response has been peeled away from our writing blocks. But a response is there, though the prince has left the stage to join his father: Falstaff's response to Prince Hal's admonishment will be, at this time, in honor of deferral,

> Tis not yet due: I would loath to pay him
> before his day.

NOTICE

15 May 1831. J.W. Goethe concludes contract with J.P. Eckermann. The latter is named editor of Goethe's last ("supplementary") works. Five percent of the honorarium to be retained by Eckermann.

10 June 1831. J.P. Eckermann receives the key to casket containing J.W. Goethe's literary remains.

Part Two

Preliminary Remarks

These pages present a case of literary parasitism. Following the course of an alien body (*Fremdkörper*) into the Goethean corpus, one lets oneself be drawn into a kind of ineluctable movement that strays beyond the boundaries of what we call literature: there can be nothing simply and exclusively literary where the parasitical asserts itself. The necessity of this straying or drifting, which accounts for certain risks taken in the analysis here attempted (without however reducing or controlling them), is already present, prior to any interpretive intervention, in the adventure itself that met Goethe and his oeuvre. Johannes Peter Eckermann's arrival, his finding his way to Goethe, is an event at once literary as it were, (i.e., intrinsic to the work of which it is a part) and biographical; nothing, not even Goethe's sovereign will, could limit its effects. In this sense, rather than having priority assigned to the specificity of this event, be it literary or biographical, it seems far more compelling, when reading the texts which bear its mark, to view the problem as one of closure—this, precisely, is the problem that Goethe and Eckermann, throughout their shared venture, seek to resolve only to have it raised constantly, without end.

The most natural move would be, no doubt, to try to locate the origin of the shared venture in Goethe himself, in other words, to accord him the precedence that is his due. In this light it would seem that Eckermann came to occupy a place that Goethe had prepared for him, thus readily inserting himself into the closed economy of Goethe's life-and-works. Eckermann would be but Goethe's instrument who guarantees his crowning achievement and the closure of his destiny. But the two roles to which Eckermann is assigned when he arrives on scene already disclose in Goethe's desire—his desire for totality and completion—two contradictory inclinations. First, Eckermann's services are engaged, or rather, he is adopted for the purpose of readying those manuscripts which Goethe cannot manage singlehandedly to render publishable. In this sense Goethe wants to complete an oeuvre, by means of Eckermann, that would be greater than himself, in excess of him; he wishes to meet a necessity whose key he does not, by his own admission, hold. On another register, Eckermann meets Goethe's needs by retaining his spoken words, by recording and conserving these words in the notes which are to become the posthumous tomes of *The Conversations*. Still within the domain of Goethe's desire, one soon discerns that Goethe will have granted Eckermann the position of witness. And responding to

Goethe's desire responsibly, Eckermann prepares to deliver an image of Goethe to the world that did not adequately pierce through Goethe's works; in effect, he creates a "Goethe" that will be greater than his oeuvre. To be perfectly executed as personality, to be completed as oeuvre: the name of Eckermann, his companion of the final years, signifies this double desire in Goethe, the desire for completion that divides and denies itself. In a more profound sense, it is a sign of what we can call the logic of incompletude. Eckermann, then, will be Goethe's secretary, he will hold the secret to the monument named "Goethe," to its closure—and even if this secret is that "Goethe" as totality does not exist.

But if one persists in viewing the desire which motivates Eckermann's venture as that of Goethe, then there would be nothing, beyond its paradoxical nature, truly mysterious about the case. In taking Goethe's point of view, one is bound to make of Eckermann a mere transition between him and himself, one is bound to cancel him out in a circular economy while repeating over and over the forgetting that Goethe had requisitioned: the forgetting of Eckermann. Traditional criticism has largely pursued this course. In compliance with Goethe's requisition, studies treating the *Conversations* or texts completed after Eckermann's arrival suggest the presence of this foreign element to be both necessary and troublesome. One is impatient to go through Eckermann, like going through a secretary, in order to reach or return to Goethe. Everything takes place as if the ingratitude toward Eckermann, of which the institution of Goethe studies is guilty, were inevitable; in order to believe in Goethe, it is necessary to chase Eckermann toward the outermost limits of the Goethean corpus—it is necessary literally to *persecute* him.

If, however, there were something mysterious—if we are dealing with a genuine enigma—then it would have to come from Eckermann's desire, discoverable in fact only from Eckermann's perspective. It was therefore necessary, in order to read and interpret the great narrative of this parasitical relationship, to adopt the point of view of the other, and to take his side. What did Eckermann want? His personal history, prior to the moment he makes his vows, devoting himself to the master, furnishes some indications on this subject. The loss of a close relative, most particularly, and his inability to complete what psychoanalysts call the "work of mourning" (*Trauerarbeit*) appear to render Eckermann an eternally haunted figure. The presence of the familial phantom could well explain Eckermann's compulsive need to substitute for his own self (*Ich, moi*) that of another. In this context the psychoanalytic theory of the phantom founded by Nicolas Abraham and Maria Torok is an indispensable sustainment. But this story is still or already that of Goethe. Understanding Eckermann, if only slightly better, is submitting Goethe to that test of alterity which he had himself chosen by appealing to an outsider for help, by calling in a stranger. His life and work welcomed Eckermann; they now demand the acknowledgment of the share that is no longer simply Goethe's.

Vita (outline)[1]

Before my time, during his first marriage, my father had a small trade, a *Handel*—but he was brought down, as the rumor went, because of (his sons and because of) his goodhearted trust in everybody, and was left in poverty. In my time, when he was already old, he looked for work by walking through villages and the moorland . . . and became a peddlar. When I was big enough, I would accompany him on these tours and help him to carry a bundle, and I remember this time as a very happy one for me. . . .

[Plans for an autobiographical novel discarded, 1820]

Cover Letter

The author of these poems was born on 27 September 1792, at Winsen.

[Error: Official records indicate E.'s birthday as 21 September]

The Pas de Deux or *Was* is Goethe

In winter he would hawk rough quills, "pens" in Moon's translation, which he brought to Hamburg "when there was the opportunity of a ship." Eckermann continues. "As soon as I was sufficiently grown up, I accompanied my father in his wanderings from village to village and helped him carry a bundle." When he had grown sufficiently to help the father carry a bundle, which he has just described as a "light, wooden box on his back," Eckermann knew that "this period belongs to the most precious memories I have retained of my youth." Despite the hardships, poverty, fatigue and insatiable hunger of which it reminds him. This corresponds to the period of Eckermann's preconscious existence with regard to poetry and art. "Luckily," he writes, "even a dark longing and striving for such things could not take place in me." He was a latecomer to the pleasures of the alphabet and did not learn to read or write before the age of fourteen. The story of his institutional education runs like a pedagogical rendition of *Gulliver's Travels*. Eckermann did not attend the Gymnasium until he reached his early twenties, and therefore among the students he stood like a giant, ignorant but friendly and well-meaning. Later on, of course, little Eckermann would be en route to visit the giant of German letters with whom he would continue his education and who, in compensation for his meager stature, would arrange to have Eckermann receive the title of "Doctor." But before Eckermann could read and write and long before he became Dr. Eckermann, something happened at the family table. He was, as usual, lodged between both parents. As usual, the sibling pairs are not entirely present. Papa had just returned from Hamburg, bringing with him a packet of tobacco to which an image of a horse was affixed. "When I had pen and ink and a piece of paper at hand, an irrepressible drive ['ein unwiderstehlicher Trieb'] to copy" this image overwhelms the child: "My father had embarked upon his narration of Hamburg while I, unnoticed by my parents, became completely absorbed in drawing the horse." Upon finishing, he had the impression that "my imitation was completely like the model, and I enjoyed a happiness hitherto unknown to me." The hypermimetic child then "showed what I had made to my parents who could not help praising me and wondering about it." When his father's bundle turns into his tobacco pouch, Eckermann proves capable of carrying this, too, doubling it, returning to the father the other half, displaying finally what he has made on the family table. And spends an agitated but joyfully sleepless night. He recognizes that "from this time onward, the drive toward sensuous reproduction, once awakened, never left me." This tableau, another version of Ostade's "Good Man and Good Wife" plus little Eckermann, joins motifs that will never cease recurring. However crude the primary object prompting Eckermann's awakening may seem, however bizarre the moment of mimetic gift-giving looks, the horse at least can be retained as the very sign of the drive ["Trieb"] itself. In these waking hours, Eckermann's menagerie grew steadily. Some time after this primal scene ["unnoticed by my parents"] that released Eckerman's reproductive energy, he learns to write and shows promise not only of a good hand ["nicht allein eine gute Hand"] but also in drawing up written essays ["Abfassung schriftlicher Aufsätze"]. As Nachbildung merges into acts associated with Abfassung, Eckermann begins to practice his hand in writs and judgments ["Klageschrift und Urteil"]. His first major exercise in writing, while this still remains a secondary drive, will be focused on legal procedures involving life-sentences and convictions, in short, on acts of criminal justice. In the winter of 1815, Eckermann's creative drive is linked primarily to painting. This phase of his *Lebenslauf* leads him to walk for forty hours in the snow to reach the house of Ramberg, who is to be his master teacher. As June approaches, however, "I was no longer capable of manipulating the stylus, for my hands trembled so." His hands give way, by reason, he surmises, of a "long guarded secret anxiety [that] had probably contributed to hastening the outbreak of the illness slumbering within me." Another mimetic perversion, perhaps, for he has just told us that "I drew completely the whole anatomy of the human body, and was not tired of always repeating the difficult hands and feet." Thereupon his own hand becomes fragile and impotent, as it were, in June, he tells us, about eight years before the June day upon which he will extend his trembling hand to another master.

When Goethe was speaking today at table, of the numerous presents which had been sent to him at Dornburg in honor of his birthday, I asked him what the packet from Abeken contained. "It was a remarkable dispatch ['Sendung']," Goethe said, "which really gave me great pleasure. A darling woman with whom Schiller took tea, conceived the happy idea of writing down his utterances: Sie hat alles sehr hübsch aufgefasst und true wiedergegeben, und lieset sich nun nach so langer Zeit gar gut, indem man dadurch unmittelbar in einem Zustand versetzt wird, der mit tausend anderen bedeutenden vorübergegangen ist, in diesem Fall aber glücklicherweise in seiner Lebendigkeit auf dem Papiere gefesselt worden. Schiller erscheint hier, wie immer, im absoluten Besitz seiner erhabenen Natur; er ist so gross am Teetisch, wie er es im Staatsrat gewesen sein würde. Nichts geniert ihn, nichts engt ihn ein, nichts zieht den Flug seinen Gedanken herab; was in ihm von grossen Ansichten lebt, geht immer frei heraus ohne Rücksicht und ohne Bedenken. Das war ein rechter Mensch, und so sollte man auch sein!—Wir anderen dagegen fühlen uns immer bedingt; die Personen, die Gegenstände, die uns umgeben, haben auf uns ihren Einfluss. . . ."* Goethe became silent. The conversation took another turn ("mischte sich anders"); I however reflected upon these remarkable words—which also touched on and expressed my innermost self—in my heart.

The scene unfolds at Goethe's table in Weimar. His house, the *Frauenplan,* is open to guests this Thursday, the eleventh of September, 1828, at two o'clock. Goethe looked very well, and was quite bronzed by the sun. Or let us say, the scene unfolds in the second entry made in the second part of Eckermann's *Conversations with Goethe in the Last Years of His Life.* And the scene, he tells us, is enfolded within Eckermann's heart. It is always contained in Eckermann's heart, in his heart's hearing, which he observes in the last lines of the Third Part to be the place of Goethe's conversations and Goethe's silence: "Goethe became silent. I however housed ['bewahrte'] his great and good words in my heart." And sometimes the scene is found to be transposed to Goethe's own heart, with tender violence, as when Eckermann writes that he has stolen into the chamber where Goethe's corpse is on witnessless display, requesting the servant to leave him alone with the body. The master servant, Eckermann, lays his hand on Goethe's breast, caressing his heart, as if to give him his last pleasure, while in deep stillness he unravels the shroud veiling the naked body of the eternal slumberer. The members (*Glieder*), he remembers and writes, are splendid. Eckermann will momentarily forget that the immortal spirit has left his earthly envelope (*Hülle*).

The question of mundane envelopes is precisely the one occupying the table guests on the eleventh of September, following Goethe's seventy-ninth birthday. Who writes, who envelopes, who contains whom in this remarkable scene which opens with the question Eckermann raises, thus opening the contents of Goethe's package? Inserted deep within the folds of the *Conversations,* this scene in fact opens and closes the text which, it appears, Eckermann has signed. "It was a remarkable dis-

---

*"She conceived everything very prettily, reproducing it faithfully, and after so long a time, it still reads well, inasmuchas one is transplanted immediately into a situation which is now passed by with a thousand others as significant, while in this case the living spirit ["Lebendigkeit"] has luckily been caught and fixed upon ["gefesselt," chained to] paper."

"Schiller appears here, as always, in absolute possession of his sublime nature. He is as great at the tea table as he would have been in a council of state. Nothing constrains him, nothing narrows him, nothing draws downward the flight of his thought; the great views which lie within him are ever expressed freely and fearlessly ["ohne Rücksicht und ohne Bedenken"]. He was a true man, and one ought to be so!—We others, however, always feel ourselves subject to conditions ["bedingt"]; the persons, the objects which surround us exert their influence upon us. . . ."

patch," Goethe is quoted as saying, as if he might be shown to be addressing, across the table, Eckermann's own transmissions—and the word *Sendung,* which Eckermann remembers Goethe to have used, is heavy with the sense of mission, as it was in *Wilhelm Meisters Theatralische Sendung.*[2] A remarkable mission that gave Goethe immense pleasure, it was here, in this place, a mission or dispatch given to Eckermann by a certain (Bernhard Rudolf) Abeken whose wife's text on—or by— Schiller was destined for Goethe. Eckermann carried a woman's text to Goethe. He specialized in carrying the pouch. It contains and carries Schiller's *Äusserungen;* it captures them "prettily" and reproduces them faithfully; and it pins down and captivates the vitality of Schiller's expression on paper. Yet if this was a faithful woman (and everything in this chain of transmissions suggests that she was faithful to him, to all of them, for she first gave the text to her husband who then gave it to Eckermann who brought it to Goethe)—if she was indeed a true (*treu*) woman, she nonetheless seems to intervene in her own faithful reproduction with an element of style and a flair for writing—prettily. Does this mean that the words spoken by Schiller were themselves pretty or that, as a true woman, she had a way of seducing Schiller's language into a pretty script? Or, if everything is indeed faithfully reproduced, would it be Schiller whose language is essentially pretty? The questions of possession, self-possession and dispossession, authorship, genre and gender, of life arrested on paper are unwrapped on Goethe's table, and by Goethe himself. A darling woman may have written the text in question or reproduced it faithfully, but the proprietor will in any case be Schiller: "Schiller appears here, as always, in absolute possession. . . ." Not necessarily in possession of the woman, but in a specific mode of self-possession, that is to say, he has not lost his "sublime" nature to the woman. Thus it appears that Schiller is in absolute possession of his sublimity, of the text that contains him *despite* the movement of the text whose style, qualified as it is by Goethe, would seem to perform contrapuntally to his nature: nothing constrains him, nothing hems him in, and nothing curbs his flight from that very text which chains him. In other words, Schiller's sublimity for once has nothing to do with Kant's understanding of the sublime, as Goethe imputes to this state no original threat or act of self-overcoming that, for Schiller and Kant, actually characterizes the sublime. There is no humiliation of the subject, no abjection. Perhaps, then, in this context it is in fact Goethe who finds himself involved in the sublime, and in some fundamental way overwhelmed. As for Schiller, the text that contains him and of which he is in full possession does not contain him, cannot possess him. Thus what lives in him can roam about freely without producing any signs of concern or reflection—without looking back (*Rücksicht*)—while, at the same time, his vitality is arrested and flattened out on paper. The vows exchanged between the sublime and the darling, the great and the pretty, the male and the female, the narrowing frame and the soaring flight, faithfulness and transgression, and so on, somehow contract a textual marriage. Schiller's flight from the domesticity of faithful reproduction made him a "true man." And one ought to be like him, one should imitate the figure who refused to be imitated or taken in by the faithful scribe. Only, one cannot be like him or like Christiane von Wurmb—for the possibility still exists that the sublimity of which Goethe speaks here flows from the woman's pen, that her transgressions are an act of faithful infidelity—because Schiller is not like Schiller, he does not seem to feel in this text restricted or contingent (*bedingt*) as "we others" are, as are we who are still influenced by persons and objects, for example by persons and objects of which we, today, at this belated birthday party speak.

Despite all the internal combinations that it fabricates, this commentary has an aura of purity for the writer; everything that follows upon it is *gemischt,* and anyway does not command Eckermann's attention or heart. Goethe has spoken or so the quotation marks that Eckermann wraps around him suggest, for Goethe is always represented in the conventional form of direct speech. And yet we learn after the last quotation mark containing Goethe's speech, that Goethe has spoken, in this case, from Eckermann's heart. Therefore it might seem that Eckermann has written what Eckermann had spoken or secretly dictated to Goethe.

And yet it is known, or thought to be known, that Goethe had dictated to Eckermann. Goethe is said to have dictated everything to Eckermann: his walk of life, his prolonged celibacy, his poverty, his enforced residence in Weimar, his pitiful survival. But what is being dictated and written on the eleventh of September is a program for the type of writing which engages Eckermann. The program constitutes a remarkable mission, and it is not entirely beside the point if the players are presented in terms of sexual difference, of traditional notions of female receptivity and male productivity, sipping-tea-writing-and-speaking, even though these distinctions are already blurred in the citation attributed to Goethe. The crossing of genders which appears to orient this program, as well as Goethe's pleasure, contains within it and begets a mark of genre which can only be found "remarkable"—that is, not found at all and not given a name to go by.[3]

Goethe himself can only identify the piece of writing presented to him as a "remarkable dispatch," whereas Eckermann usually shows him to be precise and even dramatically rigorous on the question of generic classification.

Goethe does not and cannot propose a typology that would accommodate this text; he can only suggest the uniqueness of such an enterprise. As concerns "—We others" (one must follow Goethe into his dashes and breakdowns), that is, all of us outside this Schiller/von Wurmb couple, are conditioned by other determinations, by finitude's pressure and the pressure that "people and objects" exert on us. Schiller has managed to escape these pressures; he is as great at table as he would have been (but never was) at the state council (as I, Goethe, am). In any case, his *Lebendigkeit,* as he was and would have been, has been preserved; he is unique. We others, on the other hand, are bound to certain limits and boundaries that in a sense frame us, keeping us less recognizable or alive than Schiller was kept by Karoline, in Karoline, at tea. Thus Schiller might appear here as he "always" does; yet there remains something inaccessible, mildly unsettling and certainly inimitable about his appearance and the status of his speech or her writing. And if Goethe refrains from classifying this text according to the norms with which he normally greets incoming manuscripts it is because this missive or mission must remain utterly remarkable for him as Eckermann memorizes, interiorizes, and expresses his "own" words. Whether von Wurmb's writing can be considered to be a sort of novelistic venture, a documentary, or even whether it might be subsumed under the heading of biography will be left undecided in Eckermann's recollections. (Officially it would be pinned down as biography, for it was first published by Karoline von Wolzogen in 1830 as part of the *Schillerbiographie.*) Neither Goethe nor Eckermann will resolve the riddle of textual identity; it will remain remarkable for them as they repeat the unrepeatable while maintaining the distance of "we others."

Goethe himself, however, has established a certain paradigm for the intermingling of textual voices and he situates this possibility, according to Eckermann, in terms of Schiller. When Goethe's subject of conversation turns on Schiller, the subject being reviewed is usually a breakdown in the concept of unicity, the law of the writing couple. And it turns on Schiller when he turns to Eckermann, speaking out against the damage done by solitude or by notions such as "solitary writer."[4] Eckermann listens, hearing a lesson on responsible passivity, extenuating himself before the silent, departed Schiller, a guardian of

Goethe's word on another other. Thus, even when it comes to be dissimulated by the presentation of other couples—for instance, von Wurmb and Schiller—the Schiller/Goethe couple acts as the secret, if unattainable model for the Eckermann/Goethe bond (in which Eckermann would not necessarily be representing himself). It would be absurd, Goethe asserts, to try to discern a "mine and thine" (*mein und dein*) when one is reading certain texts composed by the one and revised by the other. This is especially true of the *Xenien*. But apart from Schiller, Goethe is manifestly xenophobic about allowing another signature to coexist with his own. Or so it seems. Another, primary model for the dissolution of the "mine and thine" difference when signing can be found in scientific endeavors, which will pose a problem for our couple at a later stage.

It is perhaps necessary to point out here, where questions arise concerning the mine and thine difference in Schiller and Goethe, that Eckermann's preference for the one over the other was late in coming. (There was even then a Schiller-or-Goethe pageant. Eckermann first admired Schiller, whose picture he *traded in* for Goethe's: "I have tasted some of [Goethe] and my judgment concerning him has changed. But Schiller lives with me in my room, I revere him as the first . . . I worship him daily, etc." 24 April 1817. "I have wound a wreathe around the divine Schiller's portrait" 13 July 1817. "I was so fortunate to be able to trade off a portrait of Schiller to get possession of the beloved picture [*dieses geliebten Bildes*] of Göthe." 1820s.) The changeover was motivated, he claims, by the fact that Goethe's poetry resolutely excluded foreign names—"foreign" meaning, presumably, Greek, Italian, and so on. So Goethe's poetry satisfies Eckermann's xenophobia, whereas Schiller's does not—all of which is difficult to take at face value, particularly when it turns out that precisely on this issue Schiller/Goethe cannot be told apart, according to Goethe's dictation. For the moment, one may assume that there exists a problem on the subject of the name, or that Eckermann felt what he said he felt, namely, that Goethe's poetry would allow for the inclusion of a name that would be neither foreign nor extraneous to Eckermann. Perhaps, namely, Eckermann. At any rate, Eckermann will want to work from a perceived inside-of-Goethe in order to establish his name. The pressure which Eckermann felt to make a name cannot be underestimated. In his letters to his fiancée he discloses that he enters Goethe life and works in order to create a name for himself, a *good* one, as if his had been tainted. But Eckermann's name will never be entirely chaste, for it is from the very start impregnated with Goethe's signature. So it happens that when one is talking about Eckermann's book, one is already speaking about Goethe's work, one is already quoting Goethe.

Or else, as it may happen, one does not quite know what one is talking about if the mine and thine is formulated in the terms spelled out, for example, by the Dunne edition of 1901, entitled *Conversations with Eckermann: Being Appreciations and Criticisms on Many Subjects by Johann Wolfgang Goethe with a Preface by Eckermann and a Special Introduction by Wallace Wood LL.D.*—many subjects, indeed. Or the couple might be listed under "Eckermann" or vice versa as the *Conversations* with the one or the other or, again, in a more neutralized manner, as *Conversations of Goethe with Eckermann,* and so forth. And yet, eventually, one could speak of "namely Eckermann"— and the same one, namely Nietzsche, could tell us to read *Goethe* thus:

> Goethe sodann ist vorbildlich. . . . Er ist, als stilisirter Mensch, höher als je irgend ein Deutscher gekommen. Jetzt ist man so bornirt, daraus ihm einen Vorwurf zu machen und gar sein Altwerden anzuklagen. Man lese Eckermann und frage sich, ob je ein Mensch in Deutschland so weit in einer edlen Form gekommen ist. Von da bis zur Einfachheit und Grösse ist freilich noch einen grossen Schritt, aber wir sollten nur gar nicht glauben Goethe überspringen zu können, sondern müssen es immer, wie er, wieder anfangen.
>
> *Goethe* is exemplary. . . . As a stylized human being he reached a higher level than any other German ever did. Now one is so bigoted as to reproach him therefor and even to censure his becoming old. One should read Eckermann and ask oneself whether any human being in Germany ever got so far in noble form. [Nietzsche, *Nachgelassene Fragmente* 29 (119), Sommer–Herbst 1873, from *Sämmliche Werke,* de Gruyter Dünndruck-Ausgabe (1967–77), Bd. 7, p.686.]

If Friedrich Schlegel had censured Goethe for becoming old, it must be said that Nietzsche employs another strategy, one that shows Goethe, if not becoming old, then passing into noble form. But to apprehend the form of that nobility and the stylization of the human being, one must look away from Goethe; in fact, "one should read Eckermann." From the *Gay Science* we know what type of aesthetic surgery is required to attain such a high level of stylization: it is a "great and rare art." "Here a large mass of second nature has been added; there a piece of original nature has been removed. . . . Here the ugly which could not be removed is hidden; there it has been reinterpreted and made sublime. . . ." (p. 99). One should read Eckermann, it says. And if one reads Eckermann, one will find that he stylizes or "reinterprets" *Goethe* with a finely cut diamond. As Nietzsche saw it, when

Goethe was speaking today at table of the presents which had been sent to him in honor of his birthday, we were already addressing the question of a declining age and the fiction of the writer as a stylized human being. The age of Goethe is in danger of declining, which is why, in a sense, it will always come down to Eckermann.

Eckermann, namely, as his name promises, acts not only in his capacity as husbandman or "Ackermann" whose labor is to break and prepare the ground for receiving the seed—he is not only charged with assuring fertilization—but he is, too (as the etymology of the Ecke suggests), a "supplementary man," one eking out an existence by writing: at once something excessive, beside the point, he is an annexed appendant as well as something of a vampiric depletion in Goethe's signature. Thus, he will eventually want his book to be published as an "introduction and supplement" to, but also a part of Goethe's oeuvre. When he explains in a letter the method underlying his work he tries to oppose a notion of appendant maleness to one of female receptivity. His letter to Heinrich Laub written eight years after the appearance of the first two volumes of the *Conversations* in 1844, argues:

> Was Aufassung und Darstellung dieser Gespräche betrifft, so war dabei wohl teilweise das Was gegeben, aber nicht das Wie. Und auch das Was musste ich gewissermassen bereits besitzen, um es zu penetrieren und mit der gehörigen Wahrheit des Details wiedergeben zu können. Manche haben zwar geglaubt, meine Produktion sei ein blosses Werk eines guten Gedächtnisses, das maschinenmässig die empfangenen Eindrücke zurückspiegelt.

> As regards the conception and representation of these conversations, the What ["Was"] was indeed partially given, but not the How ["Wie"]. And I had to a certain degree already to possess the What in order to penetrate it, and to reproduce it with the appropriate truth of detail. Some people have believed that my production is merely a work of a good memory that reflects in a machine-like way the received impressions.

The couple "thine and mine," has in this instance transformed itself into *Was* and *Wie*. Now, *Was*—presumably the subject of his labor— was partially given to Eckermann. Yet he already had to "have" the *Was*, before it was given to him.

If *Was* is Goethe, as we are given to understand it is (or was), then Eckermann's *Conversations* presuppose a prior possession and penetration of the Was, the subject that Was (which remains unnamed at this point) and the ground upon which Eckermann must work. The very strange methodology that Eckermann proposes here functions to displace the possibility of assigning a strictly present tense of posses-

sion, penetration, or subject either to Goethe or Eckermann, or to
Was or *Wie*. At the same time—at this time—he more or less claims
possession of both terms of the couple of which one had been "in part
given" to him. Despite his place as receptacle of the givens and the
gifts bestowed upon him, however, Eckermann feels he must argue
against the image of pure receptivity. Eckermann must therefore penetrate and cut (*Details*) the *Was,* and, above all, he wants to cut through
the myth of his role as Goethe's micro-secretary or "machine-like"
word processor.

Regardless of the complexity inherent in the relationship of the *Was*
to the *Wie,* the writer to the writer, each to the other, Eckermann's
style is, in the end, indistinguishable from Goethe's. Scholars have
been unable to determine whether he copied from Goethe's diary or
whether Goethe reconstituted his diary from Eckermann's notes. The
radical copulation of style is one reason that the status of the *Conversations* must in part remain suspended. Some call it Goethe's last
work, or—quoting Eckermann without the quotes—Goethe's spoken
text; others have preferred to see it as Eckermann's martyrdom,
though they have shown little sympathy for the martyr. Still others,
such as Hebbel, Grillparzer, and Heine firmly put Eckermann down.
Heine, for instance, mocked him as Goethe's parrot (*Papagei*). There
is some truth to such an interpretation, but in a far more troubling
sense than Heine, the head of Young Germany (*Junges Deutschland*),
seems to have suspected when he discerned this particular aspect of
their relationship. Nonetheless it should be noted, and in homage to
Heine's own martyrdom, that on his deathbed the persecuted poet
reached for Eckermann to find strength and what the ailing ironist
terms "etwas pomadiges."[5]

It may be that solitude's ironists such as Heine and Nietzsche were
moved, and finally comforted, precisely by the staging in the *Conversations,* of the type of passivity that was inseparable from their own
lifetime activities: Eckermann staked his life on the fine lines distinguishing writing and passivity, as if he knew that both presupposed an
erasure and extenuation of the subject. Blanchot takes this a step
further, writing in *Faux Pas* that Eckermann witnessed the poet in his
solitude. The way he posed himself as participatory witness no doubt
left a deep impression on the solitary poet and philosopher who, while
claiming each other, at least from Nietzsche's view of his exceptional
affinity to Heine, cannot be joined according to the terms of contract
which binds the Goethe/Eckermann couple, however much this might,
in the end, have appealed to one or both of them. The *Conversations*

confronts us with a notion of joint ownership, a perverse textual yoke, a faint recall of the ancestral Platonic pair within which Eckermann offers himself up as a suffering Plato, doubled over before Goethe's upright Socrates-posture. Goethe in this portrait is turned into pure voice, gradually passing into noble form, as Nietzsche put it, while Eckermann the writer takes over to execute Goethe's oeuvre and life. It will be *his* desire and command that Goethe complete *Dichtung und Wahrheit*—complete his autobiography, his life; his decision will determine which of Goethe's works are to be burned or preserved, published. And Goethe will do much the same by doing the opposite for Eckermann, that is, he will not let him complete his life or oeuvre, he will finish Eckermann, for Goethe considers himself a kind of finishing school for the younger writer whose native talent for "extorting literary productions" from the old master needed, he felt, to be encouraged. Extortion (*ex-torquere*) is a violence that goes both ways, of course, often leaving us to wonder which of the two in this relationship is Tasso and which Antonio. But as in *Torquato Tasso* they may be legitimately interpreted as one entity whom Nature or the nature of writing has sundered, that is, coupled. Goethe, for his part, will make Eckermann indissociable from himself; he will lend him his name and his style which Eckermann will then bend and twist into our readings of *Goethe.* So many works of scholarship presumably occupied with Goethe will import this somewhat foreign body, this Eckermann, to lend a certain buoyancy to their claims; they will say that "Goethe said. . . ." but append Eckermann's name to what Goethe is said to have said.[6] For they have adopted a logic—sometimes Eckermann's logic, and sometimes Goethe's—of the homotextual drive that seeks to abolish the "mine and thine," "his and hers," "mine and mine," etc. The seeming unicity of style and signature imputed to the movement of extortion which the couple practices on one another passes, in these works, for "Goethe." Nietzsche, however, knew better; he knew about the intricacies of the pas de deux, and the certain vertigo that is always involved in a measured *Dis-tanz:*

> Wenn man von Goethes Schriften absieht und namentlich von Goethes Unterhaltungen mit Eckermann, dem besten deutschen Buch, das es gibt: Was bleibt eigentlich von der deutschen Prosaliteratur übrig, das verdiente, wieder und wieder gelesen zu werden? [*Menschliches, Allzumenschliches*]

About whom or what does Nietzsche write when he writes that he is writing about Goethe's writing—the best German book? He introduces the great name with *namentlich*, and though he says he is referring to Goethe's writing (from which, once again, one—he—has to look away, *absieht*), he names the *Conversations* as the most distilled and perfected form of this writing. What remains of German prose, what deserves the eternal return of the reader is, according to Nietzsche, not entirely Goethe nor Eckermann, but the name of Goethe's supreme writing: namely, Eckermann. And it is indeed with Goethe's remains that Eckermann will write the remainder of his life.

If the *Conversations* leaves behind it a residue of unresolved problems today, the questions of ownership, property, and authorship were no less ambiguous in Eckermann's writings either. In addition to his letter to Laub, the letter to potential publishers, which also constituted the basis for his contract, asserts: "One can consider this work as half *Goethe*'s ['halb und halb als ein Werk *Goethes*'] and indeed as a *spoken* one ['ein *gesprochenes*'], insofar as my merit ['Verdienst'] lies primarily only in the conception ['*Auffassung,*' also apprehension, interpretation] and artistic exposition." This time, the work belongs in part to Goethe insofar as it can be considered to be a spoken one. It is also said to belong in part to the conceiver or writer; nonetheless, the work's main merit lies in its rather total production of the "authentic" and "complete" Goethe. Eckermann stipulates in this epistolary contract that if the *Conversations* are "not added to one's reading, one will not be able entirely to have the authentic Goethe" ("den eigentlichen Goethe nicht vollständig haben, wenn er nicht auch diese Gespräche hinzufügt"). The *Conversations,* then, will let you have the authentic Goethe. At once an addition or supplement to Goethe's corpus, they also guarantee its totality. Yet, as totality, they in fact revert to the function of a half. The authenticating supplement, the authenticating signature: at one point the couple disagrees on which of them will authenticate, underwrite the other. In any case Eckermann wished his book to be published wearing the same jacket as Goethe's collected works (*Ausgabe letzter Hand*), and to serve in the terms spelled out by his contract as "introduction and supplement"—as the appendage and the ground. As if Eckermann had to make Goethe presentable to us.

An entry which he contributed, after considerable hesitation, to the Brockhaus *Conversation-Lexikon der Gegenwart* (4 volumes, 1838–1841), suggests a somewhat different appreciation of Eckermann's project, however:

Wer ihn in dieser Hinsicht näher kennzulernen wünscht, den verweisen wir auf Eckermann's "Gespräche mit Goethe" [2. Aufl., Lpz. 1837], ein

Buch, das aus neunjährigem vertrauten Umgange mit G. entstanden, und das uns den Dichter sowohl in seinem häuslichen und geselligen Leben als auch in der Werkstätte seines poetischen und wissenschaftlichen Treibens und Schaffens mit anerkannter Wahrheit schildert. [716]

Whoever wishes to know him more closely in this respect is referred to Eckermann's 'Conversations with Goethe' (second ed., Leipzig: 1837), a book that grew out of nine years of intimate acquaintance with G., and that shows us the poet both in his domestic and social life as in the workshops of his poetic and scientific activity and creation, depicted in acknowledged truth ["mit anerkannter Wahrheit schildert"].

The book in this account is guaranteed not so much by the authority of Goethe's signature, spoken or not, but by its confirmed truthfulness (whose guarantors Eckermann does not mention). In this rendering, the book acquires attributes primarily of a documentary genre, a kind of allobiography that opens perspectives on Goethe's domestic and social life, permitting as well access to his creative and scientific activities. But when Eckermann is not halving himself or halving Goethe, he expresses a sentiment of embarrassed hesitation, even as he enters his confirmed-as-true *Conversations* in the Brockhaus *Lexikon of Conversations*.

Eckermann was less hesitant when selling his manuscript. While he was content to share his proprietal rights with Goethe and to designate himself as Goethe's writing half—which in itself by no means suggests an innocent contention or desire—Eckermann's preface (*Vorrede*) to the bipartite *Conversations* documents a subtle struggle for copyrights, for the rights of ownership and authorship. "This collection of discussions and conversations with Goethe," he begins, "arises for the most part from my indwelling natural drive. . . ." Eckermann is not arguing for half ownership, but shows this work to originate now for *the most part*—he claims not half but most for himself—from something as indivisible and innate as, for example, his natural drive. Everything that follows will have been naturalized (for the most part) as Eckermann's drive and will bear the mark of his body's desire to embody. This indwelling drive, Eckermann goes on to say, compels him to appropriate: "the natural drive consists in appropriating for myself *irgendein Erlebtes* [some sort of living thing]" which seems to him valuable or noteworthy, through "schriftliche Auffassung" ("grasp or conception of writing"). Writing, for Eckermann, involves recuperating something "for myself," for the most part instinctively; it entails repetitive acts of appropriation. The thing to be appropriated is what has been lived or, more likely, what has lived. The second paragraph in the preface suggests that Eckermann's writing, in addition to ful-

filling a need for learning, furnishes him with a means both of possess-
ing and deferring possession of Goethe: "und ich ergriff gerne den
Inhalt seiner Worte und notierte ihn mir, um ihn für mein ferneres
Leben zu besitzen," "and I gladly grasped the content of his words and
noted it for myself, in order to possess it ['ihn,' him] for my future life
['ferneres leben']." The content, the inside (*Inhalt*) to be held and
appropriated is that which has lived, destined to live on in a future
whose place is more precisely *remote,* faraway (*ferneres Leben*).

Although Eckermann shows himself prepared to give thanks to
something other than himself for this book, the rights of ownership will
not necessarily go to Goethe:

> Übrigens erkenne ich dasjenige, was in diesen Bänden mir gelungen ist,
> zu meinem Eigentum zu machen und was ich gewissermassen als den
> Schmuck meines Lebens zu betrachten habe, mit innigem Dank gegen
> eine Höhere Fügung; ja ich habe sogar eine gewisse Zuversicht, dass
> auch die Welt mir diese Mitteilung danken werde.

> For the rest, I recognize that which I have succeeded in making as my
> own in these two volumes, and which I have some title to regard as the
> ornament of my life, with deep-felt gratitude toward a higher power;
> yes, I even have a certain confidence that the world will also feel grati-
> tude toward me for what I here impart.

This passage contains elements that have already taken shape elsewhere while it also allows a revealing reversal to take place. In the first
place, Eckermann introduces what is perhaps most pertinent to the
question of who signs the *Conversations* in a sentence structure that
explicitly designates a kind of supplementary force; "additionally," or
"by the way"—"übrigens"—he recognizes and knows how to make the
successful part of this work his own property, proper to himself (*Eigentum*) as in what he owns, what is his own. What has worked out well in
these volumes, what meets success, namely, is Eckermann.

Here a momentary reversal takes place; Eckermann is not the supplement or addition to Goethe and his life, but Goethe, who remains
unnamed at this point, is the addition, the decoration pinned to Eckermann: the jewel of my life. This is not to say that Goethe relinquishes
his commanding position before the beginning of the *Conversations*
proper; it is momentarily displaced and in a certain sense reversed.
Eckermann will carve a subtle argument into these reversals when, in
the introduction, he turns the adornment of his life into a hard-stoned
diamond. A moment of humble submission seems to follow upon his
offering Goethe up as his jewel; once more Eckermann offers thanks,

but not as a "pupil and collaborator ['Mitarbeiter'] of Goethe" (contract). Rather, he figures himself in the book as someone who has been guided by a higher authority, a *höhere Fügung* or destiny; as someone, finally, who can confidently expect the gratitude of the world for his word. All this is by the way.

Only after the expression of thanks which Eckermann gives to destiny and receives from the world does he announce the value and intent of this work:

> I hold that these conversations will not only shed some light on life, art and science, or contain inestimable teachings ["Lehre"] but that these unmediated sketches taken from life will also contribute specifically to perfect ["vollenden"] the image of Goethe which one might already carry within oneself from his multiple works.

This work, a contribution to that work, or rather an outer part of that work contributes to the prior one (Goethe's) a fuller image of Goethe. Eckermann aims to perfect or give the finishing touches to Goethe's image, including to Goethe's image of himself that arises from his works and is in some sense blocked by multiple mediations. Eckermann positions himself as an insider ("unmediated sketches from life") whose contribution however comes from the unbridgeable remove of an outside always endeavoring to make itself an inside. This is doubled by his position "outside" the reader, which he judges provisional, for he articulates a desire to modify the "image that one carries within oneself." The aim is to get within, if not within Goethe then at least within those who carry Goethe within themselves. In a drama, however, which claims to unfold under the sign of multiple appropriations, the masked aim perhaps, the "indwelling drive," is to get within Eckermann. Namely Eckermann: the one who began by "already carrying" an image of Goethe, carrying a bundle, carrying an other, and also, within himself, an image that needed to be modified.

Eckermann shows caution, and retreats momentarily from the notion of an inside. He does not believe that the inner totality of Goethe will have been depicted through his work. Comparing Goethe to a multifaceted diamond whose emanations reflect different colors in each direction, he concedes: "And as, under different circumstances and with different persons, he became another, so, I, too, can only say, in a very modest sense: this is *my* Goethe." He claims modesty; yet he has just authorized himself to claim his Goethe.

Eckermann's strategy here is, at bottom, to safeguard Goethe. The pathos of rescue with which Eckermann approached Goethe from the very beginning always should be kept in mind. In the first place, by announcing "this is *my* Goethe" he is immunizing his enterprise against any possible contestation that might be brought to bear on this text. In asserting a part of Goethe that is wholly his own, namely Eckermann's, he renders this work invulnerable to attack. Of course, if this were a critical work about Goethe's oeuvre, a mere interpretation, Eckermann would have to assume full responsibility for his writing; but here he establishes the status of the text as testimony and, as such, the only criteria for truth must be derived from the purely subjective effect that Goethe produced on Eckermann. At the same time, Eckermann is giving back to Goethe what is his own. For the only truth of Goethe, of this diamond, can be the different perceptions that one receives from it. The diamantine cut of this text guarantees the reception of the testimony while also saving Goethe from a scientific operation. As the object of testimony, Goethe will remain mysterious, elusive and safe from any attempt to pin him down. In this respect, Eckermann returns *everything* to Goethe. Everything I say, he says in effect, is not equal to the grandeur and multiplicity of the phenomenon, Goethe. However, the same holds for anything anyone else might say or write about Goethe, for anyone else would be perceiving another, singular facet. As an assembly of multiple facets, Goethe will never be, strictly speaking, identifiable with what one can say about him. In fact and as facet, "this is *my* Goethe." Eckermann's project is a delicate one. If this is *his* Goethe we cannot properly have any access to him; and if, then, Goethe is unknowable as a total object of any discourse, then Eckermann is also at the very beginning disclaiming any possibility for representing the true Goethe. Yet in saying 'this is my Goethe, this facet of Goethe is the reflection that I perceive' he is claiming to disclose precisely that facet of Goethe which is the only image or manifestation of Goethe to which one can ever hope to accede. Eckermann's project is therefore, from the start, or before and after the start—that is, in the preface, already entangled in contradiction. This explains perhaps why Eckermann prominently displays the notion of contradiction in this place of introducing his project. However, he refrains from identifying his own writing as contradictory, opting instead for a transfer: he directs the paired concept of contradiction and diction, of what he calls citing Goethe's epigrams "Spruch und Widerspruch" to Goethe himself. While Goethe acts as the source and containment of contradiction, he is summoned up only as an *example* of contradiction:

So, um nur ein Beispiel anzuführen, tragen Goethes einzelne Äusserungen über Poesie oft den Schein der Einseitigkeit und oft sogar den Schein offenbarer Widersprüche.

So, to give a single example, Goethe's individual remarks on poetry often have an appearance of one-sidedness and indeed often of manifest contradiction.

But the contradictory notch, whether or not merely an appearance (and his whole argument is based on appearance), is tied into the project itself insofar as the "multiple revelations" to which Eckermann will be the privileged witness "are not so easy to say:"

Es ist nicht abzutun durch Spruch, auch nicht durch Spruch und Spruch, auch nicht durch Spruch und Widerspruch, sondern man gelangt durch alles dieses zusammen erst zu Approximationen, geschweige zum Ziele selber.

It is not to be disposed of through a dictum ["Spruch"], nor through this or that dictum, nor even through dictum and contradiction ["Spruch und Widerspruch"]; rather, one approaches, through all these, merely approximations, to say nothing of the goal itself.

It may not be easy to say, but Eckermann knows this much: his project is an impossible one; his text and testimony are impossible—and yet they are true. Goethe, Eckermann in effect says, will never be identifiable with what I am about to say. This text is Goethe, but it never attains him. And Goethe is also the signatory of this text, for this is the only way he showed himself to me, Eckermann. But because this is the way Goethe showed himself, I, Eckermann have to sign.

This structure guarantees the text as Eckermann's property, insofar as it is an instance of subjective testimony. In this respect it is unique: nothing else can be substituted for this testimony, it is irreplaceable. As such, we have to assume its truth: however, to assume that it is true, we have to attribute it—to Goethe. As exclusive reader, Eckermann *is* the owner of the speech. A diamond only shows itself in this way; it is therefore the truth of the diamond. The logic of the argument runs something like this: the subjective effect that Goethe had on me was multiple appearance; therefore I tell the truth (if the object shows itself only as appearance, then that very appearance must be the truth of the object). However, Goethe is the divine source about which only one thing can be said, although none of this is really correct: therefore, everything is only approximation. Nor does this amount to a simple, innocent or even modest gesture of retreat. He reaps the benefits of this divinization of the text, rendering it superior to any criticism or refinement. My text is better than it is, my signature is even more illustrious: it is *my* Goethe. *I* have written the best German book. Eckermann casts the book into the world, wishing it well, three years after Goethe's death: "And now I bid a loving farewell to my long cherished book upon its entrance into the world, wishing it the fortune of being agreeable, and of exciting and propagating much that is good."

The singular double signature remains invisible, manifesting itself perhaps only in "Weimar, 31st October, 1835." Eckermann himself will be chained to Weimar for the rest of his life, proximate and forever only approximate to the body of works in which he invested his signature.

In his author's preface, Eckermann has exposed the double-edged assignment, repeating the terms that we saw ascribed to von Wurmb's writing on or with Schiller: "And this word [this is *my* Goethe] applies not merely to his manner of presenting himself to me, but to my capacity for apprehending and reproducing ["aufzufassen und wieder-zugeben"] him." Eckermann is sensitive to the probable loss incurred by such a task, and to the loss which may accrue to the text in the form of an addition:

> In such cases a refraction takes place, as in a mirror; and it is very seldom that, in passing through ["Durchgang durch"] another individuality, nothing of the original is lost, and nothing foreign is blended in ["nichts Fremdartiges sich bemische"].

Eckermann has managed, further, to elude the passive/active or receiver/giver couple. In effect, he eludes a structure which might have appeared to have informed his relationship to Goethe, as well as the one between Eckermann and Eckermann, since, throughout the preface, it is manifestly he who receives and gives, who fluctuates between the passive and active moments of hearing/receiving (assuming this is indeed passive) and writing/giving (assuming this is active). At this point, when "passing through," Eckermann places himself neither entirely inside nor even outside Goethe: he has traversed Goethe, an act whose travesty and violence is not lost on Eckermann. Traversing his object, he has at once taken from Goethe something that might have belonged to him and deposited something external, strange, a piece of himself into Goethe. "In such cases" one cannot bypass violation; he in any case will have gone through Goethe, violating him in order to place, or deposit, his signature on the Goethean body. The loss, the exchange of having taken and deposited, a violation or intercourse (*Durchgang*) leaves a mark of impurity (*Fremdartiges sich bemischt*), thus marking Eckermann's passage. We shall see how Goethe will have worked precisely within this economy of loss to write off or expel his loss. The loss which both parties agree may be Goethe's is recuperated in this account, that is, transferred, and poured into one of Eckermann's savings accounts, to his benefit, marking the place of his name and "imprint of his individuality." When Eckermann writes this passage on his passage, he calls representations of Goethe's body to mind, although this remains only a passageway to mind. Nonetheless, the body does claim a place here:

> The physical images of Goethe ["die körperliche Bildnisse Goethes"] in the works of Rauch, Dawe, Stieler and David are all to a high degree true, and yet they all carry more or less the imprint of the individual who produced them. And if this can be said of physical things, how much more valid will this become in the face of the ephemeral and intangible things of mind ["Geistes"]!

Eckermann's exchanges with Goethe, the *Conversations,* are founded on a premise of apprehension—a notion that will be elaborated in Eckermann's dream narrations. His grasp of Goethe always includes a moment of sensuous vertigo, a sentiment of what will be or was already lost. And Eckermann knowingly names, affirms, that something has been lost, even as he draws closer to *his* Goethe.

Eckermann's mood when drawing close to Goethe appears to be one of joy. Commanded by his "natural drive," he appropriates or incorporates "what has lived" in an apparent mode of pleasure. One of the things that has lived, and continues to live on is Goethe's voice, which guides Eckermann's writing. Yet, while it belongs to the order of things that may be considered a gay science, there is often a strain of tragedy in the homotextual condition, in its simulation of domesticity within a sameness that however prohibits absolute identity or unity; and there is an inevitable marginalization of the figure that risks and defends it, a kind of silence that overwhelms its articulation. As signatory of the *Conversations,* Eckermann, for his part, will be the center without a place, face, or facet in this text. Goethe, on the other hand, is pure facet that can be neither centered nor touched. The last to have touched Goethe, Eckermann will see to it that his Goethe remains untouchable. He is shown repeatedly to take the risk of touching the untouchable in this text (and not merely in terms of the Goethe whose manuscripts were placed in his hands for re-touching, cutting, editing, judging, etc.). His deep love and reverence for Goethe, Eckermann will write at the end of his introduction, and what he entitles self-presentation, was of an "almost" passionate nature ("meine innige Liebe und Verehung [war] fast leidenschaftlicher Natur"). There now lived in him no drive ("es lebte in mir kein anderer Trieb") other than to be in intimate proximity to him for "some moments."

The Place of an Absence

By way of introduction—though it is getting rather late for that—we can say that Eckermann created the fiction of the self-composed, Olympian Goethe. Of the *Gesamtbild* we may still carry of Goethe, he can be credited with having handed down its principal elements—although this rarely would be credited to his account. As for his own image, what can be said but that he was a shadow, a phantom, a writing hand attached to Goethe's voice? He wanted to make a name for himself; and so he wrote in a letter to his fiancée of thirteen years, long before he felt capable of giving her his name, that he wanted first to receive—to become (*bekommen*)—his name(s). It was very hot that summer. As he walked, he repeated inwardly the comforting impression that he was being guided by "particularly good forces, and that this journey would be of great importance to my success in life." He was thirty years old in June 1823: it was getting late.

In Goethe (as with Nietzsche) Eckermann was accorded a place which is not really a *place,* between the writer and himself at a moment when the signatory "Goethe" no longer coincided with—Goethe. Eckermann's first assignment, an impossible test, was to determine which of the papers in Goethe's possession were actually written by the master: by the summer of 1823 Goethe no longer knows, and asks Eckermann to find, identify, perhaps to invent his style. He was to discern, he writes, "was davon aus Goethes Feder stamme" (what therein stems from Goethe's quill). Eckermann spent the entire summer identifying Goethe in order to return to him his findings at the beginning of the Fall. Satisfied with the results, Goethe adopts him, thus sealing his destiny. We shall never know whose destiny was sealed at that moment, nor who indeed interpreted when Goethe decided that Eckermann interpreted his style and signature correctly.

The history of the *Conversations,* a long one, which we are still holding, is a history of incertitude involving among other things a constant revision of the writing couple and the breakdowns that produce a text. Of the great writers we commemorate in German letters, however—the Hölderlins, the Schillers, the Heines, the Nietzsches, the Benjamins, the Kafkas—*Goethe* was the only one not to succumb to a notion of breakdown or sufferance—a stand for which he will never be pardoned. At the same time, it is his very resistance to fragility, "hypochondria," madness, and the night (*Umnachtung*) that grants him a status of embarassingly monumental proportions among certain representatives of German culture or Germany "itself," if this can be said. (It is possible, however, that no such entity exists—neither a Germany nor a German Culture, leaving these representatives to represent an unacknowledged loss that keeps on recurring). But the noble irresponsibility that Goethe, in Nietzschean terms, can be seen to have exercised through his invention of *Welt* and *Weltliteratur,* through his worldly renunciation of suffering, starts with his rapport to writing as a relationship of writing to alterity. For Goethe, this alterity goes by many names—by the names, we could say, of sufferance itself. Thus Schiller would be one, Eckermann another. These figures act as pseudonyms for Goethe's suffering. Despite Nietzsche's protestations we still tend to read "Goethe and Schiller" in one breath while we collapse Goethe and Eckermann into a teleological beam that gives us "Goethe's own words," in his own words, uttered after his death.

The structure of Goethe's doublings might be illustrated by a modified morphology that, like Goethe's scientific writing, privileges a spiral movement.[7] While the seduction of scientific models is always at play in Goethe's works, it is only being invoked here to demonstrate that "Goethe," in an apparent citation of Faust, involves at least two souls whose deciphering remains linked to a problematics of heredity and the transmission of a legacy. The image generated by DNA might prove useful insofar as it is organized around the basic molecule of heredity (the "magic" molecule), opening a space shared by two figures within the architecture of the double helical or spiral staircase. The process by w_ich DNA passes its message from one generation to the next includes a moment in which the two sides of the helix unzip, so that each can act as a template for making an exact copy of the original (genetic) material. However, what still remains to be discovered in the case of DNA and that which has been abbreviated as "Goethe," concerns the way the hierarchical controls actually work.

Understanding "Goethe" as one term of a double helix (regardless of the futility of separating the two sides), one could begin to read from a different point of view Goethe's multiple inscriptions of seeing and being double and his insistence on the impartible couple (Faust and Mephistopheles, Tasso and Antonio, etc.) as the predominant means of passing messages on to an assumed future in this spiral movement of unzipping. Thus, if two souls live in the Goethean breast, unfolding or unzipping according to certain laws and conditions of transmission, and if there is my Goethe, then we still need to comprehend the mechanisms of reciprocal copying or dictating and, in the first place, that which the double helical upholds or protects in its double but hierarchically ordered movement.

Whether best viewed as bi-text or double helical, it would appear that Goethe himself had a hand in producing and organizing a second, secondary, and indeed more fragile part of himself. This other part or particle was to be sacrificed to the fiction of "Goethe." Indeed, Goethe arranged his survival as template of fiction and of life—as fiction of life—whose faltering or decline the Romantics would readily contemplate. It is hardly fortuitous if Goethe fastened on to Eckermann, forbidding the instinctive migrator from straying too far up the Rhine. Eckermann was to be shielded from the Romantic illness; but more importantly, he was to shield Goethe from this impertinent, rebellious generation or degeneration of writers.

As the other, shadowy side of the double helix, Eckermann in a sense became the deflecting object, the *conduit* as Nietzsche would say, that attracted the resentment of a whole generation (which, even now, hasn't stopped generating its resentment). After Goethe's departure, however, Eckermann's lot would eventually come to resemble the one reserved for widows, those creatures left behind with a body of works to become the petty functionaries of its future institution. Eckermann, always to a certain extent Goethe's void, will be severely punished for the profit he made and for the proprietary rights he exercised over Goethe's works. This profit, though never calculable in material terms, was to be viewed as something of a killing. The punishment, begun almost immediately, continues to be meted out.[8] Thus even in the twentieth century, if one deigns to mention Eckermann, this embarrassing leftover, it is mainly to exercise one's spleen or to demonstrate one's healthy capacity for disgust. In this respect, Friedenthal and other Germans have discovered Eckermann's beady eyes, for example; his nose was/is too long, at any rate, he is servile and ugly.[9] Though they do not put it quite so, he would serve as a singular exponent of Nietzsche's not so manly aesthetic beauty pageant of the "I am ugly created the beautiful."

Eckermann is ugly; he comes to us as the defective or, at least, imperfect side of the "Goethe" zipper. In addition or rather, once again, in subtraction: "Er ist ein Halber, aber er hat ein ganzes, rundes Werk geschaffen, das zu Goethes Oeuvre gehört" ("He is a Half, but he creates a whole, rounded work, which belongs to Goethe's oeuvre.") This type of halving and mutilation to which Eckermann is subject has been, I believe, largely dictated by Goethe. Perhaps it was only a sly and terribly ironic Nietzsche who could undo these nearly universal judgments, though Nietzsche would himself suffer the indignities of a ferocious widow and philosophical executor, Elisabeth—F.N.—Förster Nietzsche. There is however, as Nietzsche seems to have known, a great niche and corner separating the crudely hacking foresters from the husbandmen of legacy.

Eckermann no doubt foresaw and to a certain extend desired his partial undoing; he may even have arrived partially undone, and at any rate he could not exercise much control over a trade or *Rezeptionsgeschichte* that would at once receive and couple the ugly with the beautiful. Nor was the confusion that ensued, such as the reversibility of author and title, entirely to his disadvantage, either. His natural instinct for copying down the true and beautiful encountered Goethe's ambivalence as well, causing him some anxiety, for he kept on pushing back the date of publication, finally contracting for the *Conversations* to be published only after his death. A premature appearance of Eckermann would be problematic, unlivable: first the correspondence with the other one, with Schiller, would have to be published, followed at some point (at Eckermann's prodding) by *Faust II*—and then there was the rest of *Dichtung und Wahrheit* to write (at Eckermann's prodding), and then maybe, too . . . Goethe's strategy seemed reasonable enough. Surely Eckermann could see that the value of his book would be established only after Goethe had read it and, in a sense, affixed his signature to it. But before that could come about, Goethe would first have to judge the book "ganz in meinem Sinne geschrieben." So, in the meantime, Eckermann would have to wait—on Goethe.

Serving Time

It turns out that Goethe in fact never held the *Conversations*. Nonetheless, Eckermann managed to obtain a sign of Goethe's favorable reading in one of his haunting, haunted dreams about four years after Goethe's death. He was an exceptionally prolific dreamer before and after Goethe. During the master's final years, Eckermann occasionally used to narrate the contents of his dreams to Goethe. On one such occasion they arrived at this conclusion (the whole point was to arrive at a conclusion): they concluded one night that at least the muses agreed to visit poor Eckermann at night; his dream narrations, at least, were inspired. If this seems unkind, one can observe that the muses stayed with Eckermann throughout the long night of Goethe's absence, often torturing him, agreeing finally to disappear only when he had completed Goethe's collected works—which in the end concluded (with) Eckermann. By this time and end, he wrote that he was seized with agoraphobic and anthrophobic terror; he had built himself a cage. And having penned himself in completely, he had perhaps finally come to *objectify* the phantasma of incorporation that had been all along "guiding him," as he writes, and in the guise of "particularly good forces."[10]

But who is this dreamer and writer, this figure of writing that inspires so much suspicion, disdain, or forgetting? We don't really know: a hungry wanderer he was, a kind of transmissionary who arrived at Goethe's doorstep to construct for him a magnificent sarcophagus "in den letzten Jahren seines Lebens" (this portion of the title is frequently suppressed in the English translation). Whoever or whatever he was, even his detractors concede that Eckermann can at least be credited with having dignified the poet's passing: a strange destiny for someone who never accepted the fact of Goethe's death. Thus Eckermann lived to be the only citizen of the Weimar community not to place a candle on his window when it was felt the time had come to commemorate the great poet's departure.

The last thing that Eckermann added to the bipartite *Conversations* after Goethe's death was the "Introduction." This is where he narrates his life, or rather this is where he demonstrates that there is no discourse in the first person.[11] Apparently he had more to say for himself but he cut a good part of that out when the book finally entered the publishing stages. Perhaps this was to have been his very peculiar way of writing an autobiography, advancing himself in the last possible moment under the cover of Goethe's proper name, and then in his customary way withdrawing. Nothing would seem more preposterous, however, than to suppose that Eckermann had been writing for or about himself. In the first place, one would be hard put to demonstrate that Johann Peter Eckermann had more than a feeble sense of the "auto," except possibly for his early and extravagant capacity for automobility which moved him to travel by foot from Hannover to Göttingen to Weimar, when he hoped to catch a glimpse of Goethe (this was to mark his second attempt to visit with him). As for the "biographical," he appears only to eclipse himself in his writing or, in any case, he proves to be a master of self-abnegation, a great figure of willed passivity, whose first person is usually Goethe. But when he does come out with something on his own, it can be as disturbing as a confessed adoration for the popular song, "Du, du, liegst mir im Herzen," which Goethe, he points out, of course despised. For the greater part of the *Conversations,* then, and in particular, for the first part, he seems to assume the position of an avid listener, an adoring disciple, a silent scribe writing another's dialogue with himself, the other.

He does however present something like himself. As if his rightful place were to be the waiting room of a grand salon in which the *Conversations* proper are to be held, Eckermann politely produces his visiting card or what in fact resembles a *Lebenslauf,* a walk of life and curriculum vitae. At this juncture, he will grant himself the place of a subheading: Der Autor gibt Nachricht über seine Person und Herkunft und die Entstehung seines Verhältnisses zu Goethe "The Author gives an Account of Himself and His Parents, And of the Origin of His Connection with Goethe"—a feature which is often omitted in English or rendered simply as the "author's preface"). Putting aside for the moment the question of authorship—Eckermann will later, or rather, has earlier managed to complicate the issue—let us see what the late Eckermann, that is, the Eckermann of the "introduction" has to say for himself, or for someone else, as the case may be.

If he comes to designate his place in the space *between* the foreword and the first conversation, it is no doubt because Eckermann was in many ways a creature of the between. A neither/nor monstrosity, in the guise, for example both of child-pupil and mature writer (and neither of these), he arrived at Goethe's house at a moment which from the beginning wavered between life and death—Goethe was almost living and almost dying when ("in the final years of his life") Eckermann appears in their midst, in the midst of his living and dying, to confront the vision of a "vom Tode Erstandenen" (a resurrected corpse). Eckermann's place in destiny's decision remains difficult to situate, but it is to be found lodged between Goethe and his friends in some contexts, between Goethe and his family in others, between Goethe and "Goethe." The situation of the peculiar forms of betweenness is granted multiple inscriptions: Eckermann acknowledges a perpetual sense of being torn between Weimar and Hannover; he shuttled, he wrote, between two types of existence— that of (English) language teacher and of guest writer at Goethe's table; and he was also caught between the desire to produce his own work and Goethe's work, between being a writer in his own right, that is, and an assistant or copy-writer of Goethe. He would also divide his time, he tells us, between moods of exalted conviction and nervous depression, between moments of inspired motivation and writing paralysis. Indeed, the first momentous decision of which he writes forced him to choose between painting and writing. His predicament is one of choosing to be in between or divided and doubled (as if this were really a choice). Positioning himself thus, repeatedly writing himself (or his other) into the space of a between, Eckermann produces the sequence of leitmotifs which has in one way or the other worked its way into the very few considerations that try to discriminate between his life-and-work, his life as work. During that part of his life spent at Goethe's side he could not decide between Goethe and a woman, for example, nor as a subsection of that indecision could he decide between two women—his fiancée Johanna Bertram and the orphan, Auguste von Kadzig, a woman with whom he wanted to write a commentary on the *Farbenlehre,* which would have constituted the place of their union.

Therefore it seems quite "natural," as he was fond of writing, that Eckermann should begin to speak of himself in the introduction as having been born somewhere between: in a little town, namely, "between" ['zwischen'] Lüneberg and Hamburg, on the border between the marsh and heathlands, I was born in nothing better than a hut."

But a proper introduction of Eckermann would have to maintain a double distinguishing mark, for he is not solely a creature of the between; he was also always late. He is a latecomer already from the moment of his birth, which in part explains why he arrives only in time to fit himself in between: "As the last born child ['Zuletztegeborene'] of a second marriage, I, properly speaking, did not know my parents till they had reached an advanced age, and I grew up between ('zwischen') them." (Throughout his life Eckermann would continue to be born late, for he repeatedly indicated his date of birth to be 27 September 1792 while it was actually, according to official records, 21 September.)

Now in the introduction, Eckermann formulates a sentence that has been variously translated, rewritten—including the following version: "Two sons of my father's first marriage were still alive" (Oxenford). The major translation, Moon's, is more to the point: "Of my father's first marriage there lived two sons, of whom one as a sailor after different voyages in distant parts of the world was taken prisoner and shut up. . . . " Both translators agree that one son had been taken prisoner though they cannot quite determine his present predicament as Eckermann writes. Oxenford translates the prison term as having taken place in "foreign parts." What Eckerman seems to be saying, however, is that one of the sons—a sailor—had had to serve a prison term ("in Gefangenschaft geraten"—the "shut up" version will serve us well at a later point), but that he was now presumed dead. The other son—and here all translators agree—eventually returned to Hamburg from numerous whaling expeditions. "From my father's second marriage, two sisters preceded me, and by the time I reached my twelfth year, they had already left the paternal house. . . . " Eckermann communicates this "notice ['Nachricht'] concerning my person and origins" in the first two paragraphs of his self-presentation.

Between the marsh and heathland, living practically (but not entirely) alone between two elderly parents of declining age, lodged between two sets of brothers and sisters who more or less vanish, according to varying degrees and determinations—all this belongs to the rhizomesque genealogy that Eckermann prepares for us as he traces the "origin of his connection to Goethe." Perhaps it is not too late to suggest that, when reading Eckermann's text, one ought to take account of these family members, as does Eckermann himself, and particularly of the phantom brother, presumed dead, who served an undetermined term in prison. This brother, we could say echoing the vituperative attacks on Eckermann, "ist ein Halber"—they are, to one another, half-brothers whose connections are sealed solely through a patrilinear notion of origin. And one should try to imagine what this piece of information might mean in a text whose addressee is indicated in the dedication as being the governing mother of a fatherland, notably, "Ihro Kaiserlichen Hoheit, der regierenden Frau Grossherzogin zu Sachsen-Weimar und Eisenach, Maria Paulowna, Grossfürstin von Russland, dankbar and untertänigst zugeignet." Deferring to the state as its loyal servant, Eckermann reminds his royal reader of the term that his lost brother had served. It might be recalled here that before sending his book out on its endmost journey into the world, in the preface anticipating this introduction, Eckermann writes, almost analogously, of his term spent with Goethe. Rigorously speaking, then, this book presents itself to be read as the discourse of an effacement, a double effacement.

In general, we can say at this point that the phantom brother, who may have found an invisible place somewhere between Eckermann and Goethe in the *Conversations,* may shed some light, however dimly per-

ceived until now, on the sense of urgency that Eckermann feels in
making or saving a name of which he was almost the last hope. The
possibility of penetrating to the domain of a dictatorship governed by
this phantom, this other half "shut up" in Eckermann while he receives
Goethe's dictation, remains here a hypothesis that will have to be tested
against further textual evidence; however, in the meantime, it can be
said that Eckermann's writing—in the *Conversations* and beyond, for
example in his poetry, dream narrations, and letters—returns here and
again to the signifying chains of *Gefangenschaft,* where there persist so
many cages, seas, and sailings with which to contend. We can even say
that one of the great scandals to beset the *Conversations* is related to this
issue. When Eckermann asserts that Goethe has written nothing of note
in his first ten years at Weimar, he of course disregards *Iphigenia* and
the beginnings of *Tasso,* an omission that has horrified quite a number
of Goethe experts. But Eckermann, too, is a Goethe expert. It may be
no more than a mute coincidence, but if he loses sight of *Iphigenia* and
Tasso, perhaps this oversight occurs because the first protagonist is lost
in "foreign parts," and presumed dead, while the second speaks the
language of shipwreck which is shown always to be related to writing.

The mother lags behind. Eckermann is slow in mentioning her, as he
is in general very careful about touching on the subject of women.
Indeed, he treats them with the same discretion as he treats himself in
his writing. This time, in the introduction, the principal character
standing between his description of his father and mother turns out to
be a cow, in this case, the "Hauptquelle des Unterhalts unserer
kleinen Familie" ("main source of support [*Unterhalt-ung,* also 'discussion'] for our little family"). Such a posturing of the source and center
of familial sustenance but also of a dividing line between what is taken
to be a male and female origin will gain prominence in the *Conversations* and will be illustrated, though slightly metamorphosed, in Eckermann's exalted description to Goethe of "Good Man and Good Wife"
(one portrait of their union by von Ostade), who sit with their dog,
gathering wool. Here, as elsewhere, Eckermann tends to pose a silent,
thinking animal between two terms of a couple. In the single sentence
devoted to her, we learn that Eckermann's mother "was particularly
expert at spinning wool"; however, Eckermann hastens to return to his
father who, he claims, was frequently absent. In Eckermann's narration he is, to the contrary, very present. The father's "special trade"
involved travelling on foot at great distances from house to house; he
was a *Hausier* or peddlar. In winter he would hawk rough quills (*rohen
Schreibfedern,* "pens" in Moon's translation) which he brought to

Hamburg "when there was the opportunity of a ship." But it seems that we have already taken all this in our stride.

Eckermann, by the end of the introduction, has travelled the distance between Göttingen and Weimar on foot; the heat was oppressive, the walk was long and difficult (150 kilometers) but he felt he was guided by some unnameable force. He finally arrived at Weimar around the anniversary of Christiane Vulpius's death. Goethe was wifeless.

On Tuesday, 10 June 1823, Goethe received, or even perhaps conceived (*Empfang*) Eckermann in a heartful manner (*überaus herzlich*), leaving the impression that this day was to be counted among the happiest in Eckermann's life. The two sat on the sofa that afternoon. "I was happily flustered in his sight and his nearness, I could tell him very little or nothing." Eckermann and Goethe—"*wir*"—thus sat together for a long while in a "peaceful, tender mood" ("in ruhiger liebevoller Stimmung"). Eckermann, forgetting the faculty of speech in his glance, claiming not to be able to see enough of Goethe, presses instead his knee ("ich drückte seine Knie"), as if in silent supplication or amorous embrace. (Translations suppress this knee passage.) The imprint of this foremost entry, of Eckermann's entry into the *Conversations* and Goethe is revealed to be as touching as it is perverse; it alerts us to all the risks and dangers, as well as pleasures that attend this textual body. Eckermann is on Goethe's knee—on his knees, that is, and this joint venture begins as the forgetting of Goethe's speech, the impossibility of conversation and the overflowing excess of Goethe's presence. This excess does not however suffice for Eckermann; he cannot be satiated: "ich konnte mich an ihm nicht satt sehen." Yet Eckermann will remember the speech that he had forgotten, and he will remember that he had forgotten and not gotten enough of Goethe. What Eckermann does not remember to remember here is a dream which anticipates this moment, one which he had prior to his encounter with Goethe but which strangely recalls and reflects the scene of that encounter.

The dream, a letter tells us, took up the entire night of 19 December 1821. In the dream of their first meeting Eckermann is, however, loquacious as he embraces Goethe's legs:

> I dreamt the whole night with Goethe ["mir träumte vorige ganze Nacht bey Goethen"], I spoke much to him. I kept on putting my arms around his legs, ["ich fasste immer seine Beine um"]; but he had thick underpants on. He said he could no longer be warm any other way ("er könne anders nicht mehr warm werden"]. He was already very old, but

he liked me very much, and he fetched out of the cabinet a whole hand full of pears, which he also peeled, but only around the stem; I was supposed to eat all of them, but I told him that I would take two with me to Hannover, for my "Hanchen." Well, I would only arrive there in Easter, but they would surely keep even that long ["so lange halten"], and I slipped the two in my pockets. He also introduced Ottilie's (von Goethe—his daughter-in-law) two children to me, they were pretty and thick with bright locks, and I recited for him verses, "dass dem Vater in dem Sohne tüchtig, schöne Knaben bringst." He contended the word should be "stillst" (rather than "bringst"), but I said to him does he not know his own poem better, it must be "bringst," whereupon he conceded that I was right. He cried about contemporary poetry, saying it lay heavy upon his heart and he must soon depart; but he was counting on me and would now die more peacefully.

While in the dream, his underpants somehow protected Goethe from being directly touched by Eckermann, in the first entry there is no mention of some covering that would separate Eckermann's hands from Goethe's legs; we are simply told that Eckermann pressed his knees. Now his underpants function to signal Goethe's inability to generate warmth for himself, or the approach of death. Goethe was already very old, but Eckermann kept on grasping or rubbing his legs, to warm them perhaps, to caress them, to feel in any case that they are wrapped in a cloth-like envelope. The skin around the pear stems needs to be unwrapped, peeled in the meantime; and of the pears, he will eat all but two. He leaves the two stems in his pockets, presumably for later. Goethe hands him the fruit of the legs to eat, but two will be preserved, kept as in an invisible conserve, to be given up to someone else at Easter, in this case the resurrection is intended for the addressee of the letter, Hanchen, far removed from Weimar, herself to be conserved for thirteen years as Eckermann's fiancée, unconsummated or consumed. But the dream metamorphosis of the two legs into the two stalks soon gives way to the impression of the two little boys. Precisely where the father-son rapport is evoked in the dream—and two sons, two brothers are presented—a textual dispute arises around the problem of "bringing" or "stilling" the sons. But in his dream Eckermann is recognized as knowing Goethe better than Goethe; he corrects the poet and reinscribes the original verse, the original act of bringing sons forth to present them to Eckermann. The dream corrects the repression of the sons, bringing them back from a reading, Goethe's reading, of the necessity of silencing them.

The only thing that Goethe exposes to Eckermann in this premonitory dream is the stalk. Yet it is not clear what he was seeking to touch when he discovered, upon caressing Goethe's legs, that the fruit was covered with a protective coating. This discovery creates a disjunction in the sentence, for he writes "my arms around his legs *but* he had thick underpants." It is not clear at all that Eckermann's dream restricted itself to a phallic protrusion, especially given the possibility that "stillst" covers the breast as well. To "still" a child means to breast-feed it, and thus when Goethe yields the pears to Eckermann's mouth, of which Eckermann keeps a pair, he is supplanting the original, untouchable fruit with the breasts. Eckermann's dream can be read, then, as the narration of his averting his desire from tasting Goethe himself (the first time he writes of Goethe he asserts "ich habe einiges von ihm geschmeckt") to a memory of the female, be it his fiancée on whom he intends to confer Goethe's breast/pears, or be it displaced onto Goethe himself, who, like the legendary pelican, will feed Eckermann from his heavy heart. Eckermann accepts the feeding, taking the breasts which are offered to him. However, the devourer-child will be unable to keep Goethe warm. Eckermann dreams of the possibility that, while it excludes the prospect of his giving a lifeglow to the very old Goethe, nonetheless affords him the pleasure of assuring the master a peaceful death. The emphasis seems to be placed on a certain pathos of rescue with which Eckermann approached Goethe, yet the dream continues in this way:

> I asked him what he thought of me, whereupon he answered that if I began properly, I could one day enjoy the same renown as he did now, for my talent was not inferior to his. Even though I was in a dream, this nevertheless seemed exaggerated to me, but it gave me deep pleasure and I decided to do what I could ["das meinige zu thun"].

All these dream elements could be said to unfold slowly within the trajectory traced by the *Conversations,* where we shall observe how Eckermann treads the thin line between a notion of rescue mission and the transmission of his desire partially to supplant Goethe, or rather, to be "the same" as "Goethe." To return to the first entry, to Eckermann's attempt to "begin properly" as Goethe in the dream had enjoined him to do, we find that Eckermann has not exactly been subjected to the "*still*ing" effect of which he had dreamt, at least not in the sense of oral gratification; for here he cannot be satiated, he is still hungry and he begins to scan Goethe's face for the resources of meaning it appears to yield: "His face was so powerful and brown and full of folds and each fold was full of expression." Locating thus the speech he cannot conjure otherwise on Goethe's body, he begins by reading the folds of a face which cannot however offer full, exhaustive meaning or satiation. Removing the focus from Goethe's legs and pears, Eckermann concentrates his entry on these folds of a face which Goethe offers as his facet. "Und solche Ruhe und Grösse!" This type of reading, momentarily joining Winckelmann and Eckermann in homage to the Olympian figure, will return in the final fold of this volume where (to the dismay of scholar-realists who crave images of the decay and shrinking in the age of Goethe) Eckermann will unfold an exalted vision of Goethe's body.

Near the end of the inaugural entry Eckermann has found a place of tranquillity; he is unspeakably content, remembering a mood of appeasement and gratification. "I felt unspeakably content with him ["bei ihm"], as might someone who, after great efforts and hope finally sees his most fervently desired wishes gratified." It is as if fulfillment were attained, finally, in the beginning, as if everything to follow this moment of devoted proximity will be graspable either as a fall from this state of joyful appeasement or in excess of it. The couple has by now decided on itself according to several determinations; it is mother and child, father and child, husband and wife, husband and husbandman, textual pair, a pair of pears, and so on. And this couple's, or these couples', first separation in what will become a nine-year cohabitation (*Zusammenleben,* Eckermann frequently terms it; *Hausgenossen,* Goethe terms it), is suggested to be a kind of gentle wrenching apart of a fused body, a first moment of reciprocal extortion. Eckermann names the violence of this extrication "love": "Mit Liebe schieden wir auseinander" ("we separated from one another in love").

Eckermann, however, will first have to give up another, related drive before giving himself up entirely to Goethe. While Eckermann had planned to spend just two days in Weimar, Goethe asks him to remain at his side, to be separated only for the duration of a summer vacation. He arranges accommodations for Eckermann in Jena, assigning him a substantial amount of homework, and Goethe himself prepares for his summer transports in Marienbad. At this hour Eckermann still "felt the most vital drive to produce something new in this time, and therefore to ground my future fortune as an author" (19 June). Eckermann had entertained the hope, he writes, of writing innumerable poems as well as several dramatic works. The beginning of their encounter, however, marks the penultimate attempt, on the part of Eckermann, to envision himself as the unique signatory of a text. Goethe will henceforth deny him permission to sign his own work, even when that work promises to be relatively innocuous, such as when Eckermann was engaged by the *European Review,* an English journal, to report periodically on the state of German letters. Goethe's response to Eckermann's request to be allowed to write for the journal was one of unrestrained anger. Why Eckermann needed to ask Goethe's permission in the first place is another question; but he based his argument on financial need—he was receiving no funding from Goethe or the principality of Weimar, he had no other source of income and depended on Goethe's noontime dinner invitations for nourishment. "No. As I said, you must decline the offer; it does not lie on your path ['es liegt nicht in Ihrem Wege']. In general, beware of splintering [*Zersplitterung,* fragmentation]; hold together all your forces" (3 December 1824). In the meantime, Eckermann was to piece together the fragments of Goethe's oeuvre with no hope of remuneration, except perhaps for the "phantom of a salary," as it is said in the case of Tasso.

The implicit contract which Goethe had drawn up for Eckermann when he came to fetch him in September to bring him back to Weimar promised a far less precarious existence or at least, indeed, it forgot to specify the type of credit system into which Eckermann had bought. "You will have the best of everything, because the best resources ['Hülfsmittel'] are in my hands." Part of the terms of that contract and that system include a "quick *Bildung*" which Eckermann is to receive at Goethe's hands; "I'll take care of finding you an apartment near me; Sie sollen den ganzen Winter keinen unbedeutenden Moment haben." Henceforth, everything will be in Goethe's hand, including, namely, Eckermann. The summer was over. His entry for 15 September ends thus:

> It was blissful to be close to Goethe again, and to listen to him speak again, and I felt that my whole inner self was given up to him ["ihm mit meinem ganzen Innern hingegeben"]. If only I have and can have *you,* I thought, all else ["alles Übrige"] would be all right. So I repeated to him that I was prepared to do whatever he, after weighing my peculiar situation, should think right.

Eckermann surrenders to Goethe, gives up the idea of an *autonomos*—of the law of *autos* and of mobility—places himself in Goethe's hand, thinking that the rest, the remnants—the *Übrige*—can be put to rest, provided that he can have and hold Goethe who already has an irreversible hold on him. Indeed, the condition of being close to Goethe will be linked up inevitably with Goethe's hands—and not only as they relate to the legacy whose finishing touches Eckermann will apply, or to Goethe's last hand (*Ausgabe letzter Hand*) but also to the weighty pressures of hand-outs (*Aus-gabe*) to which Goethe subjects Eckermann.

In this context it is perhaps fruitful to point out that Eckermann has no particular qualms about designating himself as some kind of parasitic bird whose pleasure and sustenance derives precisely from eating out of his guardian's hand. His entry of 11 October 1828, develops this theme concisely. He begins by telling how the company at Goethe's table laughed at his expense: "Man lachte auf meine Kosten." Very soon after this prophetic remark (they are still laughing), one begins to recognize that *Kosten* plays on a double, anasemic significance: he pays for the general laughter at his expense; in addition, however, it appears that the company was moved to laugh on account of his taste, his manner of tasting (*kosten*) and consuming Goethe. Eckermann's rather surprising table manner is revealed to us at a Sunday dinner which gradually works its way down to dessert, consisting of biscuits and grapes: "They [the grapes] were sent from remote parts and Goethe was secretive about their origin." Goethe distributes the final goods of the repast unequally; he has saved ripeness for Eckermann: "He divided the grapes and handed me an extremely ripe branch across the table. 'Here, my good man,' said he, 'eat of these sweets and be contented ['vergnügt'].' " The other side of maturity ("extremely ripe") has from the very start been put away for Eckermann; he never ceases to remind us that, in this case, he is in fact partaking exuberantly of Goethe's ripeness. Yet there is a hint of a belated bestowing; Goethe in his infinite wisdom and sadism has reserved the overripe, rotten grape for Eckermann. But this, with all its implications, remains only a hint. Here the scene is limited to a special, secretive branch which Goethe had saved especially for him, delivering it with the injunction to consume and enjoy. True to the spirit of the injunction, and to others of this same nature, Eckermann shows himself eager to prey on the Dionysian bait. As in his poem "An Goethe," which is set in motion by the eventful gesture of "Hat mich Deine Hand ergriffen," Eckermann conjures an image of being hooked or clasped by Goethe's hand and then reeled into his proximity. The grape's origin, he has said, was mysterious. One of its origins, at least, can be retrieved as the Old High German *chrapo*, meaning a hook or clasp. Goethe gives him an extremely ripe "branch," his hand, hooking Eckermann who confides that "I enjoyed [tasting] the grape from Goethe's hand ["Ich liess mir die Traube aus Goethes Händen wohlschmecken"], and was now close to him both in body and soul ["und war nun mir Leib und Seele in seiner Nähe"]."

One among many secret enactments of a festive contractual scene
between Goethe and Eckermann, today's dessert was served before an
anonymous public. While Eckermann refrains from mentioning the
names of the "other dinner guests," Goethe's diary entry for that day
notes those present as Kanzler von Müller (who wrote the rival text,
another "Conversations with Goethe" rendition), Alwine Fromann,
Macco, and Coudray. Eckermann prefers to have forgotten these details when he puts the event to paper, focusing his attention instead on
his desire to be alone with Goethe that day, the impression of youthfulness that Goethe made on him, and the particular details of his
clothing: "I found him, as I wished, still alone, in expectation of company. He wore his black coat and star, in which I so much liked to see
him; he appeared today in quite youthful spirits. . . . " Despite the
eventual influx of dinner guests, Eckermann grants himself his wish of
remaining alone with Goethe, in the midst of company, unable in a
state of distraction to come up with the appropriate word when addressed. His mind is occupied with the lesson Goethe had taught him
before dinner, as a kind of private hors d'oeuvre. Goethe instructed
Eckermann, namely, on the status of his oeuvre: "Goethe" would
never be "popular," one should therefore renounce the wish to spread
his work among the multitude. He delivered the lesson to Eckermann,
just before the banquet had begun, anticipating the arrival of the unnamed *populus*. Goethe had pulled Eckermann aside, bringing him
near the window. "My dear child," he said, "I will confide to you
something which may help you on a great deal and should do you good
throughout your life. *My works cannot be popular [Meine Sachen
können nicht populär werden]*. Anyone who thinks and strives to make
them so is in error. They are not written for the masses, but only for
individuals who desire and seek something similar, and whose aims are
like my own ['und die in ähnlichen Richtungen begriffen sind']."
Goethe wished to say more; "but a young lady who came up interrupted him, and drew him into conversation." Eckermann writes and
wishes that Goethe wished (to say) more, but their intimacy is disrupted, as is wont to happen, by the arrival of a young lady—one,
moreover, who draws Goethe into conversation.

Eckermann, "in the meantime," has been left behind, perched on the
window, left at least with the inner certitude that Goethe had wanted to
continue imparting confidential lessons to him. Their relationship constantly faces similar disruption, mutation, and the distancing at least of
one of the partners; nonetheless, the aspect of their affiliation in which
Goethe takes Eckermann under his wing, confiding a testimony and

legacy, seems here as elsewhere to be firmly established. Goethe is handing down the law of "Goethe," designating the destination of his writing and appointing a correspondent. The singular person who corresponds to my desire and direction—whosoever undertakes to pursue the same trajectory—will be, whoever he may be, my correspondent. That person will correspond to me, he will act as my correlative and correspond with me—or rather with my writings, my writing style. The mass which adheres to itself cannot adhere to me. Goethe's law is shown to govern the very scene in which it is uttered: Eckermann stages his reading of Goethe's argument, taking pains to focus on the moment Goethe draws him apart from the inflowing mass to impart his message to him alone. In order to avoid all suspicion of being a part of any company or populace, Eckermann stresses his solitude and inwardness, his singularity of thought; he remains absorbed in thought and "Goethes Worte lagen mir im Sinn und beschäftigten ganz mein Inneres." Turned inwardly amidst the masses, but toward Goethe, Eckermann stays fixed in a mediated mode of absence. So it may not seem surprising when Goethe, in the same entry, identifies Eckermann's constitutive absence, which is only disrupted, he finds, by representation: "Leave Eckermann alone," he warns the others, "he is always absent, except when he is sitting in the theater." Eckermann is always absent except when he is absent, sitting silently in the theater while others perform.[12] In any case the company—the dinner company—leaves him to his own resources so that he may prepare a meal for the world in the imaginary theater of genius: The world, he ruminates, feeds on genius—it feeds on Mozart, Raphael, and Goethe. "And does not the world relate to such immense sources like snackers ['wie Naschende'], who are happy here and again to peck at something, so that they would be granted for a while a superior nourishment ['eine höhere Nahrung']?" The world according to Eckermann pecks at a bit of Goethe. But to Eckermann, the individual whom Goethe drew apart, goes the task of a more serious kind of consumer's rapport. At this point of the entry and dinner, Eckermann has not yet begun to peck at the grape; he is still in the main course, but the remotest hors d'oeuvre, we may recall, was served up prior to this oeuvre in the form of pears, two of which Eckermann may still be carrying.

Though it is not always set out as explicitly as in this scene, Eckermann in his customary way inscribes in his writing a double repetition of what Goethe had confided to him. His twofold repetition or re-presentation of Goethe does not necessarily underscore an instance of simple servility, however; rather it serves to give Goethe's utterance legitimacy, founding his word as law. In such an instance the lawgiver is in effect Eckermann, who codifies Goethe's law, letting it resonate outside the contextualizing and restrictive effects of quotation marks, which often appear to carry Goethe's words the way a predatory bird might carry its catch. In saying "yes" to Goethe's words Eckermann gives them a ground and releases them, somewhat paradoxically, as a sign of appropriation. They can resound as an internalized law having attained superegoical dimensions. "Yes! I continued in my thoughts. Goethe is right! He cannot, in terms of his range and greatness, become popular, and his works are only for individuals in search of something similar, and whose aims are like his own." A quotation of Goethe without quoting him, this repetition of Goethe's utterance does not repeat the sentence it revives. Eckermann has left out Goethe's *wollen* ("those who correspond to my *desire*"). While Goethe is right and one must enter a relationship of correspondence to his search, this particular correspondent crops his desire out of the picture, out of the frame of reference when it is reset. Is this omission to be viewed as something like a lapsus on the part of Eckermann, or has he intervened with his editorial hand to strike the passage of Goethe's desire? In the third volume of the *Conversations* Eckermann reminds us that Goethe considered such cancellations—the striking of a line or word—a *furchtbare Operation* reserved for the intervention of mature, practiced hands: "Mann muss ein alter Prakticus sein, fügte er lachend hinzu, um das Streichen zu verstehen" (p. 565). Whether or not his striking operation seems premature or mature, practiced, Eckermann, in his affirmative repetition, cannot repeat Goethe's desire for a corresponding, identificatory desire; perhaps it would be impossible to acknowledge or repeat that Goethe's desire is repeatable, or even already a repetition of Eckermann's undisclosed desire. As nonrepeatable, his desire would border on aberration, monstrosity. Or maybe indeed Goethe's desire for another's desire is not to be repeated, and can only be placed by Eckermann in Goethe's mouth, in the mouth of the great host whose desire for Eckermann seems to be articulated as his desire for the corresponding other to eat his grape, to attach himself to his ripe body and to find pleasure in this. As if Goethe *desired* devoration—a hypothesis that corresponds to Eckermann's deepest phantasms.

In any case, Eckermann's repetition, while leaving out mention of Goethe's desire (which no doubt was shared by Eckermann too), designates Eckermann as the unique correspondent of Goethe's desire. Goethe's writings, he reflects, are destined in particular (*im einzelnen*) for those who prove capable of passionately savouring him (*leiden-schaftliche Geniessende,* passionate gourmets). Moreover, Eckermann continues thinking, they are meant for those who search out the poet for their own heart's bliss and pain. In addition to the pleasant form of cannibalism and radical identification these works afford, they are for young poets who want to learn how to express themselves, and, too, for the *Naturforscher* who is given the great laws and who receives (*empfängt*) the indwelling methods, and so on. All the attributes which Eckermann adumbrates here, including the gentle savaging of Goethe, and to which he says "yes," will be shown, in the course of the *Conversations,* rightly to belong to Eckermann. While Eckermann remains spiritually absent from the table, his heart's language continues to feed on it:

> And so all who strive in the arts and sciences go as guests to the richly bedecked tables of his works ["den reichbesetzten Tafeln seiner Werke zu Gaste"], and their effects testify to the general source of a great light and life ["Quelle eines grossen Lichts und Lebens"].

In his absent-mindedness, Eckermann has spit out everything (almost everything) that Goethe had told him—onto the table, in front of everyone, and they are in the meantime laughing, he thinks, at his expense (*Kosten*). We are still here, on 11 October, at Eckermann's expense, astonished at his taste. In his anorectic fit, at once abstaining from eating and compulsively relating everything desirable to food, Eckermann has been closer and more present at the table than even Goethe might have suspected. While digesting Goethe's words, and in the course of memorizing and conserving the tables of Goethe's laws, before accepting the host's grape and hand, Eckermann will have set the table before us with Goethe's works. And this singular guest will consume all forty courses; he is already savouring Goethe's light and life, keeping himself alive by serving himself serving Goethe, and eating heartily. It may be, then, that every time Eckermann shows himself sitting at Goethe's table (the times are innumerable), he is narrating the specific mode in which he consumes the body of Goethe's works and conversely, every time he writes that he is reading Goethe, he is, as the saying goes, devouring him.

Instead of prescribing some kind of nestitherapy for Eckermann, Goethe, on the contrary feeds him on himself, often overfeeding him in secret harmony with the fantasmatic terms dictated by Eckermann's nightmare. Yet Eckermann has written, as early as the first entry, that he could never be satiated.

If the very dinner scene which thematizes the world feeding on genius is attended by an anonymous public whose identity Eckermann at no point reveals, this is because the other guests steal into the scene as a massive disruptive force, supplanting Conversation with conversation, the singular with the populous—but more importantly, and in the first place, perhaps because Eckermann is Goethe's only guest in the proper sense of the term. The others who double as guests, or as the mundane version of that concept are petrified by Eckermann into mute witnesses of the primal event, always verging on a consenter's crime, which establishes the covenant between Goethe and Eckermann. The covenant institutes Goethe's desire as law: "eat my body, conserve it, and make this your pleasure." One question that the entry leaves open, however, is whether Eckermann, according to his own calculation, is to be perceived as a mere "snacker" on Goethe's genius or whether he is uniquely corresponding, in responding to Goethe's greatest desire of which he had long ago dreamt, namely Goethe's desire to be consumed and incorporated, indeed, to be the name of incorporation. Goethe had begun by giving himself away as the body of his texts, for instance as early as *Werther,* "the flesh of his flesh," the first offering he made of himself to the world, when he described himself as the legendary pelican. The pelican-parent tears out its heart to be consumed by the child. As for this staging and entry of his incorporation of Goethe, Eckermann has in the meantime swept from the window conversation to Goethe's hand. Goethe has called him a child, his "dear child." Later Eckermann will explain to Goethe that certain birds are believed to swallow their adoptive parents.

Body Building

If Eckermann's predatory habits seem to correspond to Goethe's desire, it is because Goethe had spontaneously proposed himself as Eckermann's host. In fact, Goethe gives his body to Eckermann so that he can constitute it as a body. Eckermann's task, as Goethe defines it, will be to transform the fragments and remains—the bits and pieces of Goethe's writing—some of which date from the 1770s, into the body of Goethe's works. Thus if their relationship may appear at first sight to be grounded in dissymmetry—and it certainly is—this does not preclude the relationship's being always in a certain sense reversible, however. For Goethe preys on Eckermann in order to nourish his body which, henceforth, will never be entirely his own. In fact, Eckermann

underscores this aspect and the secret reversibility of their relationship
when he feeds Goethe back his own lines from a work whose completion is, according to its author, due to Eckermann. The question on 16
December 1829, is Homunkulus, that mysterious figure capable of
reading the mind and dreams of Faust when he lies unconscious. "Sie
empfinden das Verhältnis sehr richtig, sagte Goethe," whereupon
Eckermann quotes to him the text referring to the relationship of their
relationship:

> Am Ende hängen wir doch ab
> Von Kreaturen die wir machten.

This is an example of Eckermann making Goethe swallow Goethe in
order to digest Eckermann: in the final analysis, in the end, we do
indeed depend on the creatures that we have created. We hang from
them, like limbs. If Goethe created Eckermann at the end of his life, it
was because this end also depended on him. In the *Conversations* these
lines revert to Eckermann; they are presented as his lines which he
picks from Goethe's body, citing from Goethe's masterpiece in order
to establish his mastery over their relationship: "Sie empfinden das
Verhältnis sehr richtig, sagte Goethe." Thus inciting Goethe to author-
ize the legitimacy of his claims and the correctness of his interpretation
of Goethe, Eckermann likewise affirms the proper functioning of his
assimilative or digestive systems.

Eckermann had long been assimilating Goethe's body to his own and
his position has always been one of hanging on to the Goethean body,
be it in the prehistory of their intimacy, at the time he wrote *On Poetry
with a Particular Reference to Goethe,* be it as the *Kompendium* to
Goethe's *Farbenlehre,* be it as that member of Goethe's familial
branch who as early as 19 June 1823, can assert that Goethe "mich zu
den Seinigen zählt und mich als solchen will gehalten haben" ("counts
me among his own and wants to keep me that way")—or be it in the
form of the *Conversations* which was first appended to Goethe's collected works. Eckermann himself hangs on to Goethe's body, of which
he constitutes an appendage, limb, or member (*Glied*) which is at
times best viewed as a type of prosthetic device that, all Goethe scholars agree, can be dislocated from the joint legacy. Perhaps we shall
have to amend this notion of Eckermann as *Glied* in a moment, as the
movement of this narrative carries us to another body.

But to remain within the precinct of this body—of the detachable/
attachable parts and reversibility—let me just say that neither was a

notion of mutual perforation nor one promoting corporeal exchange ever directly addressed in the recorded exchanges between Goethe and Eckermann. However, in the third volume of his conversations with Goethe, Eckermann inserts an account of a dream he had narrated to Goethe. He had dreamt his dream the night preceding 12 March 1828. "I saw myself namely," Eckermann begins, "in an unknown region among strangers, but I was altogether in a good mood" (this, needless to say, is a dream). "It was a resplendent summer day spent in enticing nature," located in a place resembling either the coast of southern Spain or France, or not far from Genoa. "At lunchtime we consumed our meal at a cheerful table ['lustigen Tafel']" and then, prolonging the merriment, they walked, coming upon pleasant, bushy lowlands when suddenly they saw in the sea the smallest island on a jutting rock which hardly had enough room for five or six people, and where one could not move without the fear of sliding into the water. Looking back from where they had come, they could see only the ocean. Ahead they saw a coastline spread before them at a distance. "There's only one thing to be done, said the one to the other: we must undress and swim over there." "You can say that easily enough, I [Eckermann] said; you happen to be young and beautiful and beyond that, you're good swimmers. I however swim badly and, anyway, I don't have the kind of figure ['ansehliche Gestalt,' eminent or distinguished figure] that would allow me to appear on shore in front of strangers with any pleasure or ease." "You're a fool ['Tor'] said one of the most beautiful. Just get undressed and give me your form ['Gestalt'] and you can have mine in the meantime. . . . With these words I quickly undressed, leaped into the water and immediately felt, in the other's body ['Körper'], that I was a powerful swimmer. I had soon reached the coast and, naked and dripping, I stepped among the people with the most cheerful confidence—I was happy in the feeling of these beautiful limbs ['dieser schönen Glieder'], my behaviour was unforced, and I was immediately at home ['vertraut'] with the strangers at table." The others eventually reached the shore to join them and the only one missing turned out to be the young man "with my form in whose limbs I felt so well." Finally he approached the shore "and I was asked if I wouldn't care to see my former self ['mein früheres Ich']. At these words a certain uneasiness ['unbehagen'] overcame me, because I felt no great joy about myself ['keine große Freude an mir selber'], in part because I feared that my friend would immediately ask me back for his own body. Nonetheless, I turned toward the water and saw my second half swimming not far in our direction and, turning his head sideways, he looked up at me laughing: 'There's no bouyancy ['Schwimmkraft'] in your limbs!' he called to me. 'I've really had to fight the waves and breakers, and it's no wonder that I'm arriving so late and am last of all.' I immediately recognized the face: it was mine, rejuvenated and somewhat fuller and wider, and freshly colored. Now he stepped onto the shore and when, setting himself upright, he took the first steps, I had a general view of his back and his thigh ['*Schenkel,*' also hinged leg; limb] and was pleased about the perfection ['Vollkommenheit'] of this form. . . . How is it possible, I thought to myself, that your small body grew up so beautifully!—Did the primal forces of the sea have such a wondrous effect on it or is it because the youthful spirit of the friend permeated or penetrated our members ['die Glieder durchdrungen']? I quietly wondered why the friend didn't act as if he wanted to exchange his body once more. Actually, I thought, he looks so stately and, at bottom, it could be all the same to him; it is not all the same to me, however, for I am not sure whether I could be pieced back together in that body or whether I would shrink to my former size.—In order to arrive at some certitude about the matter, I took my friend aside and asked him how he felt in my limbs [or member, 'Glied']. 'Just fine!' he said. 'I have the same sense of my being and strength ['Kraft'] as before. I don't know what you have against your limbs! As far as I'm concerned, they are perfectly alright, and you see that one only has to make something of oneself. Stay in my body as long as you please, for I am completely content to abide in yours for all eternity ['für alle Zukunft'].' I was very happy about this statement, and insofar as I, too, felt completely as before in all my sensations, thoughts and memories there came to me in the dream the impression of a complete independence of our souls and the possibility of a future existence in another body."[13]

And the possibility of an existence in another body. The other body to whom the contents of this dream have been confided responds with the characteristic ambivalence that he seems to reserve for Eckermann's more delicate revelations. "The muses are particularly favorable to you at night," Goethe comments, "for you will surely admit that in your waking hours it would be difficult for you to come up with something so peculiar ['Eigentümliches,' also "proper to yourself"] and pretty." "I hardly understand how I arrived at that," Eckermann replies, "for in the past days I have been feeling greatly depressed, which would make the idea of so new a life seem rather remote."

It would no doubt be foolish to attempt any further analysis of a dream that so knowingly speaks, so to speak, for itself. And yet, before we slide into the dream's oceanic elements which form the place of both the dreamer's self-dissolution and self-discovery as other, we might retain the fact that this is one of the few dreams to be singled out for narration in the *Conversations*. As such, it is also the unique place exposing the terms of the currency involved in Eckerman's peculiar exchange program. On the whole, then, the dream narration spells out, in a very odd yet telling way, the deal which dictates the terms of Eckermann's membership in Goethe's corporation. As usual, the corporate body enters negotiations around a table. However, the corporation is not quite corporate yet, for Eckermann judges the stature of his own membership to be wanting, at least, to be too meager to expose himself in the company of these other powerful members. This, precisely, is what institutes the exchange system, the exchange of bodies and, in the first place, an exchange of the earth, which somehow anchors Eckermann, for the body of water which produces a menacing effect and diminishes his—if we can still say "his"—standing.

The purported motivation for the dream's central event—the exchange—is to enable self-presentation. The minimal presentation to which Eckermann aspires takes place after the exchange is effected, when he can confidently present himself naked and dripping: he is happy in the feeling of these beautiful members or limbs. But, as if this were the absolute and sole condition governing the corporate body or assuring the sensation of wholeness, one member, at this point, is missing; namely, "my earlier self." This earlier self arrives late, and as the last to appear, it occupies the position both of latecomer (as perhaps Eckermann was in coming to Goethe), and also as a source of anxious speculation. At any rate, the missing member's face is recognizable as Eckermann's, but it shows signs of having undergone some metamorphosis. As the figure of the former self stands up, it corresponds in size to the new figure: in fact, the former self is only a series of traces of itself, of which something in the meantime had been made, as it tells itself or its other in the dream. To make something of oneself means here to enter the other body—and we shall examine the consequences of this fantasmatic entry in a moment. For at bottom, there is always a way out.

To make something of oneself, then, means, among other things, to appropriate to oneself a stronger, more beautiful, perhaps almost immemorial body with splendid limbs. In short, it requires self-conglomeration, and negotiating oneself into a corporate body with members in good standing. At the same time, however, one of the members may, in one way or the other, be counted as missing, or at least presumed missing and on the way to reclaiming itself. Nonetheless the dream assures Eckermann that, to the other, elusive, figure it is all "one and the same thing" ("einerlei"). For the self that says "I," however, it is neither one nor the same thing, and he recognizes the risks involved in taking back his own, that is his alien, body, should it return to him from the waters. Such an inflation of the body, such a chart for the projected growth of the limbs or members would, if it were sustained, have protected the Eckermann of the waking hours from being designated (by himself and others) a frail spirit who is small and ugly, "le petit docteur Eckermann," who would never have dreamt of exposing himself, his body, before the guests or shareholders at Goethe's table. And since we began to account for this dream by measuring the corpus of Goethe and Eckermann, this, too should not forego mention here, namely, the vast and splendid corpus to which Eckermann attaches himself or in which he disguises himself. He dreamt, he tells us, that it was all the same to Goethe.

Eckermann himself, in conversation with Goethe, gives us a clue to where a primary dream source might be found. He supposes it to have arisen somewhere in the discussions of the previous evening. He announces that the dream must have something to do with "the forces of the ocean and the sea air"; and thus he wonders: "War es nun dass ich mit diesen Gedanken und mit einer gewissen Sehnsucht nach den belebenden Kräften des Meeres einschlief. . . . " ("Whether or not it was that I had fallen asleep with these thoughts, and with a certain longing ['Sehnsucht'] for the inspiring powers of the sea ['den belebenden Kräften des Meeres', enlivening forces]; suffice it to say, I had in the night the following, and to me very remarkable, dream.") This is Eckermann's clue. However, before we explore the implications of this longing, which longingly calls for interpretation, or the "enlivening forces" whose memory lulled Eckermann to sleep that night, we might look elsewhere in that conversation, in that previous evening with Goethe, to take account of the exchange which may have left its imprint in Eckermann's dream.

That conversation—of 11 March 1828—engaged Goethe in a reflection on genius for which, Eckermann notes, Goethe has exchanged the term "productivity." "Every divine illumination in which the extraordinary arises ['das Außerordentliche'] will always be bound up with youth and productivity." What determines productivity will not be a quantitative mass of creations but their *life* and *endurance* (*Leben und Dauer*). There was a pause after Goethe linked productivity to life:

then, Goldsmith, for instance, can be considered a productive poet precisely because the little he produced was "knowingly capable" of sustaining its indwelling life ("ein inwohnendes Leben hat das sich zu erhalten weiss"). This gave rise to a pause ("Es entstand eine Pause") during which Goethe continued to pace up and down the room. Eckermann interrupts the pause by asking whether genial productivity resides only in the spirit of an important person or whether it might also be lodged in the body ("oder liegt sie auch im Körper?"). "At least," Goethe replied, "the body has a great influence over it.—There was however a time in Germany when one thought of a genius as being small, weak and even hunchbacked; however, I praise the genius who has the appropriate body." One can well imagine how this part of the exchange between Eckermann and Goethe might have been translated into the dream had that night by "le petit Docteur Eckermann." This pause itself should give pause, as it introduces a dead moment into the question of life. Genius has something to do with youthfulness—this, by the way, is the same conversation in which Goethe makes his notorious assertion associating genius with repeatable puberty ("wiederholte Pubertät"). It may well be that the listener had already arrived at the scene equipped with a reading of genius as something "lodged in the body"—a resident phantom or alien body, a *Fremdkörper*.

Eckermann, the questioner, the listener, the writer of genius—though that genius may not be proper to him or embodied in his outward appearance—is now old by comparison to Goethe; he is doubled over Goethe, hunchbacked, writing this down, depressed. He may not know how to sustain life—his own life—he may lack the necessary buoyancy. He was perhaps never young. He was a latecomer (he was born belatedly as the last son of a second marriage, he was born to elderly parents—Goethe gets him on this, too). And Goethe cannot resist talking to Eckermann about the physical constitution ("körperliche Konstitution") of a writer who might not be solid or well—one who, on the contrary, would be subject to dejection. The productions of such a writer, he presumes, must frequently come to a standstill ("häufig stocken"); this type of writer is depressed and suffers blockage. Goethe has advice for him: "My advice, therefore, is to force nothing. . . ." Eckermann's dream that night in one sense enforced this admonition, but in the other body: "I felt very fortunate in these beautiful limbs," he dreams. "My behavior—I—was not forced." As one of Goethe's beautiful members, I do not force my writing. I am young and healthy. Elsewhere, Eckermann has told us that swimming and writing amount to the same activity.[14] Nietzsche will advance a similar hypothesis, notably when he writes that the decision to start writing is like leaping into cold water.

The beginning of the conversations from which Eckermann believes his dream to have emerged, constitutes one of the most painful entries he has made. He is ill, he is haunted by phantoms, he must force himself to go on, his energy depleted:

> For the past several weeks I have been quite unwell. I sleep badly, and have the most harassing dreams from the beginning of the night to morning, in which I see myself in very diverse states, carry on all sorts of conversations with known and unknown persons, get into disputes and quarrels, and all this in such a vivid ["lebendig"] manner, that I am perfectly conscious of every particular the next morning. But this dream-life ["Traumleben"] consumes the powers of my brain, so that I feel weak and unnerved in the daytime without thought or pleasure for any intellectual activity.

Eckermann "had frequently complained of my condition to Goethe." While Goethe does not quite offer to exchange bodies with him, he does suggest that the problem ("was Euch fehlt," what you are lacking or missing) is probably not worth the trouble of consulting a doctor (although he also "repeatedly urged me to see my physician"). Goethe can arrive at such a solution for Eckermann—consult a physician, don't consult a physician—because he has his own diagnosis to propose for his haunted companion, one that proves to be cruelly reiterable when Goethe speaks, in the context, of the enfeebled writer: "It is probably nothing but a small blockage ['Stockung,' standstill, stagnation]." Goethe recommends water with a bit of salt to the ailing writer. Besides prescribing a saltwater remedy in which Eckermann's subsequent dream will abundantly bathe him, Goethe sternly compares Eckermann to "a second Shandy," the father of Tristram, in a context which also conjures the phantom of Yorick. Goethe instructs his triste disciple that the father spent half his life angered over a door hinge, being unable to decide to alleviate his daily misery with a simple drop of oil. It's not surprising that Goethe is brought to think of a father, and not only because he considered his own father to be easy prey for bouts of "hypochondria," but because Eckermann has in a sense become very old by the time he asks the young genius, the man of repeatable puberty, for advice and counsel. Certainly, it is not all that irrelevant that Eckermann remembers Goethe naming him here as second to somebody, a late double of sorts, and even a father. Aging beyond the age of Goethe, second and unhinged; needing, moreover, to silence the creaks: the phantom keeps on returning around the joint legacy.

When Eckermann wrote this haunting passage about being haunted—by dreams, by conversation, by known and unknown persons—it was already 1842, a period in the life of Eckermann when he was invaded by his phantom, when someone else was dictating to him as Johann Peter Eckermann sat in a dark room at night, writing this down, taking dictation, in something resembling a hypnotic state. There was no more light. Among the deceased remains, a document containing these notes:

> Nachtwandlerisches Produciren, nicht den Muth gehabt, ein schiefliegendes Blatt gerade zu legen aus Furcht, die Geister zu verscheuchen. Schreibe nachts im Dunkeln. Schiefertafel. Ledernes Wams.

> Somnambular producing, didn't have the courage to straighten out a crooked sheet of paper, out of fear of shooing away the ghosts. Write nights in the dark. Slate. Leather doublet.

The dream, which is both part of and departed from the current of the *Conversations,* provides an interpretation of what can be considered Eckermann's reproductive compulsion or his hypermimetic history. At the same time, it motivates a reading of the *necessity* of Goethe's continued dictation, even after there was no more "more light" or "mehr Licht!" to be hoped for, assuming that a notion of absolute departure is, in the case of Eckermann, at all conceivable. Certain aspects of the dream have been submerged by those elements that were quickly brought to the surface of the conversation. It would be useful to consider these aspects in a new light.

Eckermann remembers the site of the dream as taking place either in Spain or France or possibly Italy, in short, a territory that is at once attached to the European continent while it remains, in the dreamer's terms, a foreign part. In the notes to the Insel edition of the *Gespräche,* Fritz Bergemann suggests that this moment of the dream narration might have originated in Eckermann's Italian Voyage. In other words, he links the dream source (though he does not make this point) to the time Eckermann left for Italy with August von Goethe. He returned to Weimar alone. It is no doubt compelling to view the dream in this light, as the story of the fatal voyage undertaken by Goethe's son in the company and care of Eckermann; however, the dream appears to narrate the impossibility of returning on one's own or arriving alone without the propulsion supplied by a greater body. This other body encapsulating an earlier self has been baptized in the primal waters of the sea. It has been detained by the sea, yet it will arrive eventually as two (my earlier self and the other), as seamen. The motif of retaining seamen, which begins to emerge here, is important throughout the *Conversations;* the retention of seamen, indeed, appears to depend on *Schwimmkraft* or writing. But we are always dealing here with seamen in foreign parts, that is, seamen gone astray—a situation which gives rise to a drive or need to retain and incorporate.[15] Eckermann appears to have in part intuited this and placed the words of superior insight in the master's mouth: "You will admit that it would be hard for you to invent something so properly your own ['Eigentümliches']"—in effect, the subject of this dream is someone else. It is perhaps even produced by someone else, for not only is it not properly your own dream, but it even knows to thematize the predicament of slipping out of one's own to retain the other as one's own, on one's own. Eckermann does not know how he arrived at this particular configuration of the dream-content which is utterly foreign to him ("so remote"). He was feeling particularly low.

When Eckermann and the other, stronger figure exchange bodies they come to resemble and duplicate one another. This reduplication takes place after they change for a swim, immersing themselves in the sea. They are not quite identical, however, nor quite twins; nor are they brothers-german but they now share the same flesh. Let us continue this line of dream-argument, this lineage. Eckermann, as his brother, was the first to arrive at the foreign island and found himself awaiting his own arrival with some dread; for the possibility still exists that his brother, as him, might ask for himself back. The earlier self is a latecomer: "dass ich so spät komme und von allen der letzte bin." This ought to remind us of Eckermann's self-presentation in the introduction to the first two parts of the *Conversations:* "As the last-born ['Als der Zuletztgeborene'] . . . one of my father's sons, after several sea voyages . . . was presumed dead." Eckermann arrives late; he arrived, and does not know how he arrived, as the late half to another half whom he in the meantime replaces. *The dread of seeing my earlier self* ("mein früheres Ich zu sehen") appears to stem from Eckermann's troubled identification with that which has vanished and has not yet returned: the brother of whom he is a double, an agent and representative—but, as such, a marked man, an agent of the living dead, so to speak. Thus *genius,* which also means "spirit," has come literally to occupy the place of a *Fremdkörper;* it is the mark of a parasitical inclusion conditioned by Eckermann's swallowing of the body presumed dead. Goethe, then, by no means provides an original instance of corporeal invasion for Eckermann; Eckermann has been the caretaker of someone who is vanishing, and who has been vanishing for a long time. Eckermann had already found a home for someone else's suffering within him when he was (at) last born. This other figure continues to agonize in Eckermann, in his dreams and in his conversations, while he assumes the responsibilities both of brother and foster parent to an alien body which has been deposited within him.

All this will be thrown up in a sense toward the end of the *Conversations,* when Eckermann teaches Goethe about birds (says he) who cannibalize their adoptive parents. Goethe, the adoptive parent, opens his ears as they enter a precarious discussion about moulting, losing one's plumage (or excreting) in order to sustain *Gesang.* The phantom agitating in Eckermann and who demands that his host continually feed him—this phantom who has long before Goethe taken up residence in his body—was present at the table society, the table d'hôte, where Eckermann appeared in his own (or someone else's) dream as the guest or ghost of the host.

The paternal injunction resounding in the dream as "one only has to make something of oneself" suggests the pressure under which Eckermann will have to make waves, and outlines the procedure which he must follow in order to make a name, as he puts it, or to make something of himself. Eckermann, whom Goethe has pronounced to be in a certain sense absent is, in part, presumed dead: a case of indwelling death, perhaps, that rhymes with the indwelling life of which they often speak. He has been half-dead from the start, which was already very late. It is that part—the part that arrived late, built itself a prison as the only means of making a name for itself—which adjoined itself to the Goethean body. He joins a Goethe who, paradoxically, was destined by Eckermann always to be presumed alive.

Taking Dictation or How to Talk-Write and Rewind

Eckermann's dream (re)places him as a latecomer, returning him to a beginning and late start. Indeed, among the qualities that might serve to distinguish or situate Eckermann, his originary status as latecomer, too, meets up with decidely negative valuations. In fact, here as elsewhere in the Goethe syndrome, the scene of birth—its timing, the inherent or inherited delays, thus even the age of those to whom one is born—produces a kind of destinal determination. By indirection and analogy, Goethe will fault Eckermann on his original belatedness; but within this fault lies the very possibility of an Eckermann.

Napoleon, as Goethe is quick to remind Eckermann, was born of youthful, robust parents, of whom one—much as in Goethe's own case—was only eighteen. In line with a conception of birth linking lineage and origin, it turns out that being born to a young mother can compensate for relatively humble origins, making up in some ways for a lack in congenital nobility; when one is born *from* such a mother, the *von,* the mark of nobility, is not far behind. In other words, a child-mother, or a mother remembered as having been a child at one's birth, guarantees in the cases of Napoleon and Goethe (and later, Freud) the possibility of self-overcoming, the institution of a demonic force, and she delivers a vitality that Goethe elsewhere associates with instinctual drive (*Trieb*) and pleasure (*Lust*). The young mother gives birth to orality.

When, on 7 April 1829, Eckermann records Goethe as having delivered a talk on the drive and desire to speak ("den Trieb und Lust zu reden"), the chief protagonist is, rather predictably, Napoleon. He claims here that Napoleon was driven by a desire to speak, but "when he could not speak, he was forced to write or dictate." In the space of a delay the patronymic steps in, into writing and dictation, after the primary rapport to speech and mother's tongue has been blocked or forbidden (and we know from *Dichtung und Wahrheit* to what extent "forced to write" stems from the paternal desire, from a concept of anality). Only when his drive was numbed, then, would Napoleon write or dictate; he would establish his rule. Note that dictation does not take place as an activity identical to speech but introduces a complication into the itinerary separating speech from writing. Viewed from this perspective, the relationship between Goethe and Eckermann can not be restricted to an opposition between speech and writing—between Socrates and Plato—but is part of a complex writing apparatus of delayed performativity. The structure of dictation, which is always at a remove from the vitality of speech as presence, ensures that Goethe can continue to talk-write, that is, dictate to Eckermann after his death. It also assures, for Goethe, the stability of the demonic force that will keep him, so to speak, on the side of speaking whereas others, of diminished strength, must write. Thus, in the same passage of 7 April, Goethe gives examples of figures who were forced, when speech failed them, to shift down to writing: "Also our *Grossherzog* took pleasure in speaking, even though he had a laconic nature, and when he could not speak, then he wrote."

It is perhaps the limit imposed by a laconic nature that prevented our *Grossherzog* from dictating. For Eckermann, however, speech, he wrote, was a near impossibility, and when put upon to speak he would often utter variations on a single theme of protest, for example, "oral teaching and effectiveness is not my thing" ("das mündliche Lehren und Wirken ist nicht meine Sache"). For Eckermann to write on the side, and always only on the side of writing, of taking dictation, is already to place him second, as double and half-dead or at least presumed dead. Someone or something is dictating to him, commanding his pen; he is secondary and doubled over, someone's telescripteur. "A genius of reproduction," some would call him. But what was he reproducing?

Far from being an original instance commanding Eckermann's reproductive desire or his desire for reproducing himself in another's body, Goethe is a double in a larger series of doublings and cancellations.[16] In this respect, Goethe cannot be considered as an original or first double, but always as a substitute for another double whose apparitions are several and imitative of one another. Let us reproduce the series on rewind and fast forward. As concerns his rapport to a mimetic type of art, Eckermann's first master was the painter Ramberg. When Eckermann's ability to hold the palette knife was mysteriously impaired, he became a devotee of Körner before Schiller supplanted him. The event that was to cancel out Schiller for Eckermann was a mediated encounter with Goethe, that is, it took place, as we noted earlier, when the phantom or image (*Bild*) of Goethe came into his hands. At this point Eckermann exchanged Schiller for Goethe by trading one portrait for the other and retaining Goethe. While we seem to have arrived at the endpoint of the series, it should be mentioned that there are doublings internal to the *Conversations,* of which only one need be mentioned here: the first man of letters whom Eckermann names in his self-presentation, the first writer ever to have drawn his attention, and who would later become an object of marked ambivalence for Eckermann, was a figure whose name was a kind of double for his own, namely, Winckelmann. It is typical of Eckermann to reproduce or repeat himself within a movement of differentiation. Thus, Winckelmann is Eckermann's first writer, one for whom he acquires a sentiment of dread.[17] To Goethe fell the task of unending yet simultaneous doublings. He doubled for the future writer in Eckermann, for the food on his table—for father, bride, mother, and, most significantly, the brother for whom Eckermann also doubles. Later on we shall see how this calculus of doubling extends to Eckermann's forty birds, who double for Goethe's forty volumes, which in turn

double for . . . and so on. Suffice it to say at this point, however, that
Goethe will also eventually double for the death over which Eckermann was unable to mourn.

This brings us finally to what brought Eckermann to Goethe, to the
one who would sustain a teaching on how not to mourn or be mourned
in which a refusal to mourn is, on the part of Goethe, accompanied by
something like a massive libidinal upsurge. Eckermann reproduces several such scenes or nonscenes of mourning, but the one that would
throw light on acts of reproduction and doubling, begins upon Eckermann's return from his Italian voyage. The voyage was undertaken in
the company of Goethe's son, August, who, led by Eckermann, was to
see the sea for the first and last time. When Eckermann left the ailing
and deeply disturbed August at that site, Goethe's son wrote that he
could not foresee a recovery for himself. Nonetheless Eckermann left
him there because his mission as August's nurse and companion no
longer seemed warranted. What is important to retain here is that
Eckermann was made responsible for the son, and the question of
August's survival was in his hands. Eckermann, then, arrives at
Göttingen (6 November 1830) when, at a table d'hôte, the innkeeper
informs him that "the great poet must still experience heavy sorrow at
his advanced age for, as he had today read in the newspapers, his only
son had died of a stroke in Italy." Eckermann spent the following
nights on the way to Gotha, and then to Weimar, sleeplessly "in the
deserted country where nothing outward was adapted for distracting
and cheering me up." "The greatest anxiety," Eckermann writes,
"was that Goethe in his advanced age might not survive the violent
storm of his paternal feelings." At this moment and passage, Eckermann comes alive in his text and quotes himself speaking to himself:
"And what impression—said I—will your arrival make, since you
have been with his son [Moon's translation reads "with my son"] and
are now coming back alone! He will first think he is losing him when
he sees you again." Eckermann's sensitivity to his place in Goethe's
tragedy is revealed in the auto-conversation, in the enclosure of the
carriage from which he will alight only to establish his identity with
the perished son of which he is to be a living sign and interior
double; his arrival will serve to expose a loss. It may be that Eckermann's acute apprehension of his place in this scene is due precisely
to the fact that this scene will not have been an original one, but a
repetition of a prior catastrophe: the one in which he arrives to take
the place of a missing son, to mark the place of an absence for an
aggrieved father. And once again he arrives late to an aged father; it

is nightfall, on the twenty-third of November; Goethe had heard of his son's death in Rome on the tenth. Upon reaching the "last stage before Weimar," he remembers this:

> I felt once more in my life that human existence has difficult moments through which one has to pass. My thoughts had commerce with higher beings above me, when a sight of the moon met me, which for a few seconds came shining out of thick clouds and then hid itself again in darkness as before. Was this now chance, or was it something more. . . .

A scene of repetition ("I felt once more"), a momentary unconcealment—was it chance or perhaps something more, he wonders. "Anyhow I took it as a favorable sign and therefore won an unexpected strength." He arrived on this strength, finding Frau von Goethe "in deep mourning."

> I then went down to Goethe. He stood erect and firm and held me in his arms. I found him entirely cheerful and tranquil [this sentence is not translated by Moon]; we sat down and talked at once of clever things ["gescheiten Dingen"], and I was extremely happy to be with him again.

Eckermann concludes the entry with these words: "We spoke about the Grand Duchess, about the prince and much else; his son, however, was remembered not with a single syllable ("seines Sohnes jedoch ward mit keiner Silbe gedacht")." No commemoration, no monument for Goethe's son, he writes. Not a single question, though Eckermann had been the last to see him. Instead, Goethe opened his arms to Eckermann, who was very happy to have arrived again.

Eckermann's emergence in the passage from Göttingen through Gotha to assume the son's place in Goethe suggests a mood of joy and arrival; however, his arrival will be lived in a mode of perishing. Henceforth, to take the place of Goethe's son means to risk untimely death, to exist in the knowledge of being forgotten. In the foreword to the third and most clouded part of Eckermann's passionate trilogy he describes his relationship to Goethe as that of son to father. While Goethe may have gained a reputation for having been harsh with August, their relationship, Eckermann asserts, "was singular and very tender." It was a relationship, he continues, of pupil to master and of one in need of *Bildung* to one abundantly endowed in *Bildung*. Goethe drew Eckermann into his circle, enjoining him to take part in the spiritual and physical pleasures of a higher existence ("an den geistigen und leiblichen Genüssen eines höheren Daseins teilnehmen"). Again, Eckermann's understanding of a superior *Dasein* includes a notion of physical pleasure whose specificity he does not however impart—except, perhaps, in the end.

The place in which Eckermann adopts himself as Goethe's son, the third part of the *Conversations,* has opened on a heavy note. He has had to overcome great obstacles, he writes, "Mein Fall war sehr schwierig." His case, his *Fall,* resembled that of a mariner ("glich dem eines Schiffers") who could not sail with today's wind, but who has had to wait in extreme patience for the wind to motivate him. The two prior parts of the *Conversations* were written because he could "to a certain extent go with good winds, for at that time the freshly spoken word was still resonating in my ears and the lively commerce ['der lebendige Verkehr,' also the vital traffic or intercourse] with that wondrous man sustained me in the element of an inspiration through which I felt myself carried as if on wings. Now, however. . . ."

Now, however, the Voice was silent, the good fortune of those personal contacts ("jener persönlichen Berührungen") were no longer entirely there. Eckermann has had to wait patiently until the "living Goethe was there again," until once more "I heard the particularly lovely sound of his voice which cannot be compared with any other." The winds that would carry Eckermann along, that would command his course and direct his intercourse were not at all times breathing inspiration, or to change the course of his narrative slightly, the dictaphone could at any moment break down, or the tape could stall, and put an end to the speak-writing from which Eckermann drew his inspiration. And when these breakdowns occurred and the winds stopped blowing, Eckermann would be in his deserted country again, his pen would dry up. It was as if Eckermann had perished in Goethe's absence. Sometimes, when Goethe would return to him, Eckermann would begin to show signs of life again. He can be reanimated: "The living Goethe was there again . . . my spirit was kindled by his ("mein Geist entzündete sich an dem seinigen"). The most intimate harmony reigned between us; he stretched out his hand, which I pressed, across the table." Eckermann's language is telling; it is telling us not to be certain about which of the two is alive in this sentence, for example: "So war ich ihm in voller Lebendigkeit wieder zugesellt. . . ." (Thus fully alive I once again joined him. . . .") If it appears presumptuous at this point to suppose Eckermann presuming himself as dead, then he dissipates any such doubt in a subsequent paragraph when writing of the months that would pass "when my soul was dead to him" ("für ihn tot war"). It died through contact with daily life, which, not being Goethe's life, is rather daily death. These were "annihilated times" ("nichtige Zeiten"), when Eckermann would have to await, in solitude and silence, the return of the past or a momentary consolidation of the past present—"where all that was past became present to me in full livingness." In the other present, the daily dead present, it is impossible to consecrate a moment to a beloved departed ("eines geliebten Toten gedenken"). The rare and beautiful hours come to us only in those peaceful moments of intense contemplation, when we believe to possess a departed loved one, or lover, in the freshness of life ("dahingegangenes Geliebte in der ganzen Frische des Lebens").

But to what does Eckermann trace this moment of coming to? What brought his soul back to life, wherein lay the motive of his coming alive to Goethe at certain unpredictable times? By what remote control system did the dictaphone begin to dictate again? According to Eckermann, all this is motivated by a single signal and consideration: "I was dealing with a hero whom I could not allow to sink." (Earlier, in another context, Goethe had explained to Eckermann how J.C. had prevented Saint Peter's sinking: you must not doubt your ability to walk on water. Here, however, Peter Eckermann keeps his Goethe from sinking or disappearing in the waters.) Goethe is a hero whose life must be sustained, he may not vanish or be presumed dead. Whether Goethe is to be understood as the ghost ship which Eckermann is steering ("My case . . . resembled that of a mariner") or a heroic figure held alive in a vessel under Eckermann's command, the waters will often unite with Goethe, keeping him buoyant in Eckermann's fantasmatic life.

"Was Sollte ich Tot Sein?"

About four years after Goethe's death, and half a year after his book appeared—it came out at Easter—Eckermann had beautiful nightmares in which "I normally saw him as someone who was alive" ("und zwar sah ich ihn gewöhnlich als einen Lebendigen"). "I held all sorts of conversations with him and always left him in the happy conviction that he was not dead" ("dass er nicht tot sei"). This time, that is, the night before, Goethe had appeared to him immensely "gay and fresh with life" in his house, with his son. Inwardly, Eckermann felt somewhat ashamed that he had not visited Goethe in four years and that, despite his repeated dreams of him, he basically believed the widespread rumors of Goethe's death. In other words, whereas Goethe was generally presumed dead, Eckermann had believed him actually to be dead. The dream conjectures that Goethe and his son had been exposed in the meantime to "the outdoors, the wind and storms" ("der freien Luft und dem Wind und Wetter ausgesetzt"). Eckermann could not prevent himself from disclosing to Goethe the rumor of his departure ("Hinscheiden"):

> People think, I called out laughing to him while I grasped his hand, that you're dead. But I always said it wasn't so, and now I see to my great delight that I was right. Isn't it true: you're not dead? "Those fools!" said he looking at me in a mischievous way. "Dead? Why should I be dead?! ['Was sollte ich tot sein?!']—I was away on voyages. . . ."[18]

Retaining his position in the dream as absolute source and judge, only Goethe, according to such logic, can pronounce himself dead. However, Goethe, as usual, is not inclined to commiting himself to self-effacing performative acts. He pronounces himself living, speaking; he is henceforth only partially departed on trips which are hardly comparable to the duration of Eckermann's corresponding guilt trips.

Eckermann could not resist asking Goethe what he "has to say about my *Conversations?*" Goethe's judgment: not bad. Someone had even said, he reports, "that in the *Conversations* my personality appears in a better light than in my own texts." Goethe wanted Eckermann to solve this riddle for him, which he does in the dream, by saying "it comes from the southern lighting" ("von der südlichen Beleuchtung"). While Eckermann was happy to receive Goethe's approbation, he later writes, he finds the expression "it comes from the southern lighting" unplumbable.

In the dream, Goethe goes now to his office in the house, leaving Eckermann to speak with his son about their Italian voyage. (This would perhaps be one source of the "southern light.") At this point in the conversation with August, Eckermann begins to open a long brown box—a casket (*Kästchen*)—where he stores different manuscripts. These he shows to Goethe's son. They are sketches, full of corrections, destined for future *Conversations* with his father, he dreams. Eckermann was planning to write them out, he explains, "in good time." Enter Goethe, who looks over his son's shoulder, sees the manuscripts, and takes them out of his son's hands to go over them. He would like to take a closer look at them, however, and takes them with him into his office, leaving his son alone with Eckermann once more. Eckermann in the meantime takes pleasure in noting that a more intimate relationship "than the one earlier in life" obtains between Goethe and his son. At this point, Goethe returns with his judgment: "A detached, torn fact, a naked expression does not mean much" ("Ein abgerissenes Faktum, eine nackte Äusserung will nicht viel heissen"). Eckermann should see to it, rather, that readers are given the details of the situation, and drawn into what is interesting about the object. This way the readers will experience an illusion ("Täuschung"), as if the asserted truthfulness were real: in such a mirroring, the reader would be enabled to believe he were experiencing ("miterleben," living with) the subject for a second time. In the already published texts, Goethe concedes, Eckermann has succeeded to a large degree in doing just this. Eckermann feels regenerated, charged ("angetrieben") by Goethe's words, happy to see his earlier accomplishments to a certain extent sanctioned by Goethe ("gewissermassen sanktioniert").

The tropological movements that prevail over his writing resurface in Eckermann's dream-conversations, which situate his manuscripts and a certain motif of castration in the open casket. In English, *casket* can mean both a coffin and a book containing choice selections; in German, *Kasten* also means the hulk of a ship; the objects held together by these containers are in constant need of revision or repression for, once again, we have something naked and externalizing (*Äusserung*) that cannot be abided. Goethe has read a manuscript and responds in the dream as if something had been torn off from him, detached. Yet to repair the tear, another cut must be made. Eckermann is advised to initiate the operation of the *detail* (*tailler*, to cut). The particular cuts of the situation harbor that which is interesting. They will give rise to the illusion or deception (*Täuschung*) of some reality that would confirm in the reader the experience of reliving a subject, or living again with a subject, for a second time. Writing, therefore, is dedicated in Eckermann's dream to the possibility of such a repetition. The dream names writing as that thing which is stored away and yet carried out when the other is presumed dead. Which does not mean that the in part departed will not return to pronounce a judgment. On the contrary.

The most stirring revision that the dream-narration has thus far made resides perhaps in the fact of Goethe's newfound intimacy with his son. In fact, Eckermann himself enjoys an unknown intimacy with the long lost son of his "father." He is the figure to whom the casket with the texts are in the first place presented. And everything remains fixed to keep this intimate triangle intact: "in this way we lived through the night, and it seemed odd to me that apart from Goethe and his son, neither someone from his family, nor one of his friends and relations ['Angehörigen'], or even a servant was to be seen."

The population increases in the second part of the dream. It is daybreak. Eckermann sees a small boat whose passengers he presumes to be smugglers. Eckermann engages the young Goethe in conversation, while the old man ("der Alte") "keine Lippe öffnete." People are busy on the other side of the shore. There is a great ferry. A lovely stork flies close by and, as with most of Eckermann's ornithological observations, this one proves to be an exemplary provider; he is said by Goethe's son to "fly already looking for frogs for his young ones." Without transition, he calls, "It is time, dear Father." "You still have unfinished business," Goethe says to Eckermann, who agrees, "I still have some things to do on this side" ("ich habe diesseits noch einiges zu tun"). And with these words Eckermann gives Goethe his hand. Goethe approaches the ferry, his lips remain sealed: it seemed that speech ("das Reden") was forbidden. Also, he did not extend his hand to Eckermann.

Something peculiar about the other passengers captures Eckermann's attention. Without exception they all carry packages and baggage while his Goethes have nothing, in general giving the impression that they had no physical needs ("keine leiblichen Bedürfnisse"). Eckermann watches them go as long as he can: "I wasn't sorry that they were going," and, "at the moment of departure I didn't perceive even a trace of emotional stirring in me; everything was as if it had to be this way. They left in a southeasterly direction."

A dream about living-death, we shall let it dream on in this text to commemorate Goethe's silence at the end, his unextended hand in consequence of the dreamer's concession to the story of Goethe's death. Eckermann, in any and every case, is left behind with their packages. Another source of remorse to which Eckermann's dreams relentlessly return him: the personality of Goethe is more true to life in Eckermann than in Goethe; he gives birth to Goethe's true Personality—the one that will survive the contingencies of his personality—he nurtures it, keeps it alive, and signs its existence (which is also a way of letting Goethe sink in his own texts). In Goethe's terms, all this would involve Eckermann in a major act of usurpation or exchange of textual bodies, for Goethe held the presentation of one's own personality to constitute an integral part of the work of genius—the fictions of personality and authorship are to coincide in one signator. The scenography of the dream drifts southeasterly, at daybreak, to Italy. The lighting gives off a deathly hue; in a way, in the dreamer's way, Goethe blames Eckermann for bringing death, and for carrying corpses. The son and Goethe are at stake in the *Conversations,* whose unpublished manuscripts, buried in the casket, are like a drafted monument, conceived in a state of ruination: torn down, naked and undraped, contextless and doubled with revisions. At least the dream allows Eckermann a reprieve; he was not sorry that they were going.

" 'You're Breaking My Arm,' I Cried."

The manuscripts to which Eckermann's dream refers are no doubt bound up with the beginnings of the third part of the *Conversations,* which he began to organize at that time. The dream appears to arise from a text, unspoken in the *Conversations,* that elucidates a particularly painful dimension of Eckermann's relationship to August von Goethe. On 22 June 1827, Eckermann writes a letter to himself. The account of this self-addressed letter was discovered by H.H. Houben and given in full in his seminal though largely unknown work, *J.P. Eckermann: Sein Leben für Goethe,* dedicated to Eckermann's nephew, Herr Oberstleutnant Gustav Bertram (1925). Beyond the link they establish to the dream, the following passages will do much to clarify a catastrophic aspect of Eckermann's life in Weimar. Until now we have been writing mostly in the mode of Goethe's "Neptunism," which grew out of his aversion to theories of catastrophe and "Vulcanism." It took an Eckermann to turn Neptune into a site of volcanic eruption. This unforeseen event erupts discreetly, splitting Eckermann's decisive destination.

"Something unfortunate ['Unglückliches'] happened to me which may have aftereffects and important consequences for me. For this reason, and because I have no friend to whom I can pour out my heart, I want to confide everything to this piece of paper and thereby obtain immediate relief." The day before yesterday, Eckermann explains to himself, on Wednesday, 20 June, he had been a guest of the Goethe house. The table was set for five guests. Among the subjects of table conversations he lists, Eckermann's contribution offered "that even the first murder took place as a deviation in the veneration of God." He does not comment on this further, but one wonders whether it is a question of chance or subtlety that has Eckermann leading up to the important event thus. Eckermann himself does not make this point, but it seems that he had turned the conversation to the story of

Cain and Abel—or to another First Murder. After exhausting several other topics of conversation, Eckermann is sent from the table by Goethe to see something that the elder apparently believes to be scandalous. He is sent out to look for the object in the company of August von Goethe, who has already seen it. We learn no more about the object in question than that it consists of two paintings. Houben's note tells us that, as yet, the mysterious paintings have not been identified. Eckermann only goes as far as saying that the "totally inane emptiness and nullity of the object immediately met the eye, just as the painter's skillfulness in its execution was not to be denied." Eckermann and the younger Goethe repeat, to one another, in a light vein, that Goethe is trying to punish them with this object. Before viewing the paintings, however, Eckermann had been led by August to two other rooms of the house and was made to guess whether the object might be found in them. "I went with Herr v. Goethe in the rooms. As good friends that liked each other since many years, we went arm in arm and joked with each other." (Remember that the entry begins with: I have no friends.) From the description that follows, it would appear that "we joked with each other" means that Eckermann was the butt (as usual) of his good friend's jests. " 'I had to look until I found the incredible things ['Wunderdinge'],' said Herr v. Goethe, 'and so should you, too, big Doctor,' " and so on, leading Eckermann on. When they reach the third room the young Goethe says, " 'It's going to have to be here. You see, I thought it would be in this box ['Kasten'], only it wasn't there but here!' " They joke about the twin paintings and start going back. In the last room, in the midst of some witty talk the young Goethe exclaims " 'I am now big, Doctor, and I defy the entire world. I always carry it ['ihn'—this is unclear but probably refers to the sword that goes with the *Kammerherrn* uniform] at my side, and so if someone gets in my way, it is bare ['bloss,' naked] . . . Nothing is sacred ['unverletzlich,' invulnerable, unwoundable].' 'Nobody?' I [Eckermann] said. 'My father, of course, I make an exception for him because piety comes into play and that's something so big that you aren't allowed even to touch ['verletzen'] it.' I praised him and wanted to open the door. 'Not yet!' said Herr v. Goethe."

Eckermann wants to open the door; he seems to sense that if filial piety is too strong a force to allow the son to take a plunge at the father, it prescribes nothing that would prevent him from wounding a substitute figure, an emissary or limb of the father—for example another type of family member in service of the head of the family, to whom Eckermann is irrevocably attached. This is the limb or member that the young Goethe would not show himself adverse to severing, if only to paralyze the father. Young Goethe is now big and, within the economy of his sarcasm, so is Eckermann who is about to be cut down to size. Provisionally, however, they return to the table, where Goethe is about to open a *portefeuille* with drawings. Eckermann is eager to look at them. "I wished to stay near to him and listen to his words." But the young Goethe signals him to follow, wanting to show him something else. Eckermann follows "half going and half held back" by the open doors through which he can still hear Goethe's commentary on the drawings. " 'I want to show you something, Doctor,' " the younger repeats, and exposes some landscapes of the Duchess Egloff-stein. " 'I am very grateful to you for this pleasure,' " Eckermann says and presses Herr v. Goethe's hand. " 'You see, Doctor, I like you,' he said, grabbing my left arm which he pressed and twisted violently, so much so that I feared that I would have to scream loudly. 'You're breaking my arm,' I cried, 'for God's sake, stop it!' The excellent ['treffliche,' on the mark] friend let go and laughed. 'That would be a good joke, Doctor, if I were to break one of your arms!' "

"For God's sake" is hardly an unusual turn of speech; nonetheless it returns us back to the preliminary report—and all preliminaries—to God, and to the notion of a deviation in the story of the first murder. We can begin to make out what Eckermann's usage of "joking" was leading up to. The good jokes are not over, however. Eckermann's arm is unbroken, but now the young Goethe asks a favor of him, he wants Eckermann to break his word, to tell a lie: "There now, Doctor, do me a favor. Lie for once! Be outright scandalous ["Seyd einmal recht schändlich. . . .]!" Needless to say, Eckermann cannot lie, he cannot oblige Goethe's son by telling the Duchess that he had viewed her drawings "behind my father's back, without his knowledge—and don't tell her I showed them to you." Interestingly, the first part of the request would not constitute a lie. What Eckermann does not seem able to say is that he would have seen something secretly ("ganz ver-stohlen"), behind "Father's" back, in a sense, having stolen something from Goethe. Eckermann's only response to the son of Goethe, now his sibling, is to point out that with the viewing of the Duchess's drawings, doubling for Father's drawings, "we have been indemnified ['entschädigt'] for those other images with which Father wanted to punish us, but his punishment did not entirely succeed." However, where Goethe does not entirely succeed in his punitive role, August rises to the occasion. The punishment that consists in wrenching Eck-ermann's arm will have been a prelude in the scene of anguish to which our unfortunate Abel is subjected.

The punishment lies in the sundering of another para-sibling pair,

the living and the dead, Goethe and Schiller. It all begins with Eckermann's failure to recognize a citation, a line from Schiller—a drasti-
cally appropriate line to miss, since the drama that ensues will situate
Eckermann as its hapless referent and destination. The line whose
source Eckermann is asked to identify runs, "Against stupidity even
the gods struggle in vain" ("Mit der Dummheit kämpfen Götter selbst
vergebens"). When Eckermann identifies the author as Shakespeare,
the young Goethe's capacity for damning reactivity begins to reveal
itself; he accuses Eckermann of thinking that *Schiller would not be
great* ("gross," big) *enough to speak in such a spirit:* So it happens that
August begins to think that Eckermann does not measure up, who
thinks that Schiller does not measure up, and so on—stemming from a
scene in which the Gods and Goethes struggle vainly against stupidity.
Eckermann's response to the reproach: "These words hit the nail on
the head and I surrendered" ("ich gab mir gefangen," I let myself be
caught or imprisoned). The prison sentence which he asks for himself
quickly dissolves into a death sentence, however, which is issued by
the Father's other son: "You are a grand person and I like you, but the
fact that you do not want to recognize Schiller makes me want to kill
you!" Eckermann attempts a few jokes on the order of the "I still have
things to do on this side" that emerged in the aforementioned dream:
"It would be a shame if I should die because of Schiller, for I would
still like to do this and that in the world" ("noch dieß und jenes in der
Welt thun"). In this case, the German allows us to hear that Eckermann still has to "do" this side, as in *diesseits, and* the other side,
jenseits, in this world. This may be the sentence that Eckermann is
serving here and elsewhere; he has to do time in both worlds simultaneously—this world and the beyond, the Old World and the New
World, for instance, into which his half-brother vanished. At any rate,
big Eckermann is beginning quickly to diminish in stature as the scene
deteriorates into a storm of injuries. But first Eckermann has to expose his skill in producing what Freud later identifies as the "cauldron
logic." "It would be a shame if I should die because of Schiller, . . .
Anyway, I *do* recognize him!"

Whether or not Eckermann recognizes Schiller, August claims to
recognize Eckermann: " 'You have no organ for [Schiller]. There are
some people who in a given way eternally remain caterpillars as long as
they live, and that's what you are in terms of Schiller. You are limited
['borniert,' ignorant, narrow-minded]! (He stepped towards me and
designated with his finger a line across my forehead). One just has to
take a look at you here to see that you are limited and will never grasp

Schiller.' This was insulting and I felt that my blood was rising, but I controlled my feelings out of respect for the place in which I was." Eckermann is no Tasso; he does not forget the sacredness of the space in which he receives an insult—and, anyway, he has no sword to wield, as does the young Goethe who has already expressed his willingness to plunge at anything but his father.

The scene continues. Eckermann tries to defend his preference for Goethe over Schiller (the argument will not stop with this pair), offering that Schiller's early dramatic works are crude. August v. Goethe stops him from robbing Schiller of what he considers to be his rightful place: "You are talking about the *Robbers* and I admit that, but his later works are the pride of German literature. In his first things, my father also committed sins." " 'Maybe against art,' I said 'but never against Nature. Your Herr Father was healthy and born perfectly ['vollkommen geboren,' fully, completely born], whereas Schiller only became what he is through culture ['erst durch die Cultur'].' 'In order to become something,' said Herr v. Goethe, 'he also had to be something. . . .' "

Poor Eckermann, arguing for birth over becoming, and in the name of a healthfulness he would never himself enjoy. All this to save Goethe, in this case, from his natural son and Schiller, "the pride of German literature." We know from his first letter of introduction to Goethe that Eckermann's aim and felt duty had always been to save Goethe. And here he is also defending the living against the dead poet. A close friend to August v. Goethe, Karl von Holtei, wrote in his memoirs: "For him, Schiller stood next to Goethe—yes, perhaps *over* him. Woe to that person who would allow himself in Goethe's house to raise the living one to the detriment of the dead one" ("Neben Goethe stand ihm Schiller,—ja vielleicht über jenem. Wehe demjenigen, der sich in Goethes Hause beikommen lassen wollte, den Lebenden auf Kosten des Todten zu erheben"; Houben, 293–94). Houben speculates that Holtei was aware of the scene that took place between his friend and Eckermann, and in fact, may have been referring to their clash in his memoirs. So whereas Eckermann was friendless and had to address the event in the absence of any immediate other, August had a friend to whom the story could be told (the friend is the one who writes the friend's story, who, for example, remembers a conversation). Eckermann will always be in a state of partial exclusion from all such pairings.

This scene does not restrict itself to the remembered, recorded acts of violence. Rather, it closes with a curious assertion—one that Eckermann in the end will have appropriated to his own purposes, as if the pain of the wound could only be deadened through a second writing that surpassed this self-addressed entry. Here is how Eckermann balances the account that he had opened for himself in confidence: " 'In order to become something,' said Herr v. Goethe, 'he also had to be something; he was a raw diamond that now shines as a polished stone. But he indeed had to be a diamond in order to produce such rays as he now does.' I was pleased with this image ['Gleichnis'] and conceded it to him." A diamond concession is about to be formed.

Although Goethe's own diary makes no mention of this scene, it was clearly brought to his attention. Eckermann stayed away for four days, and on the fifth he seems prepared to renounce another invitation to the paternal household: "Excellency! I doubt whether I dare come to table today, for I have not had the fortune of reconciling myself with your Herr Son" ("mit Ihrem Herrn Sohn zu versöhnen"). It is as if Eckermann would fail to come to the table if he could not be made sons with the son ("Sohn zu versöhnen"), if they could not be in some way brothers. "Nonetheless, I am long since favorably disposed towards him again and hope that this tension ['Mißverhältnis,' misalliance, missed relationship] will be appeased." Apparently Goethe saw to it that it was—that thay were *versöhnt*—for Eckermann promptly appeared at Goethe's table on that same day, 27 June.

The remarkable itinerary of the *Gleichnis* and other similarities that cause Eckermann to concede to his aggressor and to break off his account, reroutes the history of his story and auto-conversation, disclosing the secret passage to an open wound. For Eckermann will have taken the dagger thrust at him by Goethe's son to reinscribe it with diamantine precision in the foreword (which comes much afterward) to the first two volumes of the *Conversations*. Despite the immense space between the event and the dream, it will reemerge where Eckermann declares that "this is *my* Goethe," that is, my Goethe, the multifaceted diamond, the eternal living that triumphs over the dead. Eckermann wrenches the diamond placed on Schiller's casket by Herr v. Goethe to exchange vows with the father, his father of German literature. All this takes place behind Goethe's back; it is *verstohlen,* a secret revision of the *Robbers.*

Within the framing propositions of Eckermann's diary account, this maneuver, conscious or not, is already accounted for. The first murder, it began, originated as a straying from the veneration of God (*Verehrung Gottes*). The scene which comes to be enacted symbolically as a repetition of the primal fratricide, begins as the boys stray from the father's table—and Eckermann traces the detour taken on the part of the natural son, in the first place, in the *Verehrung Goethes.* However, if Eckermann has represented himself as a kind of disabled Abel, this is primarily because his role is more correctly to be understood as that of Cain. August, it will be recalled, had etched something on his forehead, which may be interpreted as the mark of Cain ("He stepped toward me and designated with his finger a line across my forehead"). August had designated his killer ("and I felt that my blood was rising")—Goethe's "other" son, his excellent friend and brother. Eckermann does away with August on at least two occasions: when he leaves him to his lot in Italy, coming away alone, and in the *Conversations,* when taking August's *Gleichnis,* he claims my Goethe, the diamond (foreword) and later, he names his Goethe his *father* (third volume), thus effectively displacing the place of a somewhat more legitimate son or brother.

To be sure, Eckermann cannot be held responsible for the death of August v. Goethe, but this does not mean that he did not feel himself to be in some way culpable. He suggests as much when he goes to see Goethe on his return from Italy (only now, on Eckermann's arrival, would Goethe recognize the loss he had incurred). Yet, even now, he triumphs in this fantasmatic murder, repeating it through other means in the public account, and naming Goethe in a certain sense his willing accomplice: "Goethe was altogether cheerful and peaceful; he spent not a single syllable on his son . . . and I was blissful to be with him again." To round off the account with something that may be only a matter of coincidence or chance, we might add here that on the day of their separation, when Eckermann left August behind, the latter broke a limb. It was not quite an arm, but the *Schlüsselbein;* the key is in the clavicle.

There exists another version of the First Murder, the one which Freud later interprets for us, invoking the name of Goethe. Eckermann leaves (the) room for this interpretation, in his dreams and his writing, though his case suggests more complications than can be accounted for in a single paradigm of the remorseful son. Eckermann has arrived at Goethe's doorstep to attend to the ceremony of Goethe's death, though his desire articulates itself in wanting to save Goethe.

In a certain way, Eckermann provisionally survives Goethe. Closer to death than to life, his survival is dramatized in the earlier dream of Goethe and his son, as well as in other sources available to us. Before looking into the other sources, the most prominent of which is the *Conversations* itself, it may be useful to recapitulate certain key moments in the Goethe-Goethe dream-narration. One source of that narration may be found in Eckermann's waking dream, the letter he wrote to himself when he felt cut off from the possibility of any *Ge-spräch,* at a painful remove from the Goethes. Certain motifs linked to the violent encounter with young Goethe recur in the dream, for instance, the claim he makes for still having something to do in this world. In the self-addressed letter, Eckermann reasons with his aggressor that it would be a shame for him to die on account of Schiller, "for I would still like to do this and that in the world." In the dream, he agrees with Goethe that "I still have something to do in the world ['diesseits']." Whereas Eckermann feels ashamed in the dream for not having visited Goethe's house for four years, he sends a letter of apology after four days. I might add here that one point in the *Conversations* that has jarred critics concerns his report of Goethe's early encounter with Schiller. Goethe, Eckermann asserts, felt that Schiller, on account of his frailty, would not live longer than four weeks after their first encounter. Why Eckermann has Goethe betting with such precision on the terms of Schiller's finitude still remains a mystery, though the four-day murder scene in which August invites the complicity of Schiller to get Eckermann may have something to do with this calculation. With regard to Eckermann's apparent aversion to Schiller in the episode, we should note that Schiller is limited conceptually to the title of his Sturm und Drang drama, the *Robbers.* In the dream, it seemed right that Goethe and his son would depart with the smugglers, leaving Eckermann behind. The dream may have smuggled Schiller into the scene of departure, supplanting the original triangle of the dream with an even more original triangle— namely, Goethe, August, and Schiller—or double pairing (Goethe and Schiller, August and Schiller). All this seemed right to the dreamer. It may also seem right to recall now that the *Robbers* is the drama of two estranged brothers.

The dream appears to want to set other things right as well, for instance the relationship between father and son, which in "earlier life" was rather a *Mißverhältnis*—the term Eckermann uses to describe his relationship to August in his letter to Goethe. The distribution of roles is clear in the dream, as are the separations and distinctions: Goethe and his son are intimately linked, tender, and both are readers of Eckermann's drafts. Whereas the narrated episode begins with Goethe's son showing something to Eckermann, in the dream a reversal takes place according to which Eckermann shows something to the son: a box or casket containing the handwritten text, the manuscripts which Goethe will interpret as something that has been torn off, *abgerissen.* Yet, if the two objects as such—the one (which turns out to be two, the twin paintings) in the drawing room and the one in the dream—are to be in any way compared, then there would be something shameful, as with the drawings, or scandalous in their content, though "the artist's skillful execution might not be denied." It is upon Goethe to punish, judge, or correct this. While the episode has Goethe's son saying that the lost object was not to be found in the *Kasten,* although he first believed it to be there, the dream reinterprets August's suspicion as having been right. Here Eckermann has custody of the *Kästchen,* the box or casket— the crypt.[19] It has been transferred to his care, but he wants to show it to them. The *Kästchen,* he assumes, has some essential bearing on Goethe and his son, on his adopted father and brother, who at the dream's beginning were presumed dead, though Eckermann did not *really* believe this.

Growing out of It

If Eckermann felt he had to save Goethe from the very start, and has to save him in this case from his son and Schiller, he still has to save Goethe from his own anxious form of surviving him, and from the drifts of his parricidal writing. For there is some of that in the *Conversations.* But regardless of seemingly reliable evidence, such as strict chronology and Eckermann's survival anxiety, it is finally inaccurate to assert Eckermann's survival of Goethe. Eckermann's dream-fulfillment consisted in realizing that their departure and his remaining behind with their remains is the way it must be. It is not clear, however, that this is the way it was. Allowing the dream of *Schwimmkraft,* in which he exchanged bodies with a distinguished figure, momentarily to conflate with the dream just related, the boat dream, let us consider the probabilities for Eckermann's survival. The odds, it appears, are against him.

If Eckermann dreams of the possibility of an existence in another body—and he has told Goethe that this *is* his dream—then he forever runs the risk of being removed or excreted from the other body, that is, of being subject to a particular form of survival from which his name might be inseparable. Eckermann has adjoined himself to the Goethean body. His survival of the body to which he is attached resembles what the German language would designate as *weiter* rather than *überleben.* Eckermann's so-called survival after 1832 cannot be grasped in terms of life or death, strictly speaking, but rather as another delay—his final delay, in fact, for Eckermann was even a latecomer to his own death. When George Elliot writes of her visit with Eckermann in 1844, she astutely notes that she had seen him before his "*total* death." Perhaps this partial and incalculable death, this delay that supplants survival as such, needs to be called by its name: namely, excrement—that which continues to grow after a body, according to biological determination, ceases to live. The first meaning that *excrementum* takes is that of any appendage or outgrowth on the body, such as hair, nails, feathers, and so on; it is related to the Latin *excrescere,* to grow out, to rise. Goethe himself seems to have intuited immediately Eckermann's place in terms of supplementary growth. His several letters and diary entries from as early as 10 June 1823, refer to Eckermann as something that has "sich an mir herangebildet" ("grown on me"—letter to Minister of State Schultz) or "Da er sich an meinen Sachen herangebildete," (H1, 132) or, again, in a letter to his publisher, Cotta, "weil der junge Mann sich . . . an mir herangebildet hat" ("as he has grown up to my level in formation and education"). (On another note, it should be added that Goethe half-jokes at length with Eckermann in the *Conversations* about the mispronunciations of his own name when it is said with a *K* sound, as in Cotta, or the plural Coethe, thus making it resonate with another sense of *excrementum*). Nor is sliding from the publisher's name to Goethe's evocative of an altogether arbitrary movement, for the thematics of publishing, *herausgeben,* or being forced to retain a publication, is related, as everyone knows, to the structure of excretion.

Nor should the history of Eckermann's own complicated attachment to hair and feathers be left entirely out of the picture: when he first encountered Goethe he had to burn his hair to accommodate the style that was agreeable to Goethe; and his last temptation and wish was to cut a lock of hair from Goethe's corpse ("Ich hatte das Verlangen nach einer Locke von seinen Haaren, doch die Ehrfurcht verhinderte mich."). When he first encountered Goethe's image, moreover, he fixed his sight on the movement of his hair (in the portrait he detects the *Locken Wehen*). Any consideration of Eckermann's relationship to his "proper" name (namely, excrement) would have to take this into account as well as his pathological preoccupation with feathers, and particularly the fact that after Goethe's death he lived in a cramped room with forty-odd birds (including birds of prey) whose droppings would fall on his papers; all this belongs to the issue of *excrementum,* a topos that will have to be recycled later on in this reading.

But the other meaning, more familar to us, need not be systematically excluded and also has something to do with a type of survival, as an early and largely unpublished poem of Goethe's tells us. The poem in question not only thematizes scatological survival, but is itself carried along by such a movement. This is *Werther's* void, entitled "The Joys of Young Werther:"

Die Freuden des jungen Werthers

Ein junger Mensch, ich weiss nicht, wie,
Starb einst an der Hypochondrie
Und ward denn auch begraben.
Da kam ein schöner Geist herbei,
Der hatte seinen Stuhlgang frei,
Wie's denn so Leute haben.
Der setzt' notdürftig sich aufs Grab
Und legte da sein Häuflein ab,
Beschaute freundlich seinen Dreck,
Ging wohl eratmet wieder weg
Und sprach zu sich bedächtlich:
"Der gute Mensch, wie hat er sich verdorben!
Hätt' er geschißen so wie ich,
Er wäre nicht gestorben!"

The Joys of Young Werther

A young man, I do not know quite how,
Once died of hypochondria
And was therefore also buried.
There a beautiful spirit came by,
He had to relieve himself
As one must after all do.
He went to his necessity upon the grave
And deposited there his load,
Observing amicably his dirt
And went thence breathing a sigh of relief
And spoke to himself, reflectingly:
"The good man, oh, how he has ruined himself!
Had he taken a shit as did I
He would then not have died!"

Excrementum is that which allows the *Geist,* which strictly speaking belongs neither to the living nor the dead, to survive—or, at least, to sustain its peculiar stirrings. As *Dreck,* this dejection is *not* ugly, hideous, or repulsive in any way; on the contrary, the "beautiful" *Geist*— thus, one aesthetically valorized—looks upon his droppings in a friendly manner, without averting its gaze, to leave relieved, breathing, living on. This is not to say that we are interested solely in constructing an image of *Dreckermann* per se, but rather in showing, among other things, the place that Goethe himself had made for *excre-*

mentum as something that follows a work, in this case, as something following the sorrowful self-elimination thematized in Werther.[20] The choice presented in this poem is precisely one between self-elimination and elimination (*schießen* and *scheißen*), of doing oneself in or relieving oneself outwardly.

Perhaps it is not even necessary (not yet) to dramatize the conditions of Eckermann's "life" after Goethe's biological death to suppose that he belongs at once to the class of the young hypochondriac who no longer lives while he is also a delayed *Erzeugung* (production, generation), as Nietzsche would say, of Goethe's *Geist*—and thus a sign of his maker's survival. This would be just one of the ways Goethe left Eckermann behind.

Excrementum, then, is the name which Goethe leaves to the company of a work, as its guardian and as a mark of its death, marking the end of a process but also the beginning of another one, one that begins with the droppings on the grave, if we also consider that this substance has fertilizing properties as well. But what is to be fertilized here is above all that layer of ground covering the buried opus; it is precisely the ground under the legacy, from which the posterity and the legend of the work will spring. And since the question of *Geist* or *Genius* has already solicited a certain notion of productivity in relation to the body, we might remember, too, that the production of excrement presupposes the proper and healthy functioning of all sorts of assimilative systems: this process not only holds for the making of a work, but also for the type of *Bildung* in which Eckermann and Goethe seem to be engaged. This brings us back to the large question, which is never held at a distance from what Eckermann writes or Goethe says, of the relationship between property or (self-)possession (*Eigentum*) and the extraneous or foreign (*das Fremde*) that pertains to *excrementum* in both senses I have developed: first as something growing out from the body and from which it is most easily detachable, belonging thus to that body and removable from it to become foreign matter; and in the second sense, as the end-station or destiny of what has been taken into the body to be discharged, secreted or excreted. For Goethe, Eckermann's place in *excrementum* allows for two possibilities which are intimately linked: it allows him to rid himself of his texts, destining them for publication (excretion), and he can also relieve himself of his thoughts at table by talking to Eckermann who, as pure listener, asserts his position as excretory device.

At the same time, it would not be difficult to demonstrate that Goethe wholly absorbed Eckermann in order to assure the afterlife of the work which for him is already buried. And at this point Goethe himself should be assimilated to a notion of oeuvre, as a work surviving its empirical signatory, for, in his own words, he had "risen from the dead" at the time Eckermann finally presented himself. But those who would designate Eckermann as Goethe's last work no doubt agree with an excretory interpretation of work—namely, excrement: a farewell gesture, any body's last gesture; but also namely Eckermann, who must grow out of Goethe's work, which he must assimilate after Goethe has assimilated him to his systems. Eckermann is to fertilize the work whose condition of survival he is: he will permit Goethe's *Geist* to move freely from the graveyard of his productions. As Goethe's outgrowth or delayed death, as his charge and discharge, Eckermann relieves Goethe of the responsibility toward those works he had more or less completed, though he felt they were not ready to be published as part of his complete works. We can think here of Nietzsche's notion of ennobled irresponsibility which, in this case, permits Goethe's spirit to move on to other projects, such as *Faust II*, or *Dichtung und Wahrheit*. And thus Goethe's ghost moves on, into the fists and limbs of Eckermann, dictaphoning the rest of his corpus to the one who has known to exchange bodies, though they would not always correspond to the distinguished *Gestalt* of which our somniloquist had dreamt.

The Farbenlehre or "When Pac Man Eats a Power Pill, the Ghosts Become a Transparent Blue Color"

If Eckermann's task and "dirty work" is to secure Goethe's posterity, to remain behind with the work, at its graveside, this does not mean, however, that Eckermann will not stir to rebel against his lot. As an outgrowth of Goethe, as his follower, pupil, and sometime son, Eckermann will not always be something on which Goethe can cast a friendly glance. This becomes especially clear in the case of the *Farbenlehre* (Theory of Color), a work which initially left Eckermann baffled. Let me interrupt this argument for a moment to recall that Nietzsche preferred the *Conversations* to *Faust* and to *Dichtung und Wahrheit*. In a note he wrote with unbaffled certitude that "Goethe, in his Color Theory, was wrong" (1876 or 1877). I am led to suspect that Nietzsche took particular pleasure in reading this section of the *Conversations,* and not only in order to oppose Schopenhauer, who sided with Goethe. Nietzsche, needless to say, takes the part of Eckermann.

Now before asking him to write the compendium, Goethe organizes another property transaction when he directs Eckermann to appropriate the theory ("Lehre") as his own ("zu eigen zu machen"), promising that what he passes on to him ("das Überlieferte") will first come to life in Eckermann's care. All this is recorded in the entry for 1 February 1827. Here Goethe predicts that "this science will soon be your property" ("Eigentum"). He leaves Eckermann in possession of this work, but something begins to take root which Goethe did not exactly foresee; namely, "an unsuspected difference" arises ("und so grieten wir in eine unvermutete Differenz") which, given the gravity of the matter, Eckermann feels obliged to impart.

The question that interests me here is not so much who is right in the course of this development—the question could be resolved in a word, Nietzsche's for instance—but rather Eckermann's need to assert precisely the *Differenz* between his own careful ("sorgfältig"), superior insight over Goethe's observations. As we go over some of the elements of this difference, we should not forget that the subject at hand is a *Lehre,* that is, the stakes here involve not only Goethe's teaching of color but his status as teacher, as master of *Bildung,* a status which Eckermann however continually affirms. In this light—in the light of the one submitted to *Bildung*—it is noteworthy that Eckermann's privileged instrument of verification most often is *Kerzenlicht,* a funereal beam that he casts over Goethe's corpus. Indeed, given everything that science meant to Goethe and his passionate crusade against Newton, this is not a matter of indifferent *Differenz.*

The problems first arise when Eckermann takes a look at the *Farbenlehre* in order to test whether he would at all be capable of meeting Goethe's "friendly request" ("Aufforderung," challenge, demand). While considering the phenomenon of blue shadowing in an empirical light, he comes to realize with "some surprise," however, that Goethe's argument is "based on error." He describes how he arrived at this conclusion, making his case increasingly solid: "in order to be absolutely sure . . . and now there was no further doubt," and so on. "The color was there, outside of me, independently, and my subject[ivity] had no influence upon it." Goethe had classified this phenomenon as a subjective manifestation, and it is perhaps not exactly fortuitous that Eckermann will seek to diminish subjective power in Goethe's theory at the same time he tries to affirm his own subject. It is equally important that in the act of refuting Goethe, of risking parricidal writing, he can fathom an "outside." In the days that follow, Eckermann finds the opportunity to confirm the truth of his hypothesis, for example, when walking alone in the fields, the sun shone through the vapors and "in this case, according to Goethe's teachings, the freshest blue tonality was supposed to emerge. It did not however emerge. . . ." After several more days of experimentation, Eckermann establishes that "Nature could not confirm" Goethe's argument "as true"; the corresponding paragraphs thus "urgently required revision." Eckermann does not stop at this: "I encountered something similar with colorful double-shadowing" which, after anxious observation, he was compelled to dismiss. However, this time, he does not limit himself to his experiments, but calls upon Shakespeare to bear witness to the gravity of his predicament. Although reference to *Romeo and Juliet* may not seem scientifically compelling, Eckermann probably could not have taken a more deadly aim at Goethe.

If Shakespeare's couple meets a tragic conclusion, the couple united in this tome now faces doom as well. For Shakespeare is the only name to which Goethe, in the *Conversations* and elsewhere, ascribes powers of mutilation. Eckermann could have found no higher tribunal to sit in judgment of Goethe: Goethe claims he had been forced to rid himself of Shakespeare, also spelled "Shakespere"—to get him off his body ("vom Hals schaffen")—in order to be able to write at all. Eckermann knew this only too well; as early as 5 January 1826, he had scribbled on one of his papers that "Shakespeare alles andere verleidet" (brings everything else to ruin or sorrow). In yet another conversation, Goethe warns Eckermann not to hold Tieck as his equal. This, Goethe explains, has nothing to do with him personally, just as he has nothing to do with the fact that Shakespeare is greater than he. Things just turn out that way. So there may be no end to Shakespeare, as Goethe's essay on that subject argues ("Shakespeare und kein Ende"), but his would be the name of Goethe's end or limit. Eckermann's strategy of including Shakespeare in a demonstration that, with the exception of this reference, remains purely empirical, belongs to the logic of his crime, to his assertion of an outside, the possibility of independence and the doubt he casts on the "double shadow":

> Das Resultat meiner Beobachtungen ging demnach dahin, daß auch Goethes Lehre von den farbigen Doppelschatten nicht durchaus richtig sei, daß bei diesem Phänomen mehr Objektives einwirke, als von ihm beobachtet worden, und daß das Gesetz der subjektiven Forderung dabei nur als etwas Sekundäres in Betracht komme.

> The result of my observation led to the conclusion that Goethe's doc-
> trine on chromatic double shadowing was not entirely correct, that in
> this phenomenon there is more of an objective dimension than he had
> observed, and that the law of subjective claims therefore can come
> under consideration only as something secondary.

Eckermann is dealing in law, in Goethe's law of subjective claim,
which he will allow only a secondary position. Doubles, shadows, sec-
ondariness: this all sounds desperately familiar.

Goethe disregarded too many things; given his fixation on what has
once been recognized as law ("am einmal erkannten Gesetzlichen")
and his way of presupposing his law/the law, even in such cases where
it appears to be concealed, he could very easily be misled (*verführt,*
seduced) into making large syntheses and perceiving a law of which he
had grown fond ("ein liebgewonnenes Gesetz") even in a place where
an entirely different law was operative.

Therefore: "when Goethe mentioned his *Farbenlehre* today and
asked me what was happening with the Compendium we had discussed, I would have gladly concealed the points developed above, for
I was unsure [embarrassed] about how I was supposed to tell him the
truth without hurting ['verletzen,' wounding] him." Eckermann was
embarrassed about telling Goethe the truth—a truth which he however
freely imparts to his readers. And this truth cannot be told without
inflicting a wound on Goethe, one whose proportions Eckermann will
disclose only at the end of this entry.

He does tell Goethe, for he had no other choice, he writes, that after
careful observation, he finds himself in the position ("Fall") of having
to deviate ("abweichen") from Goethe. Goethe, it appears, begins to
gain in stature in Eckermann's rendering of the scene, for "it is not
given to me to develop a subject of great length in oral conversation
['im mündlichen Gespräch'] with any clarity . . . I would do that later,
in writing." Later, in writing . . . "However, I had hardly begun to
speak when Goethe's lofty and cheerful nature grew clouded ['verfin-
sterte'], and I saw only too clearly that he did not appreciate my
objections." Eckermann saw too clearly; he saw too clearly in his
experiments with light and shadow, and he sees too clearly when
Goethe's brilliance is clouded over, darkened. As you see, the experi-
ment is now being carried over to Goethe; and if Goethe appears too
obscure in his writing, and Eckermann can so easily give umbrage, it is
also because conversation is at stake. Having asserted his inferiority in
oral conversation (*mündlichen Gespräch*), Eckermann will now shift
the sense of the mark to announce the possibility of triumph: "it can

happen, however, that the mature ['Mündige'] are overprecipitous whereas the immature ['Unmündige'] find it." Goethe flushes and returns with mockery: "As if you had found it! With your conception of colorful light, you belong in the fourteenth century, and besides ['im übrigen,' in what is left—as usual] you are trapped in the deepest dialectics." Perhaps Goethe wants Eckermann to get out of the trap of a master/slave dialectics, the deepest which could afflict the couple; in any case, he makes Eckermann's immaturity a question of age, of the dark ages, injuring him with his charges of obscurity. But "the only thing which is good about you, is that at least you are honest enough to come out with what you are thinking." That would be the only thing good about Eckermann.

The stakes are high, and Goethe does not refrain from naming them. Eckermann's deviation in his veneration for Goethe already has a place in intellectual history: " 'Es geht mir mit meiner Farbenlehre gerade wie mit der christlichen Religion. One believes for a while to have faithful pupils and before one turns around they deviate and form a sect.' " Eckermann is indeed about to take the form of a sect, to be cut off (sect, section, cut) from Goethe's body, to be ex-communicated. " 'You are a heretic just like the others, for you are not the first to have deviated from me. I have become estranged from the most excellent people because of disputed points in the *Farbenlehre*. . . . With * because of . . . and with * because of. . . .' He named for me a few important names." It is understandable that Eckermann would prefer to leave stars in the place of names (his letter of 14 July 1836, remembers one of the stars as being Schopenhauer; we can assume other shooting stars to be the physiologist Johannes Müller, the Berlin philosopher Leopold von Henning, and a later addition to the list of heretics, the Berlin physicist Thomas Seebeck). It seems less evident, however, that Eckermann would have to omit mention of the passages that have been disputed by the stars. To be sure, this would have introduced an order of positive historical contention which Eckermann consistently evades. The deep dialectician has restricted the scene of judgment to three terms and to an essentially symbolic dispute; it is to remain, in this context, a family affair between Goethe, Eckermann, and Shakespeare—the father, we might say, the son, and so on.

Goethe, then, has severed relations with the most excellent people, among whom Eckermann may or may not count himself, precisely for the type of objections that Eckermann raises. The immediate consequence of Eckermann's heresy is indeed a form of ex-communication: they had finished eating (for they always eat) and conversation ceased ("das Gespräch stockte"). Yet if conversation was blocked, the *Conversations,* it must be said, has rarely flowed so freely, for this is also among the lengthier "conversations" that Eckermann would record: an instance of interrupted intercourse sustaining Eckermann's desire to write (*conversatio*). Now arrives the moment of sublime triumph, in which the younger becomes the master, at once the elder and the child, in short, the part who is not suffering:

> Goethe stand auf und stellte sich ans Fenster. Ich trat zu ihm und drückte ihm die Hand, denn wie er auch schalt, ich liebte ihn, und dann hatte ich das Gefühl, daß das Recht auf meiner Seite und daß er der leidende Teil sei.

> Goethe got up and stood by the window. I went over to him and pressed his hand—for even when he chewed you out, I loved him and anyway I had the feeling that I was right (lit.: that right was on my side) and that he was the suffering party (lit.: part).

This is the magnanimity of power: if Eckermann concedes to Goethe in this manner it may be due to love, as he suggests, but it is most certainly because he has justice on his side: he is right, and this right surpasses Goethe's threat of vengeance. Goethe has been judged—by Shakespeare and by Eckermann—justice is on his side, but the other part or member (*Teil*) suffers. The trial is more or less over. Thus, "it was not long before we conversed and joked about indifferent matters." The *Differenz* appears to be suspended, the division repaired. Yet, when Eckermann leaves, promising Goethe a written version of his objections—he reminds Goethe that if he would not concede to him his right, it was simply a consequence of the awkwardness of "my oral delivery"—Goethe cannot refrain from saying a few things about heretics and heresy as Eckermann was in the door. Goethe throws his comments at Eckermann "halb lachend, halb spottend." Half and half: the halves are beginning to multiply again with the nonsuffering half on which Goethe casts half scorn, half laughter, half inside, half outside Goethe's house. If Goethe is himself divided, it is because "Goethe" is as such divided, as Eckermann proceeds to explain:

> If it should seem problematic that Goethe could not easily tolerate opposition regarding his *Farbenlehre,* whereas with his poetic works he showed himself to be wholly gracious, accepting each well-founded objection with gratitude, then perhaps the riddle ["Rätsel"] can be resolved when we consider that as poet he received the fullest gratification from the outside ["von außen her"], whereas in the case of *Farbenlehre,* this largest and most difficult of all his works, he experienced nothing but blame and disapprobation.

Eckermann is still wandering in the parricidal path. He understands and explains patiently why it was particularly painful for Goethe to meet any opposition concerning the *Farbenlehre*. It is a question of the outside, and Eckermann puts himself entirely in line with this outside-of-Goethe which repudiates his most difficult work. And this outside comes at him from all sides, for the better half of his life, forcing Goethe into the stance of a reactive warrior who is not afraid to cut to the quick. Nor is he afraid to amputate. Eckermann, as we noted, runs the risk of being cut off. At the same time, he qualifies Goethe's reactive instinct as natural: he evokes a reading of what has been traditionally associated with male instincts. Yet, bringing Goethe to certain conceptual limits of aggressive masculinity, he will, as we shall see, immediately and without transition, drive him to the "other" side of sexual difference as it is here presented. This is how Eckermann begins his winning retreat:

> Ein halbes leben hindurch tönte ihm der unverständigst Widerspruch von allen Seiten entgegen; und so war es denn wohl natürlich, daß der sich immer in einer Art von gereizten kriegerischen Zustand und zu leidenschaftlicher Opposition stets gerüstet befinden mußte.

Armed for battle on the field of science, Goethe is the warrior whom Eckermann challenges, if not to a fight quite to the end—though his end is always in sight—then at least to a "natural" duel on Nature. But the difference between the painful duality taking shape here and the mass of other conflictual pairs who have fought over this particular text is that Eckermann does not belong to the legions of slavishly uncomprehending opposition: he stands his ground alone, he is honest, as Goethe has said, and forthright; he does not, for instance, hide among the ranks of that army raised by Ressentiment. In Nietzsche's terms, *he also knows how to be an enemy.* This, of course, is precisely what makes him a most dangerous opponent.

Yet Eckermann has just told us that, in the case of the *Farbenlehre,* he has been in effect all along describing and engaged in a riddle ("Rätsel"); and when riddles are at issue, the myth of Oedipus does not always lag that far behind. However, this wanderer, as we shall see, will find a devious, if not ingenious solution to the riddle, thereby bypassing the path which he has been hitherto pursuing, the parricidal path upon which he has nonetheless and, it would seem, irrevocably entered. The detour that he takes, the deviation from the site of the First Murder, the solution and resolution of the riddle is in fact simple: Goethe, it turns out, is, in this case and connection, not the father but the mother, the *good* mother: "He was, in connection to the *Farbenlehre*, like a good mother" ("Es ging ihm in Bezug auf seine Farbenlehre wie einer guten Mutter"). A good mother, that means a mother to whom no violence has been done, not by Eckermann namely, for it was precisely his earlier recognition in the episode of the "unsuspected difference" that stopped and deadened the urge for intercourse. Goethe, the father, will not have been killed, and Goethe, the mother, will retain her integrity. As for Eckermann, he will certainly not have to pay for what was almost a crime. He can write against the Father without remorse. Or so it would seem.

"A City Like Berlin"

When Goethe crosses over to motherhood in Eckermann, the *Mann* rises to the challenge, beginning to put in question Goethe's claims for the auto-nym, much in the way woman's self-sufficiency or narcissism would later be a source of anxious inquiry for Freud.[21] In this part of the exchange, Goethe asserts his unicity, at least as concerns the sciences, thus:

> "I have no illusion about anything that I have accomplished as a poet," he would say repeatedly. "Excellent writers have lived with me, more excellent ones before me, and there will be still more excellent ones after me. However, I take pride in being *the only one* in my century to know what is right in the difficult science of the *Farbenlehre,* and I therefore have the consciousness of superiority ['Bewusstsein der Superiorität'] over many." [italics mine]

Eckermann is up against Goethe's consciousness of being on top, and he will not forego the temptation of challenging the assurance he displays in this position of his singularity, uniqueness, and self-presence. If Goethe was the only one in his century ("his" century spans what historically has been considered two centuries, but Goethe is already citing the *Goethezeit*) to know what was right, then Eckermann was the only one to know that what Goethe thought was right would only be right, in a genuine sense, after Eckermann rewrites it. Goethe had after all conceded the rights of other excellent writers after him, and he had placed the *Farbenlehre* in Eckermann's care. Eckermann, it appears, could not allow the text, whose unique and unified author Goethe now thought he was, to escape his signature as well. This would be another aspect of the "unsuspected difference"—a newly asserted difference between himself and Goethe—that Eckermann in this case could not allow to abide.

The dance of unsuspected difference rejoins a notion of sexual difference when, on the next day (20 February 1829), "Goethe came over a bit to my view with respect to the blue shadowing on the snow." The frigidity in Goethe's yielding gesture should not escape us, for Goethe himself speaks of his motherhood, but also of what this implies for the one who presumes to be the man: " 'We are like women,' he said; 'while they are giving birth they are resolved ['verreden sie es'] not to sleep with the man, and before you know it ['ehe man sich's versieht'], they are pregnant again.' " One can suppose this to mean that, for us women, giving birth represents an ordeal such that it seems preferable to abstain from intercourse. Goethe skips the part that would explain exactly how he suddenly finds herself pregnant again; pregnancy is something that befalls him as if by chance, as if no man were involved, in other words, by some sort of auto-insemination.

Goethe's manner of articulating this resolve and his desire for birth-control is peculiar, for he invokes the term *verreden* where *versprechen* might be expected (to promise or make a slip of the tongue as in *sich versprechen*). Be that as it may, *verreden* in this context is made to communicate with *versehen,* indicating that slips of speech and sight are still at stake in the drama linked to the *Farbenlehre.*

Eckermann appears to induce this slippage, preferring *reden* for *sprechen,* precisely to distance Goethe's resolve not to sleep with the *Mann*—the husbandman, and Eckermann—from the site of conversing (*sprechen*) or the possibility of conversations (*Gespräche*) that are to stem from his pen. Both Eckermann and Goethe are now struggling for legitimacy from positions of negated or excluded difference. On the twentieth of February Goethe feels that childbirth is such an ordeal for two reasons other than the one previously suggested. In the first place he has had to struggle to bring his child, the *Farbenlehre,* into the world despite Eckermann's attempt to obscure it. Secondly, while Goethe, in Eckermann's words, was a good mother, he at the same time prides himself on being an unwed mother "whose love for a superb child increased that much more, the less it was recognized by others." The *Farbenlehre* would be another of Goethe's not-so-legitimate children placed somewhat grudgingly in Eckermann's care. (Goethe has also, for a long while, imposed or relinquished the status of unwed mother to Christiane Vulpius, who gave birth to their illegitimate child August, likewise entrusted to Eckermann.)

Goethe's diary entries for the nineteenth and twentieth of February

merely indicate a "discussion with Eckermann about manifestations
related to color" and "Noon Dr Eckermann. We discussed the details
to be taken up. Nothing less than what is to be done in a work of
editing the *Farbenlehre*." No hint of his expectancy or the imminent
staging of a paternity suit. For Eckermann at least, it is essential that
Goethe be the mother of the *Farbenlehre*. The whole scene as Eckermann has described it lends itself to a reading of a rather familiar
family episode according to which the Father arrives, late, to find fault
with the child and later, when Mother, "the suffering party or member" looks gloomily out the window—after their silent meal—he comes
over to her and, in a conciliatory gesture, takes her hand, though he
knows that he was right. This, however, would not be enough to
explain the tension that is being concealed by the conciliatory gesture.
By nearly universal consent, motherhood can be looked upon as a
complicated thing. It has been argued elsewhere that the mother is as
such always double, for she harbors an alterity within what can be
called, for the sake of convenience, an already heterogeneous "self."[22]
Goethe represents himself to be a single mother, a single double therefore, and thus the question arises for Eckermann of where he would fit
in as a supplementary alterity, somewhere between Goethe as single,
and—in his capacity as mother—as double. Being a single mother,
Goethe is not obligated to relinquish his name, but can pass it on
unrevised to his child. However, the child, according to Eckermann,
requires revision—a different conception of its conception, if not a new
name.

The urgency of Eckermann's remonstrations suggests the necessity
for another split in Goethe's self-conception, and this is expressed in
terms of a right and desire on Eckermann's part (the suffering part or
member) to make certain paternity claims, if only peculiarly belated
ones. Eckermann wants his name, as do some fathers—whether adoptive or not—to belong to the child as well; the *Farbenlehre,* after all,
was to be his property, Goethe had promised, and in some way linked
to his proper name. Born out of wedlock, it should be accorded full
legitimacy—it should receive a recognizable civil status as a product
(*Erzeugung*)—only through Eckermann's participation. While the
Conversations largely accords Eckermann these rights, that is, by
something resembling performative rights ("On this date, on these
pages, I, Eckermann, hold the *Farbenlehre* to be mine"), the question
of Eckermann's name, and the very possibility of the enunciation "I,
Eckermann" is never a simple one. It is possible that from the very
beginning the name(s) of Eckermann could not have been as singularly

impressed on a text as Goethe's name was. There is something in what we have been calling Eckermann that makes impossible his wish to oppose the unicity of Goethe's name with his "own," or with a sense of what is proper.

The destabilization of Eckermann's name occurs in another context that will help us illuminate the problem he encountered in dealing with the *Farbenlehre*. He creates this context in a letter written to Goethe from Geneva which was written on 12 September 1830 (part two of the *Conversations*). As this letter occasions a curious slip of the pen, it requires some commentary. Once again Eckermann begins an address to Goethe by reverting to his incapacity for genuine oral delivery: "In general, oral teaching and effectiveness is not at all my thing. It is a métier for which I possess as little talent as training ['Ausbildung']. I lack any gift whatsoever for speaking, insofar as every living *Visavis* normally has such an overpowering, violent effect upon me, that I forget myself. . . ." Eckermann cannot speak, but only be spoken to; and he writes this to Goethe from a distance. Yet his chosen genre obliges him to face a living *Visavis,* to forget himself in the crushing livingness of the other. Now it would appear that in writing this letter, Eckermann is less susceptible to forgetting himself. But the letter continues, explaining, "my entire nature impels me now to go beyond myself ['aus mir heraus'], and to have an effect on a larger circle, to win influence in literature and for my further happiness; finally to make a name for myself." Eckermann does not write "a name for myself," but *"a few names* for myself" ('mir endlich einigen Namen zu machen') thus making, by error or by some compulsion "to go beyond" himself, the name he wants to make divisible, disseminative, or in any case, something(s) implying radical indeterminacy. The juxtaposition in his sentence of "finally" with the "few names" creates an odd sign of determination, bordering on the comic: with resolute finality, Eckermann will pluralize his name for himself—or, assuming him to be the destination of his letter, for the one who signs his letters to Eckermann alternately as "J. W. v. Goethe" or "Goethe" (Eckermann reduces his signature in the exchange that he publishes here to the initial *E.*) It is not clear how to go about analyzing Eckermann's serialization of his name. On the one hand, Eckermann always writes in the plural, for and through someone else, in the name of the other Eckermanns perhaps. But since he is addressing Goethe here, he may be involved in the double gesture that gets articulated, when it comes to *his* name, as denial, for doubling or multiplying a name is also in some sense cancelling or neutralizing it. This is Eckermann, opening a joint ac-

count despite himself, "for myself," presumably addressing himself to
the great name, albeit from a distance, where violent effects of the
living Voice are supposed to be attenuated. Writing to the great name
on the subject of making a name, or two, his desire to resist or efface
the great name with something like his own, great name, may be too
great to elude a bungled discursive action at this point.

His apparent lapse constitutes a double, contradictory gesture on
another register as well. On the one hand it implies a break from
Goethe (he wants to make a name for *himself,* not for you, Goethe).
This is complicated by the fact that to make names for himself he has
to go beyond himself, that is, to a certain extent, beyond Goethe,
beyond Weimar (as he writes from the safe distance of Geneva). On
the other hand, in a hypothesis derived from an anasemic reading of
the phrase, it would suggest a desire for coupling (*einigen,* unite) his
name with that of Goethe, in which the wish to go beyond himself
would mean to grow into Goethe. In both cases Eckermann desists
from establishing a privilege for the singular property of the proper
name. In order, finally, to make names for himself Eckermann in the
first place must go beyond himself, leave himself behind and, as his
letter suggests, leave Goethe behind. He will hardly venture any of
this, of course, and Eckermann may never have made enough names
for himself, though he does in the same letter prepare to leave himself
behind.

A few paragraphs later in this published version of the letter Eckermann explains that his life has come to a standstill. The winds are not
blowing, he "would like his life to take a fresh course again." He adds
that his health is now feeble, shaky, "and I would gladly leave something good behind, so that my name in the commemorative memory of
humanity might for a while be sustained." Eckermann, then, can only
conceive of his name in the singular when he projects his death—that
is, the "fresh course" that his life would take after his deathful existence, one that had long ago come to a standstill.

At any event, the response he draws from Goethe a month later will
prevent Eckermann and his others from having an immediate effect on
a wider public, and will impress on him rather the necessity of adjoin-
ing Goethe's signature to his feeble, shaky one. The publication of the
Conversations, Goethe writes, must be delayed, health or no health:
". . . I do not wish an imminent publication of (your manuscript), but
I would gladly go through it with you and would like to rectify it. Its
value will increase if I can testify that it can be construed entirely
according to my wishes and my sense of things ('ganz in meinem

Sinne']. I shall say no more. . . ." There was certainly no more to be said. While Goethe has often enough been viewed as a tough mother, it is not clear in this instance why he was so sure that Eckermann's text would require rectification, although once again the emphasis seems to be placed on rights (*rectus*) .

Goethe no doubt understood what was at stake, as Eckermann understood that Goethe understood in his dream, where Goethe does finally get to look over the manuscripts, four years after his death, and rectify the passages that were already crowded with rectifications and revisions. For one thing, he would certainly have wanted to amend the *Farbenlehre* episode we have treated.

The letter to Goethe, published in the *Conversations,* hardly seems to motivate Goethe's drastic measures, his putting off publication indefinitely (Goethe changed the date of the projected publication a few times; first he felt he would die in 1830, which seemed an appropriate moment for Eckermann to publish; after 1830, he pushed the date back until "after my death.") However, if Goethe's response seems full of uncharacteristic reactivity, it is because the letter actually sent to Goethe is not identical to the letter Eckermann tells us he sent to Goethe. In the passages I have cited, and in others that can be found in the published version, Eckermann places emphasis wholly on his desire for a *literary* career. This in itself, as we have seen and Eckermann has shown us, would hardly have provoked Goethe to block the publication of his manuscript. The letter, whose receipt Goethe acknowledges, however, exposes at length the sender's passionate committment to *science*. Literature is not even at issue.

In a way that should remind us of Nietzsche's *Ecce Homo,* Ecke Mann begins, "wie ich mich kenne und was ich darüber denke" ("how I know myself and what I think of this"). He begins with the beginning, that is, with his boyhood which until now was thought, as all other documents and testimonies assert, to have been spent in a state of blissful illiteracy. "As one can imagine, I had as a boy a great inclination toward the sciences; however, in the conditions in which I found myself, I could not pursue such a direction. Rather, I saw myself placed before the necessity of taking up work *im Schreibfache* [writing, copying] early on." Eckermann describes the history of the suppression of that scientific drive. He still has not attained ("bei weitem nicht erreicht"), as he would have liked to, the goal, set in boyhood, of his scientific education ("meiner wissenschaftlichen Ausbildung"). So this is what Eckermann wants, writes he to Goethe from Geneva: "Now I would prefer a city, which would be both the residence of a great power ['eines grossen Reiches'] and academy. . . . I would like to study and be active in a big city like Berlin, and from time to time come to Weimar to rectify myself at your side and to take part in your highest creations. That is how it stands with my wishes for the future. Most immediately I attach great importance ['am Herzen liegt'] above all to the completion of those papers I so often mention." Eckermann now needs a big city, an institutional site for his scientific education, he would commute to Weimar on a part-time basis to rectify himself at Goethe's side, to take part, part-time of course, in Goethe's highest creations, and in the meantime he would like to finish with those papers which he mentioned, though he can't really speak, which is why he is writing about them. This is the manuscript, the first step in Eckermann's project for the future establishment of Eckermann, whose completion and thus also inception, Goethe will delay.

Eckermann probably foresaw the inevitability of Goethe's stalling techniques, and suggested that his end was nearing (the more he would impress on Goethe his end, the closer he would get to commencing): "Additionally, my health is weak and shaky, I cannot be certain of my long stay in this existence, and I would like in the case of a change ['Verwandelung'] to leave something worthy behind, so that my name in the commemorative memory of humanity might for a while be sustained." He concludes—and this is his conclusion, his end—that without Goethe's approval he would do nothing. The rest of the story is (effaced) history: there was no shuttle taking Eckermann from Goethe to the big city institutions, only a couple of round-trip economy fare tickets—no real out, outside-of-Goethe, or outliving Goethe. And even years after Goethe's death, when the solitary Eckermann begged the principality of Weimar to have his little grant transferred to Hamburg, the town decided that he was not to leave—someone had to assure Goethe's continued presence. The only way out for Eckermann was, as per prescription, down and out.

The year of the letter, 1830, ends with the promise of Goethe's recovery. Shortly after August's death, he was, like Eckermann, "not far from death," inaccessible—and speech was forbidden to him ("das Reden ist ihm verboten") as in Eckermann's dream. But by the final entry for 1830, his "eternally agitating spirit cannot rest, and he is already thinking of his works again." From Goethe's seclusion Eckermann receives a message, like a command from the deceptive silence of a grave. The message reads: "Pls. be kind enough, dear Doktor, once more to go through the enclosed poems, which are already known. And put the enclosed new ones in order, so that it makes a seemly whole ['damit es sich zum Ganzen schicke']. Faust will follow!" He sends (*schicken*) the poems to Eckermann to develop them into a totality, and if Eckermann thinks that this is the end station, there is still Faust and the future, Goethe's future. Thus before beginning the section headed 1831–1832, Eckermann comes to the end of the year and the page, submitting: "An eine Redaktion meiner Gespräche mit ihm war nicht mehr zu denken; auch hielt ich es für vernünftiger. . . ." ("Editing my conversations with him was no longer in question; also, I held it to be more reasonable this way"). Thus Eckermann furnishes himself with a response to the letter he had written to Goethe, echoing Goethe's decision and letter in which he said the conversations were not to be made public yet; and Eckermann held this to be more reasonable, he writes.

A point might be argued concerning the importance with which Eckerman invested the *Farbenlehre* and science in general (something that he in a sense discovers belatedly to have been his boyhood desire, before circumstances forced him into the business of copy editing). The point is a vanishing point regarding the missing place of science in the *Conversations*. When he finally publishes the *Conversations,* whose delay was to a degree Goethe's punishment for that interest, he represses the abundant references to scientific texts, drives, or institutions in the letter of rupture, substituting them instead with the passage announcing his desire for making a few names, which is perhaps a desire to splinter *Goethe's* name. The threat of Eckermann's encroaching scientific apprenticeship outside-of-Goethe, perhaps at the side of "deep dialectics," that is, Hegel in Berlin, had pushed the master into halting publication of Eckermann's copy writing. Goethe had argued, at that time, for the necessity of applying his signature, as a kind of guarantor, to any of Eckermann's endeavors; he had imposed the master-name as the condition for the possibility of valorizing Eckermann ("its value would increase only if . . . entirely mine"). When Eckermann reproduced the letter for the *Conversations,* he had long abandoned the hopes held out for him by Berlin and science; he was writing under Goethe's name, but without the guarantee of having Goethe for a cosignatory (for Goethe, as we said, never held the *Conversations,* he had no chance, outside Eckermann's dreams, of rectifying them). Goethe's name was to survive Eckermann, his signature was to cover for Eckermann's life and works. In this context it should not be forgotten that, according to his letter, Eckermann planned to die before Goethe—which, taken at face value, would make any delay in publication an act of killing the text.

When Eckermann produces the letter of rupture for publication, then, he knows he is writing within the deadline Goethe had given him. Writing in the space of a delay, unrectified and unauthorized by the one in whose name he writes, Eckermann can in a sense only advance his name as so many false names, with each inscription undercutting his signature in a mask of pseudonymity which the several names would grant him. He is by now a ghost writer, that is, a writer who hides, unrecognized, behind another name or perhaps several other names. His paternity claims have not been heard—the question of his name arises in conjunction with the *Farbenlehre*—which is why he continues to this date (28 August 1984) to agitate as the spirit of an unappeased father. However, this is getting ahead of ourselves, for the *Farbenlehre* episode has hardly been resolved but merely disrupted.

By 20 February 1831, the second anniversary of Goethe's sudden pregnancy, there is an opening, a reconciliation, a renewed possibility for a union and hope for the peaceful coexistence of two hypotheses. A place is made for the double signature. Eckermann has long since returned to the table from which he rose to leave:

> With Goethe at table. He disclosed to me that he had tested my observation concerning the blue shading in the snow—and recognizes it as being right ["richtig"]. "However, both can be active simultaneously," he said, "and the impetus stimulating the yellow light can strengthen the appearance of the blue." I agree entirely and am happy that Goethe at last concurs with me."

Both can be active simultaneously, one can strengthen the appearance of the other, one agrees that the other concurs, they are both right, Eckermann is happy that Goethe finally comes around to his side, disclosing, opening ("eröffnet") himself.

Only after this concession or amalgamation of the two readings has taken place does Eckermann begin to write of actually reading the *Farbenlehre*. Goethe has opened himself to Eckermann, who, on 26 February 1831, begins, in his own words, to "grow into" ("hineinwachsen") the text. A comparison of the passage intended for publication with that found in his diary would be fruitful. The diary version reads:

> Ich lese bei Tag viel in Goethes Farbenlehre und freue mich dass ich diese Jahre her durch vielfache Übung mit den Phänomenen in das Werk so hineingewachsen bin, dass mir nun jeder Buchstabe lebendig ist und es fast als mein Eigenthum betrachten kann. Ich bewundere wie es nur möglich gewesen ein so reiches Werk zusammenzubringen. . . .

These days I am reading quite alot of Goethe's *Farbenlehre* and am pleased that this year, due to extensive practice with the phenomena, I have grown into the work to such an extent that now every letter has become alive to me and I can consider the work almost as my property. I wonder with admiration how it was even possible to put such a rich work together. . . .

Now for the less immediate impression Eckermann wished to make:

Ich las heute viel in Goethes Farbenlehre und freute mich zu bemerken, dass ich diese Jahre her, durch vielfache Übung mit den Phänomenen, in das Werk so hineingewachsen, um jetzt seine grosse Verdienste mit einiger Klarheit empfinden zu können. Ich bewundere, was es gekostet hat, ein solches Werk zusammenzubringen. . . .

Today I read quite a lot of Goethe's *Farbenlehre* and was pleased to notice that this year, due to extensive practice with these phenomena, I have grown into the work to such an extent, that I can now perceive his great achievement with some clarity. I wonder with admiration at the cost of putting such a work together. . . .

Eckermann's primal statement regarding the *Farbenlehre,* made on 19 October 1823, read: "the object, however, was something entirely strange, external ['fremd'] to me." Here, a good eight years later, the notion of growing into the work is retained in both the private and public versions of his readings. However, what goes underground in the private entry for that date concerns the letters, each of which *now* comes alive, inviting Eckermann to consider this work almost as his own, as his property, for the dead letters come alive to Eckermann, perhaps only to him, which is also the condition for his growth.

Whether we are dealing with inner or external growth, *incrementum* or *excrementum,* it is always a matter of something, namely, Eckermann, that has been added to a work or that affixes itself to a corpus which he recognizes to be a living one. In view of such an inappropriation—in this instance, the corpus seems to be appropriating him—it becomes *almost* his property. One could say that the "life" which he perceives in the work becomes a property of Eckermann. He grows into the work to the extent that every letter shows signs of the life which his ingrowing gives them. The passage (of Eckermann into the work and life of Goethe) was not to be published by Eckermann, who instead transfers "my property" to "his great merit." In the course of this transfer of property, of giving Goethe his due by recognizing his merit and profit ("Verdienst"), the question that arises in many a property transaction arises here as well: that of cost, investment as well as a certain notion of cutbacks or renunciation. Eckermann does not place his interest in what the bringing together of this work may have cost Goethe; he shows interest rather in what it would cost someone who would want to emulate or forge, in any case someone who would like to do the same in the manner of or after ("nachtun") Goethe. Who would this be?

> Only a person of great moral strength could carry this through, and whoever wanted to emulate [Goethe], would have to rise to the occasion. All that is indelicate ['Unzarte,' also rude or tactless], untrue and egoistical would have to disappear from the soul, or Nature, who is pure and true, would scorn him.

Eckermann has learned his *Farbenlehre;* he has accomplished the *Lehre* and *Bildungsprozess*—a necessity which his encounter with this theory had always implied. By now, everything that may have been indelicate on his part, *Unzart,* or in some way rude or tactless—for example his confrontations with Goethe on this subject—and every "untrue, egoistical" gesture will have been subdued, sublated, and stored up in his memory bank. The immediacy of Eckermann's rebellion or his resistance to theory, the immoderate acts of an appropriation that had not yet learned renunciation—all this would have had to disappear from his soul and his text. Eckermann is making amends, he is rectifying and paying for his part in the bringing together of this text; in sum, he presents himself here with the bill of *Bildung*. And if this sequence of error had not been effaced, if he had not in fact attained to the "great moral strength," then the purest and truest of teachers, whom he now calls Nature, would scorn him, as in fact Goethe had done in the anterior stages of his education, which included moments of greatest estrangement and alienation. The process is long, and as Hegel warns in his book of *Bildung,* one, like the *Weltgeist* itself, must show patience. "If people took all this into consideration," writes Eckermann, "then they would gladly devote a few years of their life to it . . . they would gain respect before lawfulness and come as close to the divine ['dem Göttlichen'] as is possible for a terrestrial spirit." Precisely the question of law, and a certain disrespect before Goethe's law, had in the first place estranged the terrestrial spirit of Eckermann. This passage traces Eckermann's path from a certain concept of lawlessness to respect before the law and a mediated proximity to Goethe. Eckermann also keeps a cautious distance from poetry, which promotes, he claims, subjectivity: "In contrast, one is too preoccupied with poetry and suprasensory mysteries, which are subjective and yielding things that do not challenge one further but rather flatter and, in favorable instances, leave one as he is." Poetry is loose, and seductive, s/he gives in easily, immediately, teaching very little. His conclusion: "Therefore I praise commerce ['Verkehr,' intercourse) with Nature, who in no way looks favorably upon our weaknesses and who either makes something of us or will have nothing to do with us." One can recommend a reading of "Nature" as Goethe's pseudonym—as the teacher and master who brings the manifold text of teaching, of the *Farbenlehre* together, making something out of us or having nothing to do with us, in other words, ex-communicating us—or, as it may happen, refusing to have intercourse with us, as Mother Goethe and Mother Nature tend at times to do.

Hypnotics

Whereas their relationship to Nature and the natural sciences implies for Eckermann an arduous process of *Bildung,* moments of great estrangement from Goethe, and delayed incorporation, all of which will find its most unsettling articulation in Eckermann's ornithological concerns, their relationship to poetry presents an altogether different picture. Though Eckermann may display some skepticism toward poetry when engaged in writing on science, it is essentially here that he reaches a spontaneous accord with Goethe—and it is here that saying and writing "we," "our," or "ours" seems least problematic. However, the limits dividing poetry from Eckermann's pathological branch of science are not always fixable, and even when he says "this is poetry" one cannot be sure that he is referring to what is commonly considered poetry.

Goethe and Eckermann live poetry in the citational mode, reciting to each other dead letters, feeding each other with these, releasing verses from their forgotten cages in ways that always signal a certain danger, for it is something like reliving a finality that has never ended. One day, for example, Eckermann recites to Goethe Mephistopheles' lines, reminding his master that "in the end we do indeed depend on the creatures we have created." It is as if everything about their relationship had been previously recorded, strangely reviewed and reflected in Goethe's poetry. When Eckermann and Goethe cite and recite (Goethe's) poetry to one another, they are usually involved in a kind of hypnotics, playing out modulations of unconscious transmission and telepathy.

In scenes of poetic delivery, the gift of giving the poems is more often
than not placed in Eckermann's hands. In the actual staging of these
moments Eckermann is shown to return to Goethe his gift so that
Goethe can take pleasure in giving back to Eckermann what he has
taken—thus giving back, in fact, another reading of Eckermann. On 5
April 1829, "we spoke of his Italian voyage and he said to me that
among his letters from Italy he had found a song which he wanted to
show me." Goethe asks Eckermann to give him the package containing
some papers. "I gave it to him, there were his letters from Italy; he
looked for the poem and read." Goethe *wants* to show Eckermann this
poem, perhaps, indeed, because its birdlike hero, Cupido, comes to
resemble his interlocutor. This resemblance is reinforced elsewhere as
well, if one remembers the famous scene of the *Conversations* in which a
young Eckermann teaches Goethe, "old but young in spirit," to use a
bow and arrow—a skill in which Eckermann excelled. The poem, of
which Goethe remarks, "it cannot be unknown [*fremd*] to you"—
though this appeared "totally new" to him—begins with the apostrophe:

> Cupido, loser, eigensinniger Knabe!
> Du batst mich um Quartier auf einige Stunden.
> Wie viele Tag' und Nächte bist du geblieben!
> Und bist nun herrisch und Meister im Haus geworden.
>
> Von meinem breiten Lager bin ich vertreiben;
> Nun sitz' ich an der Erde, Nächte gequälet.
> Dein Mutwill' schüret Flamm' auf Flamme des Herdes,
> Verbrennet den Vorrat des Winters und senget mich Armen.
>
> Du hast mir mein Gerät verstellt und verschoben.
> Ich such' und bin wie blind und irre geworden;
> Du lärmst so ungeschickt; ich fürchte, das Seelchen
> Entflieht, um dir zu entfliehen, und räumet die Hütte.

> Cupid, loose, obstinate boy!
> You asked me for lodgings for a few hours.
> How many days and nights have you stayed!
> And now you have become dictatorial and Master in my house.
>
> I am expelled from my spacious den;
> Now I sit upon the earth, nights I am tortured.
> Your wantonness incites flame upon flame of the hearth,
> Burns winter's reserves and ravages me, a poor wretch.
>
> You have displaced and deferred my apparatus.
> I search and have become blind and insane;
> You clumsily make noise; I fear
> My soul escaping in order to escape you—veering from the hut.

While it would be foolish to insist on some sort of absolute identity of Eckermann and Cupido, it would be overhasty to ignore the contextualizing powers at play. The issues are familiar to us by now, and they have been found to permeate Eckermann's text. The extended visit, the question of mastery, the dislodging effect that such an intervention, however vital and necessary, might have on Goethe, the close alliance of eros and thanatos—all of which can be traced from the moment Eckermann touches Goethe's knee to Goethe's death, or from the instant he brings back to life Goethe's works to their completion. And Eckermann himself suggests that something like an unconscious transmission is taking place as Goethe reads. He delivers the last lines in a trancelike state, "as if dreaming"—lines which Eckermann, as if in Goethe's command, repeats again in his text: "Du lärmst so ungeschickt," etc. "Goethe had read the poem very beautifully; I could not release it again from my senses, and it seemed that for him too it remained in his mind." The trancelike episode in which the one implants the poem in the other who handed it to him, closes oddly, if sweetly: "Goethe fed me finally with a lot of honey, also with some dates that I took along." As if to double once more the connections that are made within the poem, but also within the *Conversations,* Eckermann names the substance of their harmony to be a food substance, the same substance, by the way, with which Eckermann will feed his most beloved birds.

The sweetened scent of the scene drifts into the next entry, this time acquiring Dionysian overtones, if Rhine wine can be associated with the fruit of Dionysos. On this date, Goethe does not quite converse with Eckermann, but rather, he hums, which suffices to inspire Eckermann to re-recite a portion of the verses to him. "We sat for a while at table, drinking some glasses of old Rhine wine with good biscuits. Goethe hummed insensibly ['summte Undeutliches vor sich hin']. Yesterday's poem returned to my mind again; I recited:

> Du hast mir mein Gerät verstellt und verschoben;
> Ich such' und bin wie blind und irre geworden, . . .

I can't rid myself of the poem, I said; it is altogether peculiar ['eigenartig'] and expresses so well the disorder that love brings into our lives." Goethe replies that there is in it something of "Good Man and Good Wife." "You take the words out of my mouth, I said," Eckermann says. They take and give words from each other, words referring them to Ostade's painting of the blissful couple gathering yarn. And yet, the

particular lines which Eckermann recites back to Goethe and cannot
forget, the lines which strangely remind them both of a tranquil portrait
of domesticity, evoking a mood that could hardly arise from the disloca-
tions, invasions, and evasions announced in the poem itself—these lines
with which Eckermann supplies Goethe's senseless humming convey
about as much serenity as, say, Eckermann's financial situation: you
have disarranged my apparatus, you have dissembled, obstructed, post-
poned, or delayed my apparatus or tool, you have played *fort-da* with
my phallus; I am searching, I am blind, going mad. These lines Eckermann cannot forget; and he says that he cannot understand how *Goethe*
would have come to the feeling of such a condition ("Wie Sie aber zu
dem Gefühl eines solchen Zustandes gekommen sind, begreife ich
kaum"). The poem, he feels, is as if from another time, another world;
he cannot understand how Goethe would have access to this world. So
Goethe, to explain the tact that "comes from the poetic mood as if
unconsciously," scans this line with Eckermann:

> Vŏn/ m͞eīnĕm br͞eītĕn L͞agĕr / b͞in ĭch vĕr/tr͞iebĕn.
> From my wide space am I expelled.

They speak of rhythm, and by 8 April, two days after Goethe explains the feeling and tact of expulsion, he comes to speak of the
poem as "our song" ("unser Lied: Cupido, loser, eigensinniger
Knabe") and Eckermann repeats, picking up the *eigen*, "It is peculiar
['eigen,' proper] to this song, I said, that it places one in a kind of
dreamlike mood ['träumerische Stimmung']." And it is no doubt also
peculiar that the meeting on this April day began as an affirmation of
telepathic prospects, for "Goethe was already sitting at the set table
as I walked in; he received me very cheerfully: 'I have received a
letter,' he said, 'from where?—from Rome! But from whom?—from
the King of Bavaria.' I share your joy, I said. But is it not peculiar
['eigen'] that, for an hour, during my walk, I have been vividly ['lebhaft'] occupied in thought with the King of Bavaria, and now I discover this pleasant news. Often something announces its arrival inside
us,' Goethe said ['Es kündigt sich oft etwas in unserm Innern an'].
'There's the letter; take it, sit next to me and read it.' "

There. This would be one of the frames pressing against the Cupido
episode from which emerged the various modalities of hypnotic thought.
A peculiar frame of mind: Sit beside me and read what you already
know, move with me toward that *eigen* which for us is two, ours, like the
circulation or exchange of unconscious messages, the conjunction where

minds, fortunes, and letters can be read together in unison, to the refrain of an "our" song, poem, text. It will have been our song not only because we delivered and dreamt the words for each other, scanned and adopted them, but also it is about us because of the young man for whom *eigen*sinn means a profounder penetration into what is mine, my space, my writing, my house, my mood, my unconscious which announce their arrival inside you. Or me. Let us sing to this, and drink to this, we are blind, expelled, we are expelled from the *eigensinn.*

Perhaps what is most remarkable about this scene is that it prepares Eckermann's progressive metamorphosis into a bird-like entity. And with this major regression—of "man," one is tempted to say—we enter the most peculiar dimension of the *Conversations,* the one to which Goethe cannot cease appending such terms as "problematic," "enigmatic," "uncanny," and so on.

VorGEfühL

Goethe uses a special word to suggest an opening for telepathy; he uses it against the grain as it were, for the normal usage of the word would arrest its semantic movement in "presentiment." However, Goethe's word for telepathy, which he uses with great frequency in especially troubling or indecipherable circumstances, is *Vorgefühl.* It may be a mere coincidence, an inexplicable falling together of crucial elements that makes this word act as a kind of cryptic code for Eckermann's most deeply felt attachment, namely to birds and to *VOrGEfühL.* Leaving aside the fact that Goethe's family name was actually Vogelhuber (before it was changed by an ancestor to the French Gothé)—there was a Johann Wolfgang Vogelhuber—leaving aside, then, the uncanny link between Goethe's hidden and discarded patronymic and Eckermann's obsession, let us provisionally suppose, as Goethe says in the *Conversations,* that certain things are not merely reducible to an accident ("mehr als Zufall"). Accidents can have mysterious sources, he argues, and it is perhaps no accident that mystery and secrecy (*Geheimnis*) as well as the uncanny (*unheimlich*)—especially the *unheimlich*—all play a major role in the passages that lead home, or to the question of a home. And these homes, be they found in the form of a nest, the *Frauenplan,* or even Eckermann's homeless wanderings as a child, are linked to the concept of *Vorgefühl.*

In the introduction to the *Conversations* we learn that Eckermann's father, the Hausierer (peddlar), carried on a trade in winter "hawking pens:" he "trieb einen Handel mit rohen Schreibfedern," with raw quills. This simple disclosure elicits a good number of motifs that run through, if they do not dominate, Eckermann's life and works. Indeed, it is difficult not to want to write Eckermann's story entirely from the phrasing of this disclosure, simplistic though it may seem. And it would be necessary to prompt only a few lexical deviations to make it speak. For example, if it were to be read as a poem, where *trieb* were coaxed into *Trieb,* drive, or *Handel* into the Hand which has held our attention, and is attached to the *Buch-handlung* with which Eckermann solicited Goethe. In the dark, wintered beginning there was the *rohen Schreibfedern:* excrement and writing, the appendage, the limb, the father, the feather, the drive and the trade, the exchanges and the tradewinds, the raw or uncultivated pens—as if all this could be related in and by Eckermann, in the drop of a phrase, a pen, or related by Eckermann as the problem of space and home. The movements delineated by Eckermann in the introduction tend to run from a "free nature" to home, and, more radically, if secretly, from the cage to prison, captivity, *Gefangenschaft.* Or it would be more correct to say from captivity to cage. (In *Dichtung und Wahrheit* Goethe remembers his childhood house already as a birdcage, perhaps recollecting the discarded patronym Vogelhuber, "bird sanctuary.")

If the arrival of these motifs is being announced too swiftly—as if you didn't already know them—it is only to give back the vertiginous impression that Eckermann gives while steadying his hand to write. (Also in the introduction: "But I thought about it, and as this long guarded secret anxiety had probably contributed to hastening the outbreak of the illness slumbering within me, it issued forth with its full violence. . . . June came on, and I was no more in a state to guide a graving tool, my hands trembled so. . . . if I had so dragged on, I would infallibly have become doomed to death, . . .".) Eckermann's case, if it does not seem too vulgar to use this word, by the internal transmissions of his texts and paratexts (dreams, letters, diary entries, notes, etc.), suggests him to figure as an exemplary case of cage or crypt, pointing up that, although he may have spells of knocking against his encasement, he basically has been caught from the start, immobile and penned in. And even when he is on the run or walking, his internal control tower directs him toward a place of internment. We shall see how, too, descriptions made of Eckermann by his friends could not suppress these aspects of his drama. For the moment, however, it is best to remain within the confines of his recorded captivity, the *Conversations,* which comprises an *éloge* to the most formidable songbird, Goethe of the Vogelhuber lineage. The birds with which Eckermann will spend the rest of his living death will have been evacuated only once from his small chamber, when after thirteen years of engagement, he brought his bride to live with him. On this occasion, Goethe, who never consented to seeing her, merely wrote in his diary that "Dr. E. seems to have lost his interest in birds." She died soon thereafter, giving birth to their child, and the birds returned. As for the child, he became a painter of eagles.

One of the early and rather ominous references to Eckermann's passion, which might be taken to signal a *Vorgefühl* for ensuing events of this nature, is recorded as having taken place on the first of March, 1830. For once, and for the last time, Goethe will be the principal speaker on this subject. What he has to offer is not devoid of horror. The general subject of conversation into which his observations are introduced concerns natural history. Goethe tells the story of the Englishman who kept and fed several hundred birds in large cages (*Behälter*). When a few of these died, he had them stuffed. "These stuffed ones pleased him so well that the idea crossed his mind: would it not be better to have them all killed ['totschlagen'] and stuffed; soon afterward he executed his idea." Eckermann has no comment to add to this communication; and indeed, it seems rather helplessly stranded among the far more sustained and coherent elaborations that both Eckermann and Goethe offer on other subjects. One wonders why Eckermann even included such a "naked expression," arriving almost without context or justificatory discourse (otherwise Eckermann always covers Goethe). One wonders about this, particularly given its place as a first indication, a kind of foreword to his insatiable concern for these creatures. What types of transmissions are taking place when Goethe evokes this scene of massacre?

As all subsequent passages dealing with ornithological considerations tend to stress, their discussions revolving around birds are rarely down to earth—they often come up on mountain tops, taking place, then, in the regions where, according to these descriptions, the soul takes flight into the *unheimlich*. These passages usually take place when telepathic transmissions come to pass and therefore, once again, it should not seem inappropriate to ask what might be taking place in this primal scene of their avian exchanges. Goethe is certainly striking at Eckermann's most vulnerable point, for it will be essential for Eckermann to keep his birds alive, as they kept him alive during his early wanderings—or as they will continue to live in his care as he dies after, if not long before, Goethe's death.

What might be focused on here is the other facet of the "living dead," this mode of preservation which by nature is most enduring, when the object is—paradoxical as this may seem—dead. The implicit motive behind the transformation of the Englishman's aviary into a slaughterhouse is suggested to lie in the fact that by this means he was able to preserve the objects of his great interest and studies. They are dead but not gone; they cannot take flight. He would however no longer have to feed them in order to ensure their remaining presence. It hardly seems that the motif of feeding is fortuitous in this context. Eckermann of course passes over it silently, probably gulping down his soup. In any case, this scene, while it may well be the decisive one, runs counter to the host of bird conversations in which Eckermann has the upper hand. Yet it is not entirely opposed; rather, it is the underside, the dimension and mention to be gone over in silence without being cut off from a form of uneasy memory. To the extent that birds are bound in the *Conversations* to a notion of home, they are also related to a structure of disappearance. They tend to represent both for Eckermann and for his Goethe something dangerous in nature, and still unexplained. The harbingers of an uncertain future, they also surround the event of death, always coming from elsewhere, and, as the Greeks had it, birds are bereft of proper burial, unaccompanied in the last instance by an evocation of cemetery (Aristophanes). In the *Conversations,* birds are shown in their condition of essential homelessness; they are largely shown to be caught in the predicament of imprisonment—the key kind of home with which man can furnish the bird. Yet they are the beings par excellence that are known to return— for example, they return to their young ones, they return from a guise of disappearance to nourish their young, and they return when you feed them. When they depart, in time, for a time, these birds usually follow a southerly direction, in pursuit of their ancestral path. This, at least, is what Eckermann's entry for 29 May 1831, teaches.

Within the confines of space which Eckermann allots these birds, they are shown to follow a trajectory leading from a condition of imprisonment to freedom and back: the trajectory maps out the course of a round trip flight, but also the course and discourse of exemplary parental care. On 29 May, then, Eckermann narrates that someone ("man") had recently brought him a nest of young warblers. There was also an older one among them, which had been caught, imprisoned ("gefangen") in twig branches. "Now I had to admire how the bird continued to feed its young ones in the room, but even after being released ['freigelassen'] out the window, it returned to the young ones. I was deeply moved ['rührte mich innig'] by such parental love that overcomes danger and imprisonment ('Gefahr und Gefangenschaft überwindende, elterliche Liebe'], and today I expressed my astonishment over this to Goethe." To whom is he telling this? Here is Eckermann, the chronically fed, telling his nourisher about the nature of feeding. And he is astonished. Yet clearly the position of this narration's elder, of the one who surrenders himself to double time and imprisonment—originally imprisoned, the older bird later confines himself voluntarily to another cage—belongs to Eckermann. He is the older one now who feels the multiplicity of others, offering Goethe this story, for example, which he feels is to Goethe's taste. Eckermann at the same time expresses his astonishment over parental love, placing the story before Goethe for his judgment. Before the judgment is delivered, Eckermann demonstrates very precisely the risks implied for a parental figure such as the one at hand who would fly back into imprisonment of his own volition. There is thus a sense in which Eckermann does not act, as it would initially seem, merely to "remind Goethe of his parental duties" (as Goethe would later remind Freud); but he follows a logic that has him figuring himself as the older songbird who returns in peril to feed his young, to assure their safety and survival as he abandons hope for his own.

Interestingly, the entire entry for 29 May, which contains this allegory, begins with Goethe's account of "a boy who could not get over an error he had made." Goethe disapprovingly points to the instance of self-accusatory rage, for it suggests to him an overly delicate conscience and a manifest illness of the sensibility. A paragraph later, without transition, the little boy of self-canceling qualities appears to have grown in Eckermann's narration into the old songbird, sounding notes over something that haunts and astonishes him, speaking perhaps from the place of a little boy who cannot get over a trespass of sorts, now older than Goethe and still his child or even his grandchild. As usual, Eckermann occupies a double position, doubling in this case also for the little boy of the inaugural account who was in fact Goethe's grandson, Wölfchen. Wölfchen, Goethe instructs Eckermann, typifies those who evaluate the moral self so highly that they forgive themselves nothing; they eat at themselves, they are the self-torturers who will never be appeased or able to set their minds at rest. Whereupon Eckermann's agitation leads him to volunteer his prison sentences.

As the narration evolves, Goethe gradually recovers his position as judge and chiding parent. As in the case of the *Farbenlehre,* Goethe's response to Eckermann consists in referring to the powers above (Eckermann), that is, simultaneously to God and to Goethe. "You silly fool! If you believed in God you wouldn't be so amazed." To demonstrate the truth of God's participation in this phenomenon, Goethe then quotes Goethe, recalling to Eckermann His words concerning the "omnipotent drive toward one's children" that is common to all that lives ("alles Lebendige der ganzen Natur"). In effect, Goethe has had to remind Eckermann of the living, of the law of the living, which in his astonishment Eckermann had presently forgotten. His diary entry for 29 March 1831, confirms Eckermann's passionate interest for birds. He had thought, he writes, that he could do without them; he then bought one bird and soon he began purchasing several of them, noting that he now *needs* them "in order to have something about me in my room that is living" ("damit ich in meinem Zimmer etwas Lebendiges um mich habe"). To have something in my room that lives, having returned, returning from the dead to the dead, to return them to life. That is what I need. The question returns with the birds, possibly the only living creatures in his room, the question of the phantom who appeared to us rattling his chains.

Losing One's Quills

While we are responding to the call of Eckermann's phantom, it might be suggested that some of the links which are made in his text and otherwise can be studied as part of a larger cultural symptomatology. In other words, Eckermann suggests a way by which it becomes necessary to consider the bird as a metapsychological fact. Clearly no exhaustive study of the relationship between a bio-cultural ornithology and Eckermann's writing or cryptonomy can be made here, but only the route that such an investigation might take will be plotted, slowly, in honor of Eckermann and other secretaries of the phantom. The specificity of Eckermann's case, the questions that he raises in diaries, notes, scenes of narrativities, and conversations—all of which tend to subsume birds under a larger metapsychological perspective, take wing in an episodic serial beginning on Wednesday, 26 September 1827. Eckermann unfolds his argument slowly, carrying messages on the order of a "Dichtung und Wahrheit" polarity that is meant to deliver some truths about his plumed companions. He aims in part to deflate the widespread poetry—that is, untruth—according to which birds are believed to swallow their adoptive parents. Eckermann holds this belief to be contemptibly false, misguided; he nonetheless brings it to Goethe's attention: "One even ascribes to ['dichtet an'] the good bird this story: as soon as it is fully matured ['völlig ausgewachsen'], it swallows its own parents. And thus one uses him as a metaphor for the most disgraceful ingratitude." If the practice ascribed to these good birds cannot be found to exist, the metaphor to which it gives rise does. What seems to disturb Eckermann resides in the power of metaphor, the most illusory of tropes, to sustain what ought not to be sustained, namely, in this case, a false link between devoration and ingratitude. Well, there is no destabilizing the metaphor as it carries on its disjunctive rapport to the truth of the matter; and thus Eckermann, on a figural level, enforces the slippage from *Dichtung* to *Wahrheit,* not by arguing against the concept of "disgraceful ingratitude," but by insisting that the bird, the good bird, would not typify such an attitude (what would have become of his assertion had he left out "good"?). He takes it a step further, for he continues: "I know people who still, at present [E. doubles the present: 'im gegenwärtigen Augenblick'] will not be talked out of these absurdities and hang on to it ['daran so fest hängen'] as firmly as if it were some article of their Christian faith." Eckermann knows some people who presently hang on. He is put off—one is tempted to say unhinged—by the metaphorical abuse to which the bird is subjected, something related to swallowing one's own (parents), but who knows what other metaphorical indulgences may be upsetting Eckermann as regards the bird. What has Eckermann had to swallow? Or rather, whom has he had to swallow? There is a line leading back to questions of faith and Christianity—close to the break in faith that characterized the *Farbenlehre* dispute, in which Eckermann had shown a flash of ingratitude toward the parental Goethe. When it comes to birds, however, the role of child and pupil belongs no longer to Eckermann but, we shall presently see, to Goethe. This is why Eckermann may need to rewrite the stories of the bird who swallows its own parents, particularly since in this field he will have been promoted to the rank of parenthood (metaphorically speaking).

The first series of episodes begins as an excursion from an edge to a hedge, from *Ecke* to *Hecke*—the inscription of Eckermann's name can be seen to appear on the horizon, mapping out the limits of the open enclosure in which he and Goethe are to meet, as if for the first time. It should be noted at the outset of this excursion that the pertinent entries represent the rare passages which trace an entire day's move-

ments, though according to the manuscript it is clear that Eckermann
fully invented the dialogue that follows, or wrote it according to
another law of transcription. The inaugural gesture of this semifictional
serial consists in a certain infantilization of Goethe, a clear-cut exchange of positions that Goethe and Eckermann have seemed to occupy throughout the *Conversations*. And, on the most immediate level,
this takes place in the domain of science.

The episode begins with Goethe noticing a flock of birds. He asks
Eckermann whether these would be skylarks (this is italicized in the
text: *"ob es Lerchen wären?"*). Dash. (*"ob es Lerchen wären?—"*).
Beginning with the dash, Eckermann imparts to us his thoughts in which
he addresses Goethe in the familiar *Du* form, and uses a construction
reminiscent of the "Wanderer's Nightsong": "—You great and dear one
I thought, you who have thoroughly investigated the entirety of Nature
as have few others; in ornithology you seem to be a child" ("—Du
Großer und Lieber, dachte ich, der du die ganze Natur. . . ."). There.
Eckermann has become, at last, Goethe's natural father, his father in
nature. The birds that the unfledged Goethe sees are everything but
skylarks; for instance, there are late warblers ("verspätete Grasmücken") among them. (Eckermann will eventually delete yet another
reference to latecomers, namely when Goethe, according to his sketch,
is quoted as saying: "I have reason to believe that the gull, together with
all other birds, was created very late ['*sehr spät*']".) If the warblers (and,
according to Goethe's suppressed reasoning, all these creatures) are
latecomers, we shall see how Eckermann progressively places himself in
the scene they create, scattering attributes that can be appended to him
among the birds. The skylark, for example, emits a "somewhat melan-
cholic song," he keeps away from places that are too "life-ly" ("lebhaft"), too proximate to crowds—forecasting Eckerman's later anthro-
and agoraphobia. Goethe's immediate response to Eckermann's expla-
nations lacks some of the eloquence we have become accustomed to:
"Hm! sagte Goethe." But the "Hm!" is telling, or rather not telling, a
kind of profounder dash which in his further responses will suggest that
he listens to a double discourse in Eckermann. You do not appear to be
a newcomer to this field, he adds. And now Eckermann recommences
his autobiography, focusing on this branch of study. Like the bird of
which he speaks, Eckermann's faculty for seeing and hearing will prove
to be particularly well developed: "from my youth I have pursued this
field with love . . . and have always had my eyes and ears open for
it . . . now when I hear a single tone, I can venture to say ['so getraue
ich mir zu sagen'] from which bird it comes." Eckermann returns to a

beginning, not only to the beginning of his history, his story of a passionate ornithologist, but also to the beginning of his history with Goethe
insofar as his first task and test was to recognize Goethe's voice among
the mass of notes and texts Goethe had submitted to him. That talent of
differentiating began in this field. And now we arrive at the passion of
his passion, at Eckermann's identification of, and no doubt also with,
his object: "Also, I have advanced to the point that if someone brings
me a bird, that in his captivity ['der in der Gefangenschaft'] has lost his
plumage because of mistreatment ['durch verkehrte Behandlung,' perverse mishandling], I can very quickly restore him again to full health
and feathers ['ihn sehr bald vollkommen gesund und wohlbefiedert
wieder herzustellen']." This would be Eckermann's telos and gift, his
great capacity and desire. It brings us back or, to use his terms, "advances" us to the point of many beginnings. Of the birds that are
brought to Dr. Eckermann, the extreme cases have suffered prison
terms as it were. They were not merely imprisoned or penned in, however; they were also mishandled, which is to say, they lost their feathers,
their raw quills. This, precisely, is what Eckermann dares and even risks
("ich getraue mir") saying at this point. For those birds who have met
with maltreatment in captivity, and have lost their plumage—they cannot fly home—he can promise restoration. Eckermann can repair the
damages; he can return them—to health and to featherhood, he can
return them *fully,* as if such a thing as *Wiedergutmachung* were possible.

Goethe's reaction to these assertions would seem beside or beyond
the point if we were not stressing a double reading of this passage:
" 'All this shows,' Goethe responds, 'that in these matters you have
already gone through a lot ['daß Sie in diesen Dingen bereits vieles
durchgemacht haben'].' " The Herr Rat advises Eckermann to continue the drive, or more commonly, to pursue his studies, or more ana-
semically, to expel these studies: "Ich möchte Ihnen raten, das Studium ernstlich fort zu treiben."

Goethe has not let the bit about losing one's quills slide by him. His
mind is captivated by a sole issue, one that suggests the motif of the
detachable appendage or *excrementum.* "But tell me something about
molting." He wants to know about this particularly in the case of the
belated warblers, wanting to know, further, whether this shedding or
casting off of parts of one's body is bound to a specific epoch ("an eine
gewisse Epoche gebunden"). Before we review their exchange on the
subject of molting in greater detail, it may be useful to note that the
word *Mauser* ("molting") can be traced to different roots, suggesting
that what is at stake at some level of this already doubled exchange is

the knowledge of passing away or passing on, of losing and borrowing the quill in addition to the desire, prevalent in Eckermann's multiple accounts, to protect and save.

To Goethe's anxious questioning Eckermann responds that molting is a matter of appropriate space ("gehörigen Raum"); if this should be available, then molting can be achieved here, and he (presumably the bird) can go forth with fresh plumage. However, if deprived of sufficient space, he goes forth with his old plumage to molt later in the south. A bird that comes early to us, Eckermann continues, departs late, and a bird that arrives late leaves early. Goethe attends with persistence to the question of the latecomer: is the gray warbler the last and latest bird to come to us, or are there others that come even later? The answer could prove unsettling, to Eckermann or Goethe or both, for the bird to arrive the latest is, according to Eckermann, of course the "so-called mocking-bird" (*Spottvogel*)—whose name among ornithologists is *Mimus poly-glottos*. This bird arrives at about the time of Pentecost. If kept in a cage, explains Eckermann, the mockingbird will molt at our place (*"bei uns"*), but this is also what makes it difficult to pull them through, for they are fragile and require great warmth.

The question of molting, as it is pursued here, comes down to the difference between natural and unnatural loss of plumage, the one incurred through mistreatment and imprisonment, the other through a natural process of shedding one's plume. However, for Goethe, this fall, or case, comes closer to resembling a symptom or disease, a sign of weakness. "One holds molting to be a disease, or at least it is accompanied by physical weakness ['körperliche Schwäche']." On this point Eckermann refrains from acting the *Mimus polyglottos* on an immediate scale, but not merely by disagreeing; rather, he proposes another interpretation of this symptom, as if in self-defense. "I wouldn't say that, I replied; it is a condition of heightened productiv-ity," thereby miming in effect one of Goethe's supremely held catego-ries, namely *gesteigeter Produktivität*. Indeed, one name of the stakes at hand is productivity, and we shall presently see how this becomes attached to the notions of freedom, eating, *excrementum,* and pen. Eckermann continues:

> I have had warblers who did not suspend their singing [*"Gesang,"* also poem] during the entire molting period which is a sign of their well-being. However, if a bird shows itself to be ill in the room during the molting, then one must conclude that he hasn't been handled appropri-ately in terms of feeding or fresh air and water. . . . If in time he has become so weak in his room—because of lack of air and freedom—that

the productive force fails him so that he could not come to molting, then one should bring him to the enriching [fruitful] fresh air, and molting will immediately be activated in the best of ways.

This is what Eckermann could have taught Goethe, namely that to sustain *Gesang* while one loses one's plumage, while excreting, is a sign of health. But this is precisely what Goethe already knows, as Eckermann knows from at least the time of Goethe's famous paradigm of shedding snake skins with each work. And thus to lose one's plumes presupposes, as Goethe already knows, a productive force. They have brought each other to the fresh air to hold this dialogue. Yet there are cases for concern, that is, cases concerning penned up creatures who have not been fed properly nor therefore handled properly; they can have become weak (or subject to hypochondria) from a lack or deprivation of freedom; they cannot be brought to the point of shedding, detaching, excreting with ease; this is their disease. Goethe and Eckermann have brought themselves out into the open. But, according to Eckermann's orchestration, it is Goethe and not he who shows distress over molting; Eckermann on the contrary sings praises to the necessary loss, suggesting at every point an opening for the motif of the Phoenix.

Although molting, according to Eckermann, implies no excessive loss, the bird, during this time, requires a supplement of protection. Nature of course demonstrates her habitual wisdom and moderation, insofar as a bird would not at once lose so many plumes as to become incapable of flying at least well enough to obtain its food. Goethe advances his classical penchant, asking Eckermann whether the shedding takes place symmetrically ("gewissermaßen symmetrisch"), on both wings. Yes, this would be the case, opines the other, there is symmetry. For if a bird were to lose for example three pinions of the left wing and not the same on the right wing, then equilibrium would collapse and the bird would lose mastery over his movement. There is nothing new about this centrist strategy shared by Goethe and Eckermann, nor about the rhetoric of conjunction that Eckermann is about to introduce: He would be, Eckermann explains, *like a ship* whose sails are too heavy on one side, too light on the other.

Eckermann has just retrieved the fantasy linking the bird to the ship which first appeared on our horizon in the introduction. "I see," Goethe replies, releasing the same homonymic sound waves that we receive in German and English, across the channels (see/sea). The eternal sea, Goethe, the reflecting body upon whose movements Eckermann will inscribe his secret and lost story, one that he buried in his depths while skimming the surface. And the old Goethe seems to speak of his place and Eckermann's, of his deposit as they continue their solitary voyage: "Always the old story ['Geschichte,' history]." The old story or history, we learn, comes down to Eckermann's old story where it meets the history of old Goethe, whose origins for Eckermann are "always the old bottom of the sea": " 'Always the old story!' said Goethe. 'Always the old bottom of the sea!—' " They, by now, have soared to the summit of the Ettersberg; they are looking down, into the past—the old story, covered by a mountain chain, blurred and mostly effaced but now remembered by these navigators of the abyss. The seagull, Goethe ventures, "the seagull that once flew over the sea which covered this mountain, he certainly did not think that we both would come here today. And who knows if, after many thousands of years, the seagull will not once again fly over this mountain." Everything returns to the sea, coming from the sea, the seamen, the gull, the site where the wing tips into the ocean. As for our navigating pair, they return to themselves momentarily; they are hungry. They look out over the mountain in a southerly direction, then they see the Schloß Gotha. Eckermann remembers the verse about eternal life's pressentiment. They find a place to sit down; Goethe has the servant, Friedrich, lay out the meal. "We consumed a pair of roasted hens" ("Wir verzehrten indes ein paar gebratene Rebhühner").

The avian path picks up again on 7 October 1827, though it starts penetrating to regions whose grounds become less and less secure. Goethe's diary entry for the previous day indicated that he had lunched with Rat Vogel and Dr. Eckermann, after which he fixed a rendezvous with the latter. The following day, 7 October, they travel to Jena for lunch with Knebel. "Everything went very heartily and cheerfully; however nothing important developed as concerns Conversations. The two old friends had enough with sheer humanly proximate togetherness ['menschlichnahen Beisammensein']." If they did, Eckermann did not. He exchanges humanly plenitude with conversation, as if now conversation were to exceed the living human, or any form of comfortable together-being. Thus after lunch "we made an excursion in a southerly direction." An angle of Eckermann's past returns, he suggests, although the scene may not be one of repetition or revival: "I knew this delightful ['reizende'] region from an earlier time, but everything seemed so fresh as if I had never seen it before." By nightfall the pair have found a room with twin beds in an alcove, "and we were contented to sit for some time without light." Curiously, it is only when light is brought in that shadows of the uncanny are thrown into relief: "I told Goethe a strange dream from my boyhood years, which was literally fulfilled the next morning." We might note that once again the birds—for the dream will contain birds—weave a knot tying an event in Eckermann's youth, a fantasy event, with the Goethe-period of his life, when he recalls and serves the dream-narration as a Conversation. And once again we are held in by these themes of imprisonment and abadonment, the problem of freedom and food. The dream and the event following directly upon it are framed by a sort of "preliminary report": Eckermann had raised ("erzogen") three linnets ("Hänflinge") on which his soul entirely depended ("hing," hung) and whom he loved above anything else. They would fly freely ("frei") about his room and, when he entered the door, upon his hand. However, one afternoon one of these birds flew away from the young Eckermann ("über mich hinweg") and out the window. Searching for the lost creature, he could find no trace ("keine Spur") of him. He fell asleep, sorrowful. Toward the morning hours he had a dream containing the following elements: He sees himself namely ("nämlich") looking for "my lost bird" ("für meinen verlorenen Vogel"). He suddenly hears the sound of his voice ("Stimme") and then he sees him. Now the young Eckermann must attract the bird ("ihn locke"); while he craves feeding, he is undecided about flying into his hand. It occurs to Eckermann to fetch his favorite food, rapeseed, at which point the hesitant companion descends upon Eckermann's hand to be joyously brought back to the two others. Eckermann awakens. Everything "literally"—"buchstäblich," by the book—takes place as the dream had foretold: I attract him, he comes closer; but he hesitates to fly to my hands. I run back and fetch the feed, and he flies on my hand, and I bring him back to the others.

And I bring him back to the others. A recurring narration of desire and terror. The two others awaiting the tracelessly lost one: Eckermann's enticements, bringing back the lost bird to the waiting couple—to the parents, his children. Finding him by voice, the name, my name, my lost name, flying or sailing away from me—my brother, my father, the quill peddler, my lost pen bringing it back, back through the voice, the voice that dictates what my quill will write, spill, eliminate after having absorbed the sea of ink spread before him. This is indeed highly remarkable. Said Goethe.

Now what Goethe is said to have said, what this voice on coming back to the present had to say, when the narrating couple recline in the alcove—in the vault or recess—is that we might not have the right key to such events. "Wir wandeln alle in Geheimnisse": we all travel in secrets. Goethe holds the key, he knows and names the secret of not knowing the secret, and he knows especially that Eckermann, in telling him this dream and its sequel, now before they retire, here which is already there, away from home and Weimar, he knows that Eckermann will have been on the verge of importing a "discordance ("Verstimmung"), so that it became *unheimlich* to all." To all? Someone, something else, also felt this uncanniness, they were not only two in comfortable together-being. Goethe says: "We are surrounded by an atmosphere, about which we as yet know nothing—nothing about everything that agitates within it and how this ['es'] is in contact with our spirit ['Geist,' mind]." This is the point of contact to which Goethe draws our attention in this passage—or toward which Eckermann can only entice us through the medium of Goethe's articulation voicing its need. We as yet know nothing. About that which is in contact, connected ("in Verbindung steht"). He continues: "This much is certain: in particular conditions the feelers of our soul can reach out beyond their bodily limits and a presentiment, yes, also a real glance into the imminent future is granted the soul."

Freud would place limits on this phenomenon by calling it wish fulfillment—and we have already seen how he places them at the outer limits of the *Traumdeutung*. Eckermann proceeds to recount another story which shows the feelers of the soul reaching beyond their corporeal frontiers and into uncanny corners: the story is about turning the corner ("Ecke"). He enters with Goethe a dimension that he later writes is governed by "more-than-chance" ("mehr als Zufall"), repeating, "as said, we all tap into secrets and mysteries." A soul can produce effects on others, he argues, simply by its sheer silent presence." And while Goethe speaks about the power of telepathic or more-than-unconscious transmission, he falls upon a story, which comes to him as if by chance in this context, about a young maiden in a dark room. It is possible, even probable, he conjectures that if she were in the room with a man, without knowing he was there, and he had the intention of murdering her, she would no doubt be overcome with an "uncanny feeling" about his (to her) unconscious or unknown presence ("unbewußten Gegenwart") and angst would set in. This would drive her out of the home.

Goethe tells this to the man with whom he alone is in the room. He rewrites the story of flight, connecting it with his feelers to a scene of murder—more precisely, of potential, conjectured murder—whose eventuality the girl would sense. The feeling of the *unheimlich* would drive her out of the home, releasing her from the intentions of a dark criminality. At this point Eckermann associates, freely, the horror story that has served as Goethe's example with a story of unconscious reunion—as if he were about to double the scene in which the "lost bird" is enticed to return, to forget the angst or crime from which it might have fled: Eckermann counters ("entegegnete ich") the narration Goethe had advanced with an opera scene that he knows. Note that while Goethe had fallen upon a story, creating it solely for this context and conversation, Eckermann counters his move with his citational skills, repeating what is already known or inscribed, in this case, in the opera. He "know(s) an opera scene in which two lovers who had long been separated through a great distance ['große Entfernung'], find themselves without knowing it in a dark room. They sense each other's presence, and a magnetic force draws them together." Eckermann says no more about the opera, nor does he give its name. However, dated at about the time of Beethoven's death in 1827, this passage, it seems safe to assume, refers to *Fidelio*, whose two lovers, both figuring in this scene as men (Leonore being disguised), find each other within the vaults of a prison. One of the men—the "real" one—is unconscious at the time, presumed dead. The opera ends with a prison liberation.

The Festival of Incorporation

Whereas Eckermann and Goethe are shown co-narrating stories of presentiment from the closure of a vault or alcove, the next day's entry (8 October 1827) will be framed, so to speak, by a triple mention of free space, beginning with the outdoors ("im Freien") in which a discussion revolving around a particular open secret takes place. The place of an open secret will make room for the final of the great "ornithological stories." These, it is reported, are told in the mode of "good conversation." The transition from the nocturnal alcove to the next day's nature, begins, like many beginnings, in the morning.

> 8 October 1827. We woke up early. While dressing, Goethe told me his dreams (he had travelled to Göttingen). We drank cups of coffee, then looked at the anatomical cabinet with all its skeletons. Goethe looked at their teeth. Schiller was with us in spirit. Visitation at Schiller's house. I looked out his attic window in a southerly direction. In the meantime, the noon hour had arrived . . . We ate our fish *im Freien* and then remained seated with a bottle of wine.

The day of the freedom banquet has arrived when Eckermann will speak freely, openly, to Goethe, to tell him the story of the good children swallowing their parents—he is still speaking of birds (says he). In case Goethe thought he had nothing to worry about—since for instance he is not a natural parent to Eckermann—then Eckermann's narrative devices will disrupt any such tranquility, for he begins immediately to narrate the story of a certain identity shared by the natural and adoptive parent. Eckermann's long discussion with Goethe about the habits of the cuckoo has seriously embarrassed some commentators who like to point out that he wrote this in the forties, long after Goethe's death (so what else is new?). Yet if these passages are embarrassing, if Eckermann seems to allow too much space, free-space, for what could have interested only him, and not Goethe, it is perhaps because Eckermann indeed is about to expose something in these pages from which one would prefer to remain shielded. The words imputed to Goethe are very clear on this, for they repeat that we are by now exploring the region of an "open secret," that we stand before something "highly problematic" for which Goethe earnestly strives to derive a universal law. Eckermann, on the other hand, insists on its aspect as pure aberration.

So the passage opens in the freedom of nature where we discover the two men eating fish while the young one provides the older one with the story of young ones swallowing older ones. " 'Everything I have heard about the cuckoo,' said Goethe, 'inspires my greatest interest about this curious bird. His is a highly problematic nature, an open secret which however is not any the less difficult to resolve because it is so open.' " The first example of a puzzle proposed by Goethe, however, will not have as referent any genus of bird, but rather the bee: "Just take the bee!" Whether Eckermann wishes to show how Goethe strays from the point or that he lacks taxonomical precision is not altogether clear. But what prompts the master to take the bee (as have so many philosophers of this era, following Aristotle's example) in the context of birds is not so much the famed asexuality of the worker bee, nor the relationship of the drone to the Queen bee, nor any question of productivity, but the fact of a fixed destination. He observes that "we see them flying for hours after honey, each time in a different direction." His question comes down to this: "Who however told them: now fly in that direction, there is something there for you, now fly in another direction, and so on?" "And who guides them back to their village and to their cells?" The question, then, is framed in terms of command, of teleguidance and the cell ("Zelle"). He observes, further, that "they go here and there as if on invisible lead-strings ('Gängelband')," and, recalling Faust, he concludes that their "innermost spiritual thread is hidden from us" ("inneres geistiges Band ist uns verschlossen"). That which is concealed reveals itself to be precisely the object of this entry, thereby retaining the image of bees in the same area as the flight of the *Conversation*'s birds: the inner bond, namely, the phantom connection ("geistiges Band") that commands Eckermann's writing from a position of flight which however always returns him to the cell.

Eckermann picks up the thread, returning it to the native haunts of the cuckoo and other birds. The cuckoo has a particular hold on him because of its precarious living conditions; in sum, he emphasizes, the young cuckoo not only exists "without protection" ("ohne Schutz"), but "thrives wonderfully" in this predicament. The example Eckermann takes is not without an invisible thread leading to the innermost crease of his destiny. Speaking of the nest into which the young cuckoo is dropped, "one should think," he offers, "that in the heat of the hot days of June, it would have to suffocate in such a closed off hollow." In this context of destination and destiny, of the home and the *unheimlich,* of natural and adoptive parents, Eckermann suggests that we think of those hot June days in which one runs the risk of suffocation. Let us listen once more to the last words of his introduction to the *Conversations:*

> On the way, often made difficult because of the great heat of the June day, I repeated inwardly the comforting impression that I was as if under the particular guidance ("Leitung") of good beings. . . .

The invisible lead-strings, the inner bonds had already been formed by the time of the introduction, the destiny and sense of destination already inscribed in Eckermann's course on those suffocating June days. The observations of 8 October continue: but the young cuckoo thrives wonderfully in this predicament. The question he now raises, again, had been addressed long ago in the introduction, as in his youth:

> But what kind of bird is it for whom, in the most delicate periods of youth, humidity and aridness, heat and cold—aberrations that for every other bird would be deadly ["tödlich"]—are things of complete indifference?

For others, for all others, these aberrations would have been fatal. However Eckermann survives the wanderings, outliving them to repeat them, thriving in a state of indifference to that which is deadly. Goethe's response will be, wisely: "We stand here precisely before a secret." The secret (*Geheimnis*) now turns on the law of *Heim,* the law prescribing that the relatively small cuckoo egg be deposited in another's nest; to this law, which remains uncommented, is added an amendment. It concerns a type of invisible, that is, unnatural bond in nature, constituted namely by foster parents who are found to be involved in a sacrificial *oikonomos.* Nature, Eckermann explains, has entered a puzzling calculation in managing her household: she has decided ("sich entschliessen") to sacrifice to five cuckoos at least fifty of our best songbirds. Our best songbird finds in this an index of nature's lack of scruples ("nicht eben skrupulös"); nature just has a lot of life to squander, he muses, and does this without giving it much thought. However, as he arrives at his next question, Goethe reduces the number of cuckoos to one: "Why is it that for a single young cuckoo so many young songbirds must perish?" The question, as usual, is one of loss. Why the loss, why the mad calculus of sacrifice, why must song be sacrificed to a foster child, Goethe asks Eckermann? "In the first place, I replied, the first brood perishes."

The first progeny disappears. We may remember that Eckermann was himself the "second progeny," the offspring of a second marriage in a sense commemorating the disappearance of a first progeny. This is what happens if the two sets of offspring—the natural and the borrowed, illegitimate—are made to share the same space:

> In case the eggs of the singing bird are hatched at the same time with that of the cuckoo, which is very probable, the parents are so much overjoyed with the larger bird that had thus originated ["über den entstandenen größeren Vogel"], and show it such fondness, that they think of and feed it alone, while their own young are neglected, and vanish from the nest ["und aus dem Neste verschwinden"].

This is not a dream, but a demonstration, a scientific argument. Yet all the phantasmic elements that we have seen emerge converge in these lessons given by the young Eckermann to the master and foster parent, unfolding a double program—at least a double one, if we do not allow the elements of his teachings to escape us as do the firstborn birds. At bottom, the same system of exchange is at play as the one we have observed in Eckermann's dream. Bodies are being exchanged, appropriated, and sacrificed. Song is at stake, and once more feeding is the sign of successful appropriation. These birds who are so bountifully fed by their foster parents are the same ones that are said to swallow their own parents. Their own parents, however, are long absent from this scene, since the young ones are in the custody of substitute parents. Or are they really absent? It seems, in fact, that their own parents have already been swallowed, appropriated and, to a certain degree, they have vanished—which links the disappearance of the parents to their being swallowed, this being the general structure of mourning as brought to light in Eckermann's case. In turn, the new parents continue to feed the young ones who have put away the old parents. This act of foster feeding causes the natural progeny to perish. Eckermann finds himself in this scene, relating (to) it and reconstituting it in keeping with the two—perhaps three—interminable losses that inhabit him at once, beginning with the perishing of the father's progeny, the perishing of the ship and songbird of the first brood; the song, the lost bird who perished before him, vanishing so that Eckermann, the second, the false progeny could thrive parasitically. This relation of natural and adoptive, of illegitimate and nourished, sees numerous revivals in the Goethe household.

The question remains of whether Eckermann's assumed role (articulated in the *Conversations,* legal documents, and elsewhere) as the assumed or adopted child is, with respect to Goethe, a stable one or at least one that conforms to the exigencies of the present narration. While developing this argument and demonstrating each point along the way, Eckermann himself occupies a position of master and teacher; it is upon him to transmit knowledge, educate the other—the passage began with Goethe's foolish remarks being put down to a dear child's extravagances—and his song has been largely sacrificed. Indeed, by the time Eckermann actually composes this passage, he has long seen his life in terms of sacrifice: he has sacrificed everything to Goethe, to Goethe's person, to his truth and poetry. His science teaches this doctrine of sacrifice and loss, of Nature's unscrupulous capacity for squandering life—his life, or his other life, the one that more or less disappeared early in his life, in the *Gestalt* of a brother, presumed dead, and that kept on repeating this disappearing act.

(Beyond the position of teacher and master that serves to alter Eckermann's place as Goethe's adoptive son in this narration, he also doubles for Goethe's father in a way that exceeds the local concerns of the *Conversations:* "My father was a shady character, lateborn child of elderly parents, his brother . . . died.")[23]

Eckermann's lessons continue, centering on the cuckoo's quenchless need for nourishment. "Besides, the young cuckoo is always greedy, and demands as much nourishment as the little insect-eating birds can procure. It is a very long time before it attains its full plumage ['vollständiges Gefieder'], and before he is capable of leaving the nest. . . ." And now Eckermann asserts this important factor: "But even if he has long since flown away, he still requires continual feeding . . . while the affectionate foster parents constantly attend upon their great child." The motif of continual feeding, whose threads run throughout the *Conversations* most often to connect Eckermann to Goethe, receives its "most convincing" treatment, as Goethe will say, in this cuckoo-narration. Even after his disappearance, then, this bird requires unending helpings of food. Which is why it returns.

Something that has in part disappeared is being fed, which is supposed to account for "the loss" (of so many young birds). "It is on this account that a single young cuckoo causes the loss"—a kind of obsessional focus on a single figure, a figuration of loss and retention, of canning someone in all senses, that is, to put him in an airtight can for preservation, to discharge, to make a phonograph record of—all of which suggest a parallel to Eckermann's feeding of his lost brother. Eckermann would be a foster parent to a *Fremdkörper,* an alien body that has been deposited within him. The Anglo-Saxon derivation of the word *foster* is helpful here, for it comes from a concept of nourishment—specifically, from *foda* or food. If Eckermann is to be perceived principally in parasitic terms—and this, curiously, has been his fate—it is only because he is doubling for the parasite that is eating at him (which is an honor that at times goes to Goethe). As host to his phantom brother, he is feeding something or someone that has disappeared from the sanctuary of a nest. This also explains why "the loving foster parents constantly attend upon their great child, and do not think of a second brood." Eckermann cannot think of Eckermann-himself, himself the second progeny (of his father and later of Goethe), nor even can he think of something like his own progeny, of his son, whose birth was deferred for thirteen years, the duration of Eckermann's engagement to "Hanchen." The first progeny—the one simultaneously occupying the position of brother and foster child—consumes Eckermann, motivating the sacrifice of song, and its safekeeping. As time goes by, Eckermann multiplies the feedings and droppings that find a place in his little room. The inside is expulsed onto the outside, objectifying while exceeding itself and the limits that seek to distinguish inside from outside.

The lengthy passages treating the phenomenon of the cuckoo aim at demonstrating the logic according to which the foster child enters the parental body and abode more lastingly than the natural child whom the parent is capable of sacrificing. This logic appears largely to govern Eckermann's reading of his adoption of Goethe or, more often, Goethe's adoption of him. Eckermann, the one who, despite everything, has become the more tenacious branch of the family than, for instance, the natural son. The structures of prolonged maturation, continual feeding, excremental growth ("vollständiges Gefieder") and adoptive parent are shared simultaneously by the world regulating the cuckoo's behavior and the ones which Goethe and Eckermann together create. And it can never be said with certainty, in the case of this writing couple, who has adopted whom as guardian, or which among them—for they are many and multiple—fosters the growth of the others.

The *Pflegeeltern* are shown to care for their child as a nurse cares for or looks after someone who is wanting. Whether the foster parent is identified at times as Goethe and at other times as Eckermann, it should be kept in mind that this role is associated for Eckermann with a love so excessive that it threatens to drive the caring parent to paroxysms of despair. In a passage describing the anguish involved in bestowing such care, Eckermann carefully points out that the parent—like Eckermann—is small when compared with his "great child." The petit Docteur Eckermann has this to say: the love of the foster parent "is so great that when one approaches the nest, the little foster parents, siezed with terror, fear, and anxiety ["Schreck und Furcht und Sorge"], do not know how to conduct or contain themselves. The blackcap particularly expresses the deepest despair, so that he ["er"] flutters on the ground almost as if it had cramps or were in convulsions." In German, the verb *flattern* also designates the practice of floating on a wave or, more generally, on a body of water. The spasms of pain and despair which Eckermann depicts so knowingly, and the horror evoked when the charges are endangered, participate in and are inseparable from the idea of foster parenthood. When the example tends to become specifically tied to an observable referent, as in this cuckoo case, the "parents" are always collapsed into a single masculine figure, an *er*. *Er*, heir, air: Eckermann's most original intention—at the risk, Eckermann's risk, of repetition—was to save and safeguard Goethe; he wrote to Goethe that he wanted to save him, and Goethe said yes. He had no doubt wanted to be his father's father, adopting his own father to rescue him from the despair of a lost first progeny (after which he lost everything, and grasped at the raw quill, refined, restored by J.P.E.).

And by taking up the immense responsibility of a father's father, a

Goethe's guardian, Eckermann would never become a second progeny, strictly speaking. He saw them flutter to the ground, wanted to
keep them buoyant. Eckermann clutches the quill, remnant of the lost
bird, contains and nurses them in the knowledge that from the beginning was always given in terms of absolute *Vorgefühl*.

The demonstration continues. Themes of the proper, one's own, and
property are put in Goethe's mouth. Answering his next question,
Eckermann characteristically supplies Goethe with his own concept in
order to propose a notion of membership whose purpose is to confer
upon illegitimacy a special aura of legitimate belonging. " 'Still it
seems very problematical to me, that a pair of *Grasmücken,* for instance, who are on the point of hatching their own eggs, should allow
the old cuckoo to approach their nest, and lay an egg in it' " (the
translation says "her egg" but Goethe says "his egg," "sein Ei").
Goethe thus brings the discussion back to a "highly problematic" issue, namely, to a question of what constitutes one's own and that
which is alien to one's own—what becomes a stranger or more precisely what has been produced by someone else. "Of course this is very
enigmatic," Eckermann patiently explains, "but not entirely so." For,
exactly because those who feed the illegitimate child have not hatched
him, "from this circumstance I say, arises ['entsteht und erhält sich'] a
sort of affinity ['Verwandschaft'] between the two, so that they continue to know each other and to consider each other members of a
single great family." Eckermann unravels the enigma by teaching
Goethe about another mode of origination, one that holds out a promise for maintaining itself: "entsteht und erhält sich." What is originated
and sustained in this problematic property transaction turns out to be a
type of affinity which makes claims for being even more natural than
the natural bond defining family; or at least it confirms the family in its
naturality. The family as such can grow a new member, branch, or
appendage, thus enlarging itself. What the extraneous egg actually
brings to the family is a concept of itself. As parasite and paramember,
the *Fremdkörper* constitutes the family, guaranteeing a fiction of an
inside, even though it is itself lodged on an outside. Goethe does not
buy this argument, but persists in raising what amounts to the same
objection: " 'There is something in that,' returned Goethe, 'little as
one can comprehend it. But it still appears to me a wonder that the
young cuckoo is fed by those who have neither hatched nor reared
him.' "

Once again Eckermann repeats the subtle reproach affirmatively:
"Of course it is a wonder, returned I, but still there exists an analogy."

Once again, Eckermann quotes Goethe's strategy to Goethe, rendering his argument irresistible to the master-disciple, since it is after all his own. Yet it should be noted that he bases his demonstration on a notion of *Vorgefühl:* "Yes, I have a presentiment that in this inclination there is a great law which goes deeply through all of nature." Foreseeing a great law that pervades all of nature, Eckermann begins the sentence which is presumed to clarify this assertion with "Ich." The important law will be illustrated by an anecdote whose subject is Eckermann. And we shall see by these means that when Eckermann intuits a law to prevail on all of nature, he refers neither to phenomenal nature, nor even to human nature, but to what could be called *his* (second) nature. In narrating the law behind the enigma, Eckermann places himself as the one who captures or imprisons (*gefangen*) the protagonist of this story.

The story meant to serve as an example of universal natural law begins, then, with Eckermann having captured a young linnet (*Hänfling;* the word for prisoner is *Häftling*). This points of course to one of the common paradoxes in the activity of "nature lovers": namely, one captures the object of one's most passionate interest to study its behavior more closely. This captivity tends to be viewed from two perspectives, the one according to which the interested observer— Eckermann, in this case, wishing to protect the object, in this case a bird—in fact protects it from its natural context. The other perspective might situate the cage itself as a protective environment. In any case, it is Eckermann who takes responsibility for the bird's captivity; he himself assumes the role of prison guard. It turns out that the linnet in question was "too big to be fed by man." In other words Eckermann could not himself nurture his prisoner: "I took a great deal of trouble trying to feed him for half a day; but as it absolutely refused to accept anything. . . ." The prisoner rejects Eckermann's efforts to feed him, which eventually compels the desperate warden to go through somebody else to keep him alive. At this point we discover that the outside can be made to participate in the inside, and that help can be sought in the form of an older member of Eckermann's captive community. This older figure also excelled in song: "but as it would not eat anything at all, I placed it with an old linnet, a good singer, which I had kept for years in a cage, and which hung outside my window." Now we arrive at Eckermann's mistaken judgment, his error, which begins as "I thought": "I thought: if the young one sees how the old one eats, perhaps he will also go to the food, in imitation of him. He however did not do so. . . ." The error in Eckermann's thinking lies in his mimetic expectations; when the young linnet would find itself confined with or to the elder linnet, who was as good a singer as an eater, he should normally be expected to imitate the more experienced bird or bard. This, however, did not happen. Instead, it opened its beak toward the old one, and "let out beseeching cries" ("bittenden Töne"), whereupon the elder linnet "felt an immediate compassion for him, and adopting it as a child, fed it as if it had been his own."

The mimetic model, displayed as error in Eckermann's great allegory of feeding, has thus come to be replaced with this festival of incorporation. The newcomer, latecomer, is to be accepted as a child who will hitherto be fed as if it were the elder's own. And though Eckermann's story may seem to spell out the law of feeding, it is itself a scene of vomiting that may be the work of one who has only very rarely been considered a fine singer (by the great expectorators). Like the cage that has been pushed out the window, this story projects or ejects something that has been buried within Eckermann, including, by now, his history with Goethe. Before continuing with a reading of what Goethe in this entry will call "the best ornithological story," one which intensifies the motifs that Eckermann spills out in this first story, we might first assemble some of its components.

In this story devoted to the exposition of a natural law, and presumably the law which dictates that certain birds be fed by others who have neither engendered nor raised them, Eckermann assumes the role and responsibility for capturing and imprisoning a young bird who however is not quite as young as that ("too big to be fed by man"). He shows himself, then, responsible for an act of imprisonment. Though little in this scene suggests that Eckermann feels indictable for this act, the captivated bird does reject his attempts at keeping it alive. Therefore, the universal law that Eckermann wishes to demonstrate here does not, in the first place, cover the example that Eckermann first provides; in other words, he has not succeeded in showing how it would be possible for him to feed a creature that is not his "own." He will however show that the bird can be properly fed by another of the same family, though this other one will not have engendered or raised him. This makes the linnet something like a sibling to the other one, but within an apparent structure of parental care. Eckermann will not be capable of nourishing his prisoner, whereas the good singer will. The good singer will nourish precisely that someone who is contained by Eckermann, agonizing within him, but who is not exactly him. As the repository for another's suffering, Eckermann effects a virtual identification with the prisoner he has imprisoned. He will have reenacted the predicament of the prisoner, his brother, locked in with the good singer; he is serving time—the *Goethezeit*. As warden and foster parent to this other whose destiny commands Eckermann's movements, or more precisely, his immobility and state of arrest, Eckermann always risks losing the bird, the phantom prisoner whose ventriloquist Eckermann has become.

We are still navigating toward the "best ornithological story ever." Before telling this last of a series, Eckermann multiplies the examples of adoption and feeding ("adoptiert und gefüttert"), and Goethe is shown to be a captive audience throughout the day. Eckermann seems especially keen on the adopting bird whose behavior he associates with that of a loyal or true mother ("treue Mutter"). Once again, Eckermann appears to be moving toward the maternalization of a fatherly figure, while his discourse also collapses the notion of a couple into a single figure. Goethe raises a question about the couple ("Grasmückenpaar"), Eckermann's response condenses the couple into one. The maternal father or the true or good mother earlier figured as the defender of the rights of the *Farbenlehre*. This figure, whether minding texts or someone else's offspring, fills its beak, in this case, with food which it distributes "now in one corner ["Ecke"] of the roomy cage, and now in the other corner, so that wherever a hungry throat opened, there s/he was." The space of the enclosure has been expanded to be limited only by the *Ecke,* which also serves as the name of the open repository, the gullet or the location of hunger. And just as in the scene where Goethe and Eckermann picnic, the *Ecke* is the place where hunger can be provisionally satisfied. The feeding is distributed from one *Ecke* to the other, he tells us—and perhaps, too, from one Eckermann to the other. "There is still more!" We shall not know how much time the coming "meantime" covers, but "there is still more! One of the young *Grasmücken,* which had grown up in the meantime, began to feed some of the smaller ones; of course he did this in a still playful and somewhat childish way, but still with a decided inclination ["Trieb"] to imitate the excellent mother." One of the younger males, who in the meantime grew up, is impelled by a decisive drive to imitate the mother and begins, likewise, to feed. Only the mother can be imitated, playfully.

"There is certainly something divine in this ['etwas Göttlichem, sagte Goethe']" said Goethe, "which creates in me a pleasing sense of wonder." And, "if it were a fact that this feeding of a stranger is a universal law of nature, it would unravel many a riddle." A riddle would be solved, an enigma answered. "Something of a universal law, I returned, is what it certainly appears to be" Eckermann repeats, reproducing the structure of double giving/receiving, of the feeder and the fed, ruminating over the same enigma, theirs and not theirs, together, in unison.

"For I have observed this helpful feeding, and this pity for abandoned ones ['Verlassene'], even in a wild state." He has observed it in a wild state. And he proceeds to tell Goethe about this state, when he captured (*gefangen*) young wrens—troglodytes, or recluses who creep or enter (from *dyein*) into dark openings. This best of stories in the best of German books illustrates how the wrens try to find their siblings (*Geschwister*), but Eckermann separates the siblings, wraps them in cloth and carries them with him "in the direction of Weimar."

Once again Eckermann carries two bodies as he walks toward Weimar. However, as he opens the sheet in a quiet spot, they escaped (*entschlüpften*)—rather than remaining immovably fixed, as he had for some reason expected, in their cloth. They disappeared (*verschwunden*), his search for them was in vain. Three days later he returns to the same spot "by chance" and, hearing *Locktöne,* he sees the answer before him. The sibling pair that had been separated from its family (and Eckermann) found an adoptive one "and let themselves be fed by the old robins." "I was highly delighted at this very remarkable discovery ['Fund']." There is joy when he finds the sibling pair (by chance, always by chance) which had escaped him as if the crypt had been opened—opened to allow its figures to become rediscoverable. If this story calls itself one of the best, recalling itself through Goethe as the best, it is because the anguish of the disappearance comes to be resolved by the *Fund*. And the find, Eckermann here tells us, will not be made in terms of repossession, of taking possession of the lost siblings, but by finding them in the custody of adoptive parents: "it was furthest from my mind to destroy this hospitable intimacy" ("so gastfreundliche Verhältnisse zu stören"). Eckermann would not think of destroying the mediation, he thinks; "on the contrary, I wish you the greatest possible prosperity." He will not interfere with a solution arrived at by adoption, which is the only solution, the simulacrum and doubling of natural affiliation. This "guest-friendly" mode of assimilation and feeding brings joy to Eckermann, suggesting that disappearance has to be mediated by another's friendly hosting, of a sibling pair for example, which would be neither dangerously consumed nor destroyed by the adoptive parent.

The best story has turned on a disappearance that is not sustained, in which the sibling pair that Eckermann carries with him in a shroud, a sail, a sheet, are released from his custody. And it is Goethe who responds to this story by pronouncing the life sentence, as they are about to finish their meal: "Sie sollen leben," he says, You should live, "Stossen Sie an. . . ." I drink to you. They are free, in Nature; they had conversed about the good and deep things. Goethe felt it was time.

> Whilst we thus conversed on good and deep matters over our dinner in the open air ["in freier Natur"], the sun had declined toward the summit of the western hills, and Goethe felt it was time to retrace our steps. We rode rapidly through Jena and after we settled our account at The Bear, and had paid a short visit to Frommann, we rode at a swift gallop to Weimar.

The next entry, the last one for the year 1827, begins with the appearance of an eagle: "Hegel ist hier." As he sips tea, Hegel brings the conversation to "people who are mentally disturbed" ("geistig krank"). Goethe has found a shelter from mental illness: " 'I therefore congratulate myself,' said Goethe, 'on the study of nature, which preserves me from such a disease' " ("das eine solche Krankheit nicht aufkommen lässt"). Eckermann writes on.

A Ventriloquy Kästchen

If Eckermann acts as a receptacle for something like unconscious transmission, if he had found a home for someone else's suffering within him and could serve as a ventriloquy *Kästchen* for the other's voice, he was also, at the same time, a powerful transmitter of desire. This, at least, is what we can gather from a letter written in 1883 by the Leipzig zoologist William Marshall. It took, perhaps, a zoologist to explain Eckermann to us. However, if William Marshall became a zoologist in order to explain Eckermann, this, too, is by no means a mere coincidence. By the time Marshall wrote his letter for the *Illustrirten Zeitung* on behalf of the late Eckermann, it had become a matter of urgency to neutralize the image that Goethe's grim "secretary" had produced. Eckermann's "sickly anthrophobia" ("krankhafte Menschenscheu"—letter to Ottilie von Goethe, 18 December 1834) had become known. He inspired only such observations as an Emil Dubois-Reymond could propose, namely the portrait of a grotesque "little crooked *Männchen*" with a "functionary-face and functionary stature" ("Lohnbedienten Gesicht und Lohnbedienten-Anstand," 1839). Eckermann was rapidly losing his already meager stature. But the zoologist would establish a different type of taxonomy, and one that shows to what extent Eckermann implanted his desire in those before whom he felt no shyness, namely, as with all apostles, in children. Marshall's report should serve as an epitaph here. It gathers all the elements we have had to disperse, dissect, and observe from a distance. Perhaps this would have been Eckermann's autobiography for, in the case of Eckermann, one is always looking elsewhere to find the place of a selfness.

Marshall, himself a mere child when he became attached to Eckermann, submits his subject to successive metamorphoses which suggests to us a type of reading that Eckermann commanded and that might be taken into account, therefore, when reading Eckermann. We shall not know to what extent Eckermann participated in this writing, but the sharpness of vision—one is tempted to say the bird's eye—with which the child-become-zoologist fixes him leaves little doubt as to the incorporation taking place in this writing of another's desire. He begins with Eckermann's physical appearance, dwelling for a moment on his astonishing physiognomy. "Eckermann presented a powerful appearance, rather small than big. His always smoothly shaven face had that peculiar ['eigentümlichen'] expression . . . namely, as it is often proper to seamen" ("wie er namentlich den Seeleuten oft eigen ist"). The name, the proper, the singular property of Eckermann's face will be namely the mariner. But the seaman remains only one of several properties. Marshall continues. There is something which he must point out, if only to discount its singularity with a rectifying observation:

> His forehead was wide and intelligent, and even if his strong-curved nose and the sharp bright eyes reminded one of a predatory bird, a peculiarity ["Eigentümlichkeit"] that perhaps rested on a kind of adaptation to his darlings ["auf einer Art Anpassung an diese Lieblinge beruhte"]. . . .

And even if. . . . "One will perhaps wonder, that I still know all of this with such precision but the old Eckermann always conducted himself ['trug sich,' carried himself] in the exact same way and in a way that was somewhat different ['abweichend,' aberrational] from the other gentlemen, and such a thing makes a remarkably deep impression on a child's mind."

The deep imprint of this wondrous aberration does not stop with the figure Eckermann cut. After describing his body, face, and clothes or toilette—that is, after describing Eckermann's adjustments in which physical and fantasmatic dimensions appear to merge without a wrinkle—Marshall's remembrance falls upon the apartment that Eckermann occupied:

> I still smell in my mind the odor of the menagerie that pervaded the rooms; in all corners and ends there fluttered his haired and feathered housemates, who partially were lodged in cages and partially ran around freely. And on their natural drive—which by the way did nothing to improve cleanliness or promote good air—he never imposed any constraints ["Zwang"].

There is a kind of intensified exchange of the inner and outer limits, the cages within the rooms and the open air (*freier Natur*) that invests his space, the indoor outside, inhaled nature, designated in terms of a certain filth and airlessness: the slow suffocation of Eckermann as he gives free vent to the natural drive which, as he had once asserted, motivated his writing. Eckermann kept only part of his companions in cages. (A real *Hausfrau* would not put up with these circumstances, Marshall points out).

While the zoologist withholds criticism of his aviary, he is clear on the cruelty of Eckermann's captivation, for Eckermann is clearly captivated by that which he captivates. Once, when a landlord complained about his "living" conditions, Marshall relates, "and in so doing perhaps used a rather strong expression for Eckermann's darlings, Eckermann claimed that this man was extremely dangerous, and one could expect any sort of depravity from him." And when "the outside world would attribute other properties to the marten called Ratz whom Eckermann fed honey, he would become enraged and call this malicious slander. Besides these captured children ["abgesehen von diesen gefangenen Kindern"]," Eckermann also enjoyed "the most intimate friendship" with mice, his favorite being a dirty-blonde named Isabelle. One day, after she had disappeared for a while, Eckermann found Isabelle as a dried-up mummy behind a pile of books: "die Trauer war gross" ("he mourned greatly"). Eckermann, it seems, can finally enter his great *Trauerarbeit*—which begins, as the zoologist remembers it, somewhere between a mummified love-object (*Liebling*) and his books.

Eckermann showed "great affection to youth: he always had a whole corps of young boys around him," most of whom he called "Sperlingsberger" (swallows or passerine rescuers). He would take the boys on long walks, most often to a place known as *Wilden Graben* (uncultivated grave), Marshall recalls. In his account Marshall recollects Eckermann's period of mourning, in part, no doubt, because he is himself in mourning over his own father's loss, that is, also over his father's sorrow: "My departed father, who was never very enchanted by my dedication to Zoology, had always held Eckermann responsible for this, and I think rightly so." The father and now the son place responsibility for his zoological compulsion on Eckermann; however, the son can say that "this incitement was still harmless." For this writer, despite his father's qualms, Eckermann was still harmless. It is otherwise with the others in whom Eckermann implanted this type of desire: "But with a few others, Eckermann, without wanting to, prepared painful, weighty moments ['schwere Stunden'] for several Weimarian families." How does he know what Eckermann wanted? He says he knows. Without having wanted it, then, on some level of consciousness, he somehow, somewhere deposited a devastating seed in the minds of his deeply impressionable followers. They would not write about Eckermann. In fact, they would be lost.

Just as Marshall shows Eckermann giving away all he owned to anyone who asked for something (*jedem Bittenden*), he suggests how Eckermann gives away that *Bittenden,* the beseecher or beggar, the *Hausierer* within him. The difficult hours that Eckermann prepared for several Weimar families were due, according to Marshall, to this: he was of course wild about the sea and life at sea ("er schwärmte selbstverständlich auch für die See und für das Seeleben"). The breath of life that Eckermann inspired in the children was the sea, his seaman, life at sea. This was the great moment of performativity in Eckermann as narrator; here is where he spilled over onto propitious ground:

> . . . since the mouth of he whose heart is full so gladly overspills, so he would thoroughly discuss with his young flock this theme, too. He would discuss it often and in depth; and with youth, which is always eager for adventure, the elder's inspired and inspiring words found only propitious ground. So it happened, that in not a few young heads the desire—in genuinely continental Weimar!—which was unheard of, came alive ["bis dahin unerhörte Lust lebendig ward"]. The desire to go to sea, and I can remember five young men whose determination grew into a deed. That's what old Eckermann did through his narrations! ["und von fünf jungen Leuten kann ich mich erinnern, daß bei ihnen dieser Vorsatz zur Tat reifte. Das hatte mit seinem Erzählen der alte Eckermann getan!"]

The seed, the desire, the ground is not Goethe but the sea. Eckermann sends them away to join, to retrieve the phantom brother. As for

Eckermann "himself"—for this is not so self-evident—Marshall finishes his letter thus:

> The brilliant star of his life, the personality to whom he gave himself fully without having anything to do with others, forever escaped him, disappeared ["für immer entschwunden"] on that 22nd of March in the year 1832. He was left behind, orphaned, an old child, the ward of a world ["Mitwelt"] that did not always let him perceive its guardianship in a noble sense:
>
> > Epheu und ein zärtlich Gemüt
> > Heftet sich an und grünt und blüht:
> > Kann es weder Stamm noch Mauer finden,
> > Es muss verdorren, es muss verschwinden.
> >
> > Ivy and a delicate mind
> > attaches itself and sprouts and blossoms,
> > If it can find neither family-stem nor fortification,
> > then must it dry up, it must disappear.

Es muss verschwinden.

*****

Johann Peter Eckermann died on 3 December 1854. The world, and the people of Weimar, were astonished to learn on that date that he was still alive. In his last years, Eckermann would observe legal holidays by setting free a few of his birds. It has been reported that on the last birthday of his beloved *Grossherzogin,* Eckermann let three bullfinches go.

Vogelfrei. The proscript's body, deprived of a proper grave, is offered up to the birds (1538 Chron. Germ. 174a).

NOTES

Introduction

1. Rudolf Magnus, *Goethe as a Scientist* (Henry Schuman, The Life of Science Library, New York: 1949), p. 221. Goethe has also written an essay on "The Causes of Barometric Fluctuations," which would be interesting to read in light of Rousseau's *Promenades*. Goethe's meteorological investigations were inspired by those of the British scientist, Luke Howard; hence Goethe's essay on "Cloud Formations After Howard" (1817), after which he kept careful diary notes, particularly between 1820 and 1823, on clouds and weather. In 1822, Howard sent Goethe his work, "The Climate of London." Goethe's theory basically predicts periodic changes in air pressure, which he began to discern as early as 1816 in his account of his Italian journey.

2. *Zur Witterungslehre* in *Goethes Werke,* Band XIII (Verlag C.H. Beck, Munich: 1975), p. 305: "wir werden es gewahr als unbegreifliches Leben und können dem Wunsch nicht entsagen, es dennoch zu begreifen" and, like the disclosure of Being in Hölderlin, "Die Witterung offenbart sich uns," and so forth, p. 306 ff.

3. "André Gide et Goethe" in *Faux Pas* (Gallimard, Paris: 1943), p. 316.

4. In *Reflections: Essays, Aphorisms, Autobiographical Writings,* Ed. Peter Demetz, (Harcourt Brace Jovanovich, New York: 1978), p. 63 (translation modified).

Part One

1. *Standard Edition of the Complete Psychological Works* (Hogarth, London: 1953–74) vol. VI, pp. vii–xiv. Henceforth S.E.

2. Ibid., pp. 36–39.

3. Scholarly scoptophilia ought to conduct us immediately at this point to the famous "Rat Man" case study, in which Goethe makes another appearance, both as the secret rat and source of this biting fantasia from *Faust.* The context is circumscribed by Freud as his patient's having "assumed that the rat had actually come out of his father's grave, and had just been having a meal off his corpse." Freud then cites the words of Mephistopheles when he wishes to make his way through a door guarded by a magic pentagram:

> Doch dieser Schwelle Zauber zu zerspalten
> Bedarf ich eines Rattenzahns.
> Noch einen Biss, so ist's geschehen!

But to break through the magic of this threshold
I need a rat's tooth. (*He conjures up a rat.*)
Another bite, and it is done!

Besides converging with many of the issues which will occupy us here, the "Notes upon a Case of Obsessional Neurosis" (1909, alias "Rat Man") offers another, though parallel, reading of Goethe's entry into Freud. By which opening was the threshold crossed? Briefly, when Freud delivers his narrative assertion to help Rat Man name his symptom (". . . some *rats* were put into it . . . and they . . ."—he had again got up, and was showing every sign of horror and resistance—'*bored their way in*. . . .'—Into his anus, I helped him out") he affirms what I would call a suppository logic, inserting the vital element into the narrative of the other. By similar methods of narrative insertion, the *Geheimrat* enters Freud, an effort which is to be interpreted, as Freud does, as the desire to have a baby with the father (by anal insemination—I am helping him out).

4. "The Father Complex and the Solution of the Rat Idea" in *Notes upon a Case of Obsessional Neurosis*, SE. X, p. 203.

5. Of his first visit to Freud in 1927, the prominent biographer Emil Ludwig tells the following:

> [Freud] did not seem satisfied and asked why I had not dealt with the psychological aspects of Goethe's childhood in my book on Goethe.
> "Because there are no documents," I said.
> "But there is one," he said, "and moreover in a very prominent place, just at the beginning of Goethe's memoirs." And he cited the anecdote in which the three year old Goethe, to his great delight, throws some dishes out of the window. When I asked him the meaning of this incident, he proceeded to explain it in great detail—I did not comprehend his explanation. At that time I was not aware of the fuss ["Zirkus"] which had been made about Goethe in Freudian circles.

First published in Ludwig's *Der entzauberte Freud* (Carl Posen Verlag, Zurich: 1946), pp. 177–80. Subsequently translated and published by Henrik M. Ruitenbeek, ed., *Freud as We Knew Him* (Wayne State University Press, Detroit: 1973), p. 214.

6. All Goethe quotes, unless otherwise noted, are taken from *Goethe's Werke, Hamburger Ausgabe*, Band IX (Verlag C. H. Beck, Munich: 1974).

7. Bettina was kept mute and veiled until Friedrich Kittler's astonishing "Writing into the Wind, Bettina" (*Glyph 7*, Baltimore: 1980), pp. 32–70.

8. Compare Jacques Derrida's reading of the *fort-da* scene of reading in *La Carte Postale: de Socrate à Freud et au-délà* (Aubier-Flammarion, Paris: 1980).

9. Estate of Max Schur, 1972.

10. *Gesammelte Werke*, (Fischer Verlag, Frankfurt a.M.: 1946), vols. 2, 3.

11. Freud, *Aus den Anfangen der Psychoanalyse; Briefe an Wilhelm Fliess, Abhandlungen und Notizen aus den Jahren 1887–1902*, edited by Marie Bonaparte, Anna Freud, and Ernst Kris (S. Fischer Verlag, Frankfurt a.M.: 1962, p. 277 (my translation).

12. *Freud-Legende: Drei Studien zum Psychologischen Denken* (Walter Verlag, Olten u. Freiburg im Breisgau: 1979), p. 53. Translated and modified in The Legend of Freud, (University of Minnesota Press, 1982).

13. *The Psychopathology of Everyday Life*, ch. VII, p. 212.

14. Even for Goethe, according to Eissler (K. R. Eissler, *Goethe: A Psychoanalytic Study;* Wayne State University Press, Detroit: 1963), "the unconscious goal of the *Italian* journey was . . . *genital* heterosexual gratification." (italics mine) It is Eissler's contention that "Goethe had sexual intercourse for the first time in his life during his second sojourn in Rome, after his return from Sicily" (p. 1019). I have not been able to verify this. Freud himself makes the connection between *Italien* and *Genitalien* fleetingly and with reference to a woman patient, though never with reference to his own difficult rapport with Italy (*Traumdeutung*, p. 237). I am grateful to Maria Torok for this reference.

15. See also Anna Freud Bernays, *"My Brother, Sigmund Freud"* (1940) in *Freud as We Knew Him,* ed. Henrik M. Ruitenbeek (Wayne State University Press, Detroit: 1973), p. 144: "At eighteen, Sigi passed all his examinations at the Gymnasium *summa cum laude."* The prevalence of the number or age eighteen should be considered in readings of Freud's texts: his father's date of birth, though according to Freud, on 1 April 1815, was actually on December 18. Dora is eighteen in 1900. Koller, Freud's early rival on the anaesthetic properties of cocaine and who was made responsible for the deeply felt delay of Freud's fame, was eighteen months younger than Freud. Schur indicates that Freud translated "18," via Hebrew, into "Life." Finally, an early professional traumatism that Freud relates after citing Charcot's "C'est toujours la chose génitale, toujours . . . toujours . . . toujours. . .:" Describing the beginning of his medical career in Vienna, he writes: "One day I had a friendly message from Chobrak, asking me to take a woman patient of his to whom he could not give enough time, owing to his appointment as a university teacher." Himself owing very little to the university, Freud arrives at the patient's home to find her suffering "from attacks of meaningless anxiety." Chobrak returns from his university appointment to explain that the "patient's anxiety was due to the fact that although she had been married for eighteen years she was still *virgo intacta.* The husband was absolutely impotent." The learned doctor concluded his diagnosis with the sole possible prescription for such maladies:

$$R_x \text{Penis normalis}$$
$$\text{dosim}$$
$$\text{repetatur!}$$

Freud justifies his having cited the prescription (for a repeated dosage of normal penis for the woman—this sounds familiar) by protesting "I have not of course disclosed the illustrious parentage of this scandalous idea in order to saddle other people with the responsibility for it." (*On the History of the Psycho-Analytic Movement,* p. 14). In the beginning, genitals remain untouched ("intact") for eighteen years. Freud concludes this part of his *History* on a pun: " 'Épouser les idées de' is no uncommon figure of speech, at any rate in French." These questions—the marriage of ideas, scandalous avowals of illustrious parentage, eighteen years, impotence—inform as well Freud's rapport to Goethe.

16. In "The Debts of Deconstruction and Other Related Assumptions" (*Taking Chances: Derrida, Psychoanalysis and Literature;* The Johns Hopkins University Press: 1984; p. 52) Samuel Weber demonstrates "the theory of *Schuld,* against its explicit assertions, that Schuld *is* Schuld. . . . debt as guilt, guilt as debt. And if the two words are one, it is precisely because they seek to be two."

17. See in particular "L'os de la fin" (*Cahiers Confrontation,* spring 1979, Paris) where Torok asserts: "Et je vous répondrais: *os* et *verdikt* étaient fatalement liés en Freud." When discussing these and related issues, Maria Torok suggested that Freud's reading of Goethe's title *Geheimrat* may be translated "mein Geheimnis erraten" (he has divined my secret). I am very indebted to her for having read and commented on different parts of this work. Barbro Sylwan has also written about the verdict crypt in "Le ferd-ikt" (*Etudes Freudiennes,* No. 13–14, Denoël: 1978).

18. "Disgregation of the Will: Nietzsche on Individuality," textscript for a lecture held at Stanford University, April 1984.

19. We can profit here from a note in the S.E. (pp. 637–38) which explains that

> in the original the words are addressed to the heavenly powers and may be translated literally: "You lead us into life, you make the poor creature guilty." But the words *Armen* and *schuldig* might mean "poor" in the financial sense and *schuldig* might mean "in debt." So in the present context the last line could be rendered: "You make the poor man fall into debt."

The lines were quoted again by Freud at the end of Chapter VII of *Civilization and its Discontents* (1930).

20. For one such example, consider Jean-Michel Rey's discussion of "an *uneven development* of Freudian theory" (italics mine) in "Freud's Writing on Writing," *Literature and Psychoanalysis. The Question of Reading: Otherwise,* Yale French Studies, Number 55/56, 1977, p. 303 ff.

21. Freud's proper name has been noted to be a homonym of the proper noun, joy (*Freude*). In a philological study unrelated to Sigmund Freud, it has been proposed that "Freud" qua proper noun can be traced back to dream: "Wir führen damit die laetitia-Bedeutungen von mhd. *troum* und ae. *dream* in germ. *ˣdraumaz* zusammen. . . ." in K. Ostheeren, *Studien zum Begriff der Freude* (Dissertation, München: 1964), pp. 72–73, 274 ff. Ostheeren makes a strong argument for rooting Freud in the dream.

22. The passage inspiring this practice is of particular interest (no doubt for Freud as well), ensuring the shuttle mechanism to which we earlier alluded, for it all comes down to osculation. The specific content, of which Freud makes no mention, concerns this: a curse is lifted from Goethe's mouth (*Mund*), or more exactly, Goethe defies the malediction placed on his mouth by a jealous girl-friend (thereby proferring his mouth to a new sweetheart). Ken Frieden initiates "The Interpretation of Dreams and Talmudic Aggadah" of his forthcoming book (*The Dream of Interpretation,* Cornell University Press) by privileging this utterance: "All Dreams Follow the Mouth" (Berakhot 55b).

23. Hans Christop Buch, ed., *Literaturmagazin 2: Von Goethe lernen? Fragen der Klassikrezeption* (Rowohlt Taschenbuchverlag, Hamburg: 1974).

24. Although these two texts, the *Natur-Fragment* and the essay on the *Zwischenkiefer,* appear to nurture independent aims and purposes, their relationship hinges on principles whose singular implications will not be lost on readers of Freud. At least retrospectively and in Goethe's own words, one aim of the *Zwischenkiefer* essay is to sound a kind of return to Nature. With his discovery, Goethe proved to be Darwinian in persuasion about eighty years *avant la lettre.* The *Zwischenkiefer* linked man to the natural process, to evolution, by providing substantial proof to Goethe and his contemporaries that Nature did not make "leaps" (*Sprünge*) or tolerate rupture. Prior to such findings, the presumed absence of this intermediary part was thought, in terms of structural anatomy, to differentiate man from other animals. The concept of Nature, its ubiquity and vigor, are held alive, even intensified, in Goethe's analysis of the jawbone. Thus the two texts in question can be said to belong to the same constellation of phantasmagoria for Freud. The following observation can be made with respect to the relationship governing these texts: in the case of the eighteen-year-old, Freud links the concept of Nature in the *Natur-Fragment* to male genitalia while thematizing an act of mutilation. In the *Zwischenkiefer* essay, the concept of Nature is linked to the jawbone, and the unspoken trauma we are attempting to excavate would involve precisely an act of buccal intervention (*Angriff*) of which Goethe is in some sense the author. These two traumatized areas stand in a relationship of mathematical analogy to one another.

25. The circumstances surrounding Goethe's discovery multiply certain fantasmatic connections of the type under study. Three days before the discovery was made, on 24 March 1784, the five-year-old princess, first-born daughter of the ducal pair, died suddenly of a suffocating catarrh (*Stickfluss*). Goethe himself had to arrange for most of the ceremonies and even to select, with Herder, the place in the church where she was to be buried. Although Goethe was particularly attached to the child, he makes no mention of the event of her death in his many letters written at that time—that is, not until his letter of 31 March to Jacobi, who had lost his wife, and then again on 24 April, in a letter to Knebel in which he devotes only one sentence to "the death of the little Princess." Goethe had observed the same kind of epistolary silence when his father died and when his sister, Cornelia, died. In the section of his book dealing with the intermaxillary bone and "the psychology of scientific discoveries," Eissler observes that "there is an uncanny connection between the child's death and the discovery. The organ whose pathology killed the child was, according to the official diagnosis, the throat, and the discovery pertains to a structure in closest proximity to the fatal area, namely the upper bone of the jaw" (p. 857). Even for Goethe, then, the birth of the *Knochlein* followed on the steps of death. The cause of Goethe's own death would be officially published by Ottilie von Goethe as *Stickfluss*.

26. Letter to Lavater of 14 November 1781 whose exact wording is, "zugleich behandle ich die Knochen als einen Text."

27. All quotes are taken from *Goethes Werke*, Vol. 13, Hamburger Ausgabe, ed. Erich Trunz (Verlag C. H. Beck, Munich: 1975). The translations are mine.

28. Ibid.

29. On learning from Anna that the Gestapo had stolen a considerable wad of money, Freud remarked that "they get more for a house-call than even I do."

30. Kurt Kusenberg, ed., *Sigmund Freud in Selbstzeugnissen und Bilddokumenten,* (Rowohlt Taschenbuch verlag, Hamburg: 1971), p. 43.

31. *The Unwelcome Intruder: Freud's Struggle with Cancer* (Praeger Scientific, New York: 1983). Romm is a plastic surgeon who has worked with cancer patients.

32. J. Derrida, "Télépathie" in *Cahiers Confrontation,* 1983.

33. Another reference to Goethe's attack on Herr M. (preceded immediately by reflections on the "phantasy of being carried by [a] wet-nurse") also gives reason to believe that Freud must be engaged in some defensive strategy. Repeating once again that "in the dream I based a calculation on the date of Goethe's death," he now adds: "I think, moreover, that all these dreams of turning things round the other way include a reference to the contemptuous implications of the idea of 'turning one's back on something.' " The S.E. appends this pertinent note here: "The German '*Kehrseite*' can mean both 'reverse' and 'backside.' Cf. the vulgar English phrase 'arse upwards' for 'upside down,' 'the wrong way round' " (S.E., pp. 326–27).

34. The conjunction of opera and operation emerges later again, with a slight nuance, in a letter to Lou-Andreas Salomé. After undergoing a complicated operation, Freud writes upon returning home on his sixty-seventh birthday that he was treated "like a diva from an operetta" (cited in Schur, p. 424; cf. also "A Chemist's Dream," see below).

35. In fact, the *Traumdeutung* is riddled with teeth marks. In the section devoted to "Internal Organic Somatic Stimuli," Freud describes "typical" (his quotation marks) anxiety dreams of appreciable frequency as "the familiar dreams of falling from a height, of teeth falling out, of flying, and of embar-

rassment at being naked or insufficiently clad" (S.E., p. 37). In "A Chemist's Dream" (chapter VI), the dental impressions left by Freud become more prominent. First he recounts the dream of a man who "was attending a performance of *Fidelio* and was sitting in the stalls at the Opera beside L., a man who was congenial to him and with whom he would have liked to make friends. Suddenly he flew through the air right across the stalls, put his hand in his mouth and pulled out two teeth" (pp. 385–86).

Freud's analysis of the dream skirts the mouth but lands on masturbation. The dream that Freud quotes immediately after this one suggests, at least in terms of succession, the link which he prefers to leave missing: a young man being treated by two university professors, one of whom "was doing something to his penis ["Glied," member]. He was afraid of an operation. The other was pushing against his mouth with an iron rod, so that he lost one or two of his teeth." By 1914, Freud affixes this footnote to his interpretation: "A tooth being pulled out by someone else in a dream is as a rule to be interpreted as castration (like having hair cut by a barber, according to Stekel)." His interpretation gives signs of being edgy or wanting to back down. "I cannot pretend that the interpretation of dreams with a dental stimulus as dreams of masturbation—an interpretation whose correctness seems to me beyond a doubt—has been entirely cleared up. I have given what explanation I can and must leave what remains unsolved." Nonetheless, Freud suggests this sole possibility which, however, psychoanalysis in the long run cannot accept: "According to popular belief dreams of teeth being pulled out are to be interpreted as meaning the death of a relative, but. . . ." (S.E., pp. 387–88). A footnote which he adds in 1909 to his resignation before the enigma of this type of dream will have a place in our analysis: "A communication by C.G. Jung informs us that dreams with a dental stimulus occurring in women have the meaning of birth dreams." If Freud must desist from interpreting these kinds of dreams in his name, by 1911 he has inserted the accounts of other signatories—who even cite him in the third person (i.e., "Freud has written")—like a prosthetic device. Freud takes sudden leave of his text, in this case handing it over to Otto Rank who works on a dream regarding the jawbone, with elements of teeth being crushed and pulverized but in which "the decisive factor was the birth of a child." Rank's step-in performance is not without merit and even suggests a way of interpreting Freud's mysterious fear of travelling: "The dreamer made use for this purpose of the verbal bridges 'Zahn-ziehen (Zug)' and 'Zahn-reissen (Reisen)' 'Zahn-ziehen,' 'to pull out a tooth;' 'Zug' (from the same root as 'ziehen'), 'train' or 'pull.' 'Zahn-reissen,' 'to pull out a tooth;' 'reisen' (pronounced not much unlike 'reissen'), 'to travel' " (S.E., p. 391). Whatever implications are suggested by the act of pulling teeth, it should be noted that Freud pulls or passes out of the text and expires ("Freud has written. . . .") at this critical juncture.

36. Jacques Lacan (in: *Le Séminaire II,* Éditions du Seuil, Paris: 1978) applies the tripartite formula for propyl to the three women whom Freud names in the commentary, recognizing at the base of the throat the "abyss of the female organ." Cynthia Chase's elegant interpretation of the Irma dream in Freud and Lacan was delivered at the 1984 MLA ("Anecdotes for Fathers").

37. V. Granoff, *La pensée et le féminin,* (Les Éditions de Minuit, Paris: 1976) and Patrick Lacoste, *Il Écrit: une mise en scène de Freud* (Éditions Galilée, Paris: 1981).

38. Baudelaire, like others, places Goethe out of debt's reach: "Je doute fort que Goethe ait eu des créanciers" (*Conseils aux jeunes littérateurs,* Pléiade).

39. An analysis of the prize bestowed on him in Goethe's name would have

to consider the striking ambivalence in the wording of the text read as an accompaniment to the prize.

40. The connection is far from being severed. The most recent book-length study of his radical attachment to Napoleon, and Goethe's corresponding demonology, is Hans Blumenberg's *Arbeit am Mythos* (Suhrkamp, Frankfurt a.M.: 1979).

41. When Freud returns to the dream of Goethe's attack after his initial commentary, his insights are guided by a notion of "acts of judgment" (*Urteilsakten; Urteilsäusserungen*) which he finds to be active in the dream (*T*, pp. 450–51).

42. Freud himself finally has second thoughts concerning the proper place of "propyls" in chapter VI, when explaining "the work of condensation." He appends "the following addition to the analysis of the dream. When I allow my attention to dwell for a moment longer on the word 'propyls,' it occurs to me that it sounds like 'Propylaea.' " This rendition of "propyls" now guides his interpretation; however, he quickly passes over Athens and goes to Munich, where he had visited a friend who was seriously ill: "but there are Propylaea not only in Athens but in Munich." It might be added that while the Propylaea in Munich stand as a reference to the citadel in Athens, on which they are modelled, the point to be emphasized in this mention is perhaps the fact of Freud's association of the propylaea with a friend who was seriously ill. "I made my friend's *Sache* my own . . ."

Part Two

If one were to conform to the recommendations of the Committee on Terminology of the American Society of Parasitologists, certain nuances would have to be introduced into those concepts of parasitism that have made their way into recent theoretical studies. Three types of parasitic behaviour should be distinguished according to the committee: *Commensalism,* from Latin, "eating at the same table," designates an association beneficial to one partner and at least not disadvantageous to the other; *Mutualism* is a relationship beneficial to both partners; *Parasitism,* which deviates significantly from the first two, is based on a symbiotic relationship in which one member—the host—is to some degree injured. An organism that cannot survive in any other way would be an *obligate parasite,* whereas those whose parasitism is not essential for survival would be *facultative parasites.* Further, *endoparasites* reside within the host, and *ectoparasites* stick to the surface. Cited in *Medical Parasitology,* ed. Markell and Voge (W.B. Saunders Co., New York: 1981).

1. In H.H. Houben, *J.P. Eckermann Sein Leben für Goethe* (Verlag Dr. H.A. Gerstenberg, Hildesheim: 1928, I). Eckermann will be cited from the edition by Houben, *Gespräche mit Goethe in den letzen Jahren seines Lebens* (F.A. Brockhaus, Wiesbaden: 1959). Translations are mine unless otherwise indicated.

2. On the missions and transmissions of the Wilhelm Meister texts and their childhood see Friedrich A. Kittler, *Dichtung als Sozialisationsspiel* (Vandenhoeck & Ruprecht, Göttingen: 1978).

3. Jacques Derrida addresses the question of genre, generic mark, and remarkability in "The Law of Genre," trans. A. Ronell, *Glyph 7* (The Johns Hopkins University Press, Baltimore: 1980). Many of the arguments made with regard to the postal code, missions, missives, etc., will have been stamped by Derrida's *Carte Postale* (Flammarion, Paris: 1982). Two deeply intelligent

readings of some of these codes, including sexual codes and other assumptions, are Samuel Weber's "The Debts of Deconstruction and Other, Related Assumptions" in *Taking Chances: Derrida, Psychoanalysis and Literature*, ed. Joseph H. Smith and William Kerrigan (The Johns Hopkins University Press, Baltimore: 1984) and the cryptologically inflected works of Laurence A. Rickels on Stifter, Kafka, and Artaud.

4. On 7 March 1830, Goethe is reported to have affirmed: "Es ist nicht gut, dass der Mensch allein sei, sagte Goethe, und besonders nicht dass er alleine arbeite; vielmehr bedarf er der Teilnahme und Anregung, wenn etwas gelingen soll." While *Teilnahme* means participation, it also suggests a part (*Teil*) of a name (*Nahme*) of another. In this passage, Goethe goes on to say that he owes his various ballads to Schiller and *Faust II* to Eckermann. Whereas Goethe to a certain degree invented the solitary writing subject (compare especially his philosophical drama of genius, *Torquato Tasso*), he thematized the concept as error or madness. The poetry of alterity in Maurice Blanchot's *Ecriture du désastre*, his reading of the other without unity, and his various readings of Goethe (and Eckermann) describe the extenuation of the subject in "Goethe" which might be seen in terms of a problematics of the writing couple.

5. Heine's exact words, from his sickbed, in 1851: "ein wahrhaft pomadiges, besänftigendes Vergnügen."

6. Eckermann's status in Goethe scholarship is, at best, contradictory. Though he continues to sign what "Goethe himself" is said to have said or thought, he is also a safe means by which to measure scholarly ressentiment. This may not seem too surprising when people want to be writing about "Goethe himself" and have to come up against his textual bodyguard. But it does seem exaggerated when even editors of the *Conversations* gang up on him, as in the case of *Goethe: Conversations and Encounters,* edited and translated by David Luke and Robert Pick (Henry Regnery Company, Chicago: 1966). In their introduction, Luke and Pick pick on Eckermann first by focusing on the very discoverer of the negative trope, ressentiment:

> It is small wonder that Nietzsche, with his own desire to construct affirmation on a basis of tragedy, his own profound appreciation of Goethe, and his declared belief in the aesthetic, monumentalising approach to the history of great men, should in a hyperbolic moment have described Eckermann's Conversations with Goethe as "the best German book ever written." Eckermann's book is one-sided: it is marred by a certain naïvety and pomposity; modern research has revealed its factual inaccuracies. . . . [p. 21]

Martin Walser has reversed the denunciatory trend to which Eckermann was subject in his handsomely titled playlet, *In Goethes Hand* (Suhrkamp Verlag, Frankfurt am Main: 1982). However, precisely by reversing the trend and showing Eckermann in a pathetic light—he avoids complications and further reversals—he never gets beyond a "beyond good and evil" reading of the couple, which basically keeps Eckermann in his place.

7. Goethe's Princess Leonore von Este is, as her name suggests, a patroness of thinking and being—in their relationship to a scientificity of discourse (*Torquato Tasso*). Jane K. Brown has shown how Goethe writes the spiral structure of his scientific works into his "Novelle" (in "The Tyranny of the Ideal: The Dialectics of Art in Goethe's 'Novelle,' " *SiR,* 19, Summer 1980).

8. The legal problems, court appearances, and trials that Eckermann faced through Goethe's afterlife should not be excluded from this discussion; Ecker-

mann was broken by these institutions as well and incurred sizeable debts while trying to defend the *Conversations*.

9. Friedenthal, *Goethe: Sein Leben und seine Zeit,* (Deutscher Taschenbuchverlag, Munich: 1977).

10. This can be read along the lines of "cryptic incorporation" as elaborated by Nicholas Abraham and Maria Torok in *Cryptonomie: Le Verbier de l'homme aux loups* (prefaced by J. Derrida's "Fors"), La Philosophie en effet (Flammarion, Paris: 1976) and *L'Écorce et le noyau* (Flammarion, Paris: 1978). Also see "Moi—la psychanalyse" by J. Derrida and Jonathan Culler's discussion of cryptonomy and sign motivation in *On Deconstruction* (Cornell University Press, Ithaca: 1982), pp. 190–192. Also see *diacritics* (The Johns Hopkins University Press, Baltimore: spring 1979).

11. Philippe Lacoue-Labarthe, in "L'echo du sujet," *Le Sujet de la Philosophie: Typographies I,* La Philosophie en Effet, (Flammarion, Paris: 1979), linking autothanatography to autobiography, demonstrates the rigorous impossibility of any autobiography or first-person discourse.

12. In general, Eckermann's rapport to the theater, to acting and representation—to knowing lines, as if under hypnosis—appears to be related to the effect of the phantom under study. In Goethe's own elaboration of this effect, the phantom of the father in Wilhelm Meister is focused on the performance of Hamlet. When Eckermann leaves Weimar for Italy, he is relieved to discover that there is no *Souffleur-Kasten* prompting the actors. His incorporation of the *Souffleur-Kasten* will be treated in terms of the dictaphone that he has internalized after Goethe's disappearance in 1832 (see conversation of 28 May 1830). In this regard, Jean-Luc Nancy's reading of the question of passivity and hypnosis in "Identité et Tremblement" would be an invaluable guide (in *Hypnoses,* Éditions Galilée, Paris: 1984); for example: "La passivité n'est pas individuelle: on peut être actif seul, mais on ne peut être passif qu'à deux ou à plusiers."

13. I am grateful to Rainer Nägele for having discerned a peculiarly Nietzschean moment in this dream narration in terms of the Second Tractatus, Section 16, of the *Genealogy of Morals,* which addresses the origin of humanity or the becoming-humanity of water animals (*Wassertiere*) as they first step onto land: ". . . als es den Wassertieren ergangen sein muss, als sie gezwungen wurden, entweder Landtiere zu werden oder zugrunde zu gehen, so ging es diesen . . . glücklich angepassten Halbtieren—mit einem Male waren alle ihre Instinkte entwertet und 'ausgehängt.' " In the same section Nietzsche traces the becoming of the human soul not as something that grows inside a body but rather onto the body; thus "dies ist das, was ich *Verinnerlichung* des Menschen nenne: damit wächst erst das an den Menschen heran, was man später 'Seele' nennt." In a way, Nietzsche's description of the soul recalls Goethe's description of Eckermann growing onto him, Nägele suggests, as the ennabling fiction of immortality—a belated supplement to the concept of the specifically human.

14. In *Beiträge zur Poesie mit besonderer Hinweisung auf Goethe* (Cotta, Stuttgart: 1824), p. 18: "Schriftsteller gleichen Schwimmern.—Die guten beherrschen das Element mit Leichtigkeit und haben das Haupt immer oben. Den Schlechten hingegen macht's gewaltige Mühe, ihr Kopf ist oft ganz überwältigt und überspült, man sieht nur arbeitende Hände." Please note that when the head is "overwhelmed," one sees only working hands.

15. The motif of straying seamen, suggests Peter T. Connor (University of California, Berkeley), may be viewed as something of a literary trope, beginning perhaps with *Robinson Crusoe* whose predicament follows upon a brother's loss. Another exemplary instance of trying to recuperate lost seamen, which is always

linked to the radical drifting of the patronymic, opens the drama of *Franken-stein;* the sibling epistle from which Victor Frankenstein's story is generated begins as an effect of frozen seamen. Nicolas Abraham's "The Case of Jonas" in *Jonas: Anasémies III* ought to be considered in this context (Flammarion, Paris: 1981) as well as Melville's *Moby Dick.*

16. The doublings prior to and around Goethe are not limited to these examples. Eckermann doubled up with Frédéric Soret of Geneva in order to write the third part of the *Conversations* and had an important correspondence with him concerning the proper presentation of Goethe. For instance, Ecker-mann was very shocked to read in Soret's manuscripts a reference to a bottle of wine next to Goethe's place at table. He wrote a lengthy commentary on the necessity of reducing the bottle to a glass of wine, so that readers might not get the wrong idea about Goethe. Soret immediately obliged Eckermann. Ecker-mann also created another partner in Auguste Kladzig, the orphan-actress of whom he was very fond. Their place of union was to be in a common project: they were to conceive a book on Goethe, more specifically, on the *Farben-lehre.* The desired project never got off the ground, but Eckermann's (project) proposal reproduces the coupling mechanisms related to the *Farbenlehre* epi-sodes. All these doublings reveal modalities of his relationship to Goethe.

17. Eckermann's aversion to the inaugural text of his reading list, Winckel-mann, would seem strangely phobic if one overlooked Goethe's famous essay of homage to W. In this essay (entitled "Winckelmann"—Goethe rarely if ever used a proper name as title for his aesthetic essays), Goethe poses W. as the exemplary figure of healthfulness, beauty, and, in general, Greek sublimity. In this essay one might even discern the law of Goethe's desire for an alterity in which the beautiful and the friend would grow into one another. In praise of homosexual friendship, Goethe writes:

> Die leidenschaftliche Erfüllung liebevoller Pflichten, die Wonne der Unzertrenn-lichkeit, die Hingebung eines für den andern, die ausgesprochene Bestimmung für das ganze Leben, die notwendige Begleitung in den Tod setzen uns bei Verbindung zweier Jünglinge in Erstaunen. . . . Zu einer Freundschaft dieser Art fühlte Winckelmann sich geboren, derselben nicht allein sich fähig, sondern auch im höchsten Grade bedürftig; er empfand sein eigenes Selbst nur unter der Form der Freundschaft, er erkannte sich nur unter dem Bilde des durch einen Dritten zu vollendenden Ganzen.

In *Goethes Werke,* Band XII (Verlag C.H. Beck, Munich:1978), p. 102.

18. Cited in Houben, Band II.

19. Stephan Broser induces the different apparitions of "Kästchen, Kasten, Kastration" in Freud and Goethe (he begins with Melusine) in an article of that title. *Cahiers Confrontation,* no. 8 (Aubier, Paris: automne 1982).

20. Long after the image of "Dreckermann" was constructed, Freud's hith-erto unpublished correspondence is made public. In a letter to Fliess, he anx-iously wonders if his thinking has produced nothing more than a "Dreckology."

21. See Sarah Kofman, *Le respect des femmes* (Éditions Galilée, Paris: 1982) and *L'énigme de la femme: la femme dans les textes de Freud* (Éditions Galilée, Paris: 1980).

22. Catherine Clément/Hélène Cixous, *La jeune née* (Union Générale d'Éditions, Collection '10/18,' Paris: 1975) and Jane Gallop, *The Daughter's Seduction: Feminism and Psychoanalysis* (Cornell University Press, Ithaca: 1982).

23. Cited in Thomas Mann's *Lotte in Weimar.*

Avital Ronell is Associate Professor of Comparative Literature at University of California, Berkeley, and a member of the Collège de Philosophie in Paris. She is the author of numerous articles on theory, psychoanalysis, philosophy, and Goethe.